DATE DUE

DEMCO 38-296

The Marshall Cavendish Illustrated History of

POPULAR MUSIC

Volume 12

1972-1973

MARSHALL CAVENDISH
NEW YORK, LONDON, TORONTO, SYDNEY

Reference Edition Published 1990

on

1. Vicenza.

be reproduced or
utilized in any form or by means electronic or mechanical,
including photocopying, recording, or by an information storage
and retrieval system, without permission from the copyright
holders.

Reference edition produced by DPM Services.

© Orbis Publishing Ltd.MCMLXXXIX
© Marshall Cavendish Ltd.MCMLXXXIX

Set ISBN 1-85436-015-3

Library of Congress Cataloging in Publication Data

The Marshall Cavendish history of popular music.
    p.   cm.
    Includes index.
    ISBN 1-85435-027-7 (vol. 12)
    1. Popular music — History and criticism. 2. Rock music — History
and Criticism. I. Marshall Cavendish Corporation. II. Title:
History of popular music.
ML 3470. M36 1988
784. 5' 009 — dc19   88-21076
                            CIP
                            MN

Editorial Staff

Editor	Ashley Brown
Executive Editors	Adrian Gilbert Michael Heatley
Consultant Editors	Richard Williams Peter Brookesmith
Editorial Director	Brian Innes

Reference Edition Staff

Reference Editor	Mark Dartford
Revision Editor	Fran Jones
Consultant Editor	Michael Heatley
Art Editor	Graham Beehag

CONTENTS

CONTRIBUTORS

CLIVE ANDERSON

Co-author of *The Soul Book* and contributor to *Encyclopedia of Rock*, he has also written for *Black Music, Black Echoes, New Kommotion* and other magazines.

STEPHEN BARNARD

Has contributed to *Atlantic Rock, Melody Maker* and the *Rock Files* series. He also lectures at the City University, London.

DICK BRADLEY

Completed his PhD thesis on *British Popular Music in the Fifties* at the Centre of Contemporary Cultural Studies in Birmingham, England, and has also written articles for *Media, Culture & Society*.

JOHN BROVEN

Author of *Walking to New Orleans* and *South of Louisiana,* he has also contributed to *Nothing but the Blues* and *Encyclopedia of Rock.* He writes for *Blues Unlimited* and has also compiled several New Orleans rhythm and blues anthologies

ROB FINNIS

Author of *The Phil Spector Story* and *The Gene Vincent Story,* he has contributed to the major rock journals and runs a specialist record shop.

SIMON FRITH

A lecturer at the University of Warwick, England, he has built up a reputation over the last 15 years as one of the leading international commentators on rock music. He has co-edited the *Rock File* series, and written *The Sociology of Rock.*

PETER GURALNIK

Author of *Feel Like Going Home, Lost Highway* and *Nighthawk Blues,* his articles on blues, country and rock have appeared in *Rolling Stone,* the *Village Voice, Country Music, Living Blues,* the *New York Times* and the *Boston Phoenix.*

BILL HARRY

Founder member of UK's *Mersey Beat,* he later became news editor of *Record Mirror* and music columnist for *Weekend.* He is currently an independent PR for such artists as Suzi Quatro and Kim Wilde.

MARTIN HAWKINS

An acknowledged expert on the Sun era of rock'n'roll (author of *The Sun Story*), he writes for *Melody Maker, Time Barrier Express* and *Country Music*

BRIAN HOGG

Publisher of *Bam Balam,* which concentrates on US and UK bands of the Sixties, he has also written for such magazines as *New York Rocker* and *Record Collector.*

PETER JONES

Was editor of UK's *Record Mirror* from 1961 to 1969. He then became UK News editor of *Billboard* in 1977 and later UK and European Editor.

ROBIN KATZ

After 10 years in the Motown Press Office, she now writes freelance for *New Sound, New Styles, International Musician* and *Smash Hits.*

JOE McEWEN

An acknowledged authority on soul music, he has written for *Rolling Stone, Phonograph Record, Black Music,* the *Boston Phoenix* and Boston's *Real Paper.*

BILL MILLAR

As a freelance journalist he writes for *Melody Maker* and other rock papers. He is the author of *The Drifters* and *The Coasters.*

DAVID MORSE

Author of *Motown,* he lectures at the School of English and American Studies at Sussex University, England.

TONY RUSSELL

Editor of *Old Time Music* from 1971, he contributes regularly to *Blues Unlimited* and *Jazz Journal* and is the author of *Blacks, Whites and Blues.*

ROBERT SHELTON

Has written about blues, country and folk for the *New York Times* , London *Times, Listener, Time Out* and *Melody Maker.*

NICK TOSCHES

Author of *Hellfire,* a biography of Jerry Lee Lewis, he also writes for *New York Times* and *Village Voice.*

MICHAEL WATTS

Writes on popular arts for *The Los Angeles Times* and London *Times* and is rock columnist for *Records and Recording Magazine.*

ADAM WHITE

Has written about Motown for *Music Week* and *Black Echoes,* and scripted a six-hour documentary about the company and its music for US radio. Also worked as managing editor of *Billboard* magazine in New York.

Words and Music

Rock in print: inspiration, information and innuendo

WRITING ABOUT ROCK MUSIC has always been an odd business. It is not like writing about any other type of music – or almost any other art form. Most rock writers are completely ignorant about the basic subject they are describing; they have no musical knowledge and no ability to describe in accurate technical terms what they have heard. Yet this does not stop them writing on the subject – often with enormous success. For rock writing mirrors the music in that, generally, it is a commercial activity that reflects what the audience – the readers – want.

There is a certain amount of academic, disinterested writing on rock, but in spite of the enormous popular appeal of the subject, this has never grown beyond a small body of work. There are several reasons for this, of which the most important is probably that to define a rock record in purely musical terms is often to miss some of its essential appeal; it has to be looked at as a social and economic, as well as a musical artefact, and the number of individuals able to combine the depth of analysis on all levels is very small.

The majority of rock writing, then, has been designed – like the music – for the market. It has been written because people will pay for it. On one level, this may be providing information for the music industry. Publications such as *Billboard* and *Cashbox* serve this function and are well-attuned to their market. On another level, writing on rock may be reflecting an older generation's dislike of the music and its supposed effect on a younger generation's morals, while at the same time showing a prurient interest. The daily press all over the world has always reflected this viewpoint – it has done its best to find the seamy side of rock stars' lives.

Questions and answers

Most rock writing, however, whether in the form of books, magazines or weekly music press, is essentially aimed at a public that likes rock music. This public does not need to have the music itself or its liking for it explained – it knows what it likes or dislikes. What most fans want is to identify with rock on more levels than that of merely listening to the records. Many are keen to learn about the personalities and intentions of the people creating the music.

Then again, many rock fans find that the whole idea of rock music provides a world they can escape into and identify with, far removed from mundane everyday life. They want to know what is happening, who is managing who, what records are being released, who are the bad guys or the good guys of the rock world. By providing the personalities with which some fans can identify and the general environment into which others wish to enter, rock provides a series of subjects that can be both written and read about. And this has provided

the great bulk of the subject-matter of rock writing from 1956 to the present day.

The world of rock writing tends to become very enclosed, however: the audience want to read only certain things; and the writers only produce work that feeds those preconceptions – because, after all, most writers themselves are basically fans. So there are few really provocative opinions expressed in rock writing, and few pieces of original or illuminating research. When a writer *does* produce a piece that arouses emotion in rock fans, he is liable to find himself severely criticised.

Albert Goldman's book on Elvis, for example, painted a very unpleasant portrait of 'the King', revealing the seamy side of his stardom in merciless detail, and with 'loathing rhetoric'. Some of the facts in his work have been challenged – Gordon Stoker (a member of Presley's backing group the Jordanaires) has referred to the work as 'stinking dirty, a trashy book . . . a bunch of crap'. But what the critics seem to object to most of all about Goldman's character assassination of such a rock'n'roll legend is not so much his lack of scholarly integrity as his inability to understand rock'n'roll itself.

Torrents of hate

That doyen of US rock critics, Greil Marcus, suspected Goldman's viewpoint to have been coloured by his own cultural and artistic prejudices and suggested that the puncturing of the myths surrounding Elvis had much wider implications: 'The torrents of hate, distaste and ethnic slurs that drive this book are unrelieved . . . it seems to be Goldman's purpose to discredit Elvis Presley entirely, the culture that produced him, and the international culture he helped create – to dismiss and condemn not just Elvis, but the white working-class South from which Presley came, and the pop world which emerged in Presley's wake.'

There may be ample justification for criticism of Goldman's salacious work, but Presley fans and rock'n'roll devotees also strongly attacked an earlier book that presented a more honest and sensitive account of Elvis's life. *Elvis – What Happened?* was written by three of his former bodyguards, Red and Sonny West and Dave Hebler, and appeared in 1977, four days before Elvis died. The book was viewed by many as a betrayal of trust.

The dangers in maintaining this trust, however, are that rock writing, in proclaiming enthusiasm for its subject, too often becomes an uncritical adjunct to the music world itself, unable to provide a truly effective commentary. But with the increasing amount of 'serious' rock analysis appearing in book form in the late Seventies and beyond, it would seem that a new and more lasting arm of rock writing has emerged as an adjunct to the ever-fickle music press.

ASHLEY BROWN

Rock Books

How rock found its way onto the library shelves

ROCK HAS NEVER figured as high in publishers' lists of priorities as sport, the cinema, showbusiness in general or the more specialised fields of jazz, and most publications have focused on the gaudy, superficial aspects of the rock scene or the private foibles of its leading personalities. Only in the Seventies did publishers begin to look at rock in a new light. At one time, the indifference of publishers towards pop could be blamed on the innate conservatism of the publishing establishment, especially in Britain. In the Fifties, editorial decisions were often taken by Oxbridge-educated men with a deep-seated distrust of the overt commercialism of the pop scene. The assumption was that pop, unlike jazz (which had inspired a vast and learned literature all its own), was not a fit subject for book treatment because it lacked intellectual credibility. Publishers had sound commercial reasons, too, for turning a blind eye to pop: the book-buying public was largely adult and middle-class, while those who bought pop records were mainly working-class and in their teens. Books were not part of teenage culture – music papers and teen magazines provided all the news and pictures that pop fans could want.

A trickle of books with pop music as subject-matter did, nevertheless, begin to appear as early as 1958. Most were variations of the glossy film annuals that had proved popular since the Thirties, filled with colour photographs and gossip about that year's idols. Most were American and geared to television shows – Steve Kahn's *Tops In Pops* (1961), for instance, featured profiles of Frankie Avalon, Fabian, Paul Anka and other stars of Dick Clark's 'American Bandstand'. The only British equivalents were showbusiness biographies of the likes of Tommy Steele and Cliff Richard, which portrayed their subjects not as pop stars but as all-round entertainers in the time-honoured British tradition. *The Tommy Steele Story* (1959) was a glowing account of Steele's rags-to-riches rise by his manager, John Kennedy; Cliff Richard's *It's Great To Be Young* (1960) played up his super-clean image but betrayed no sense of pop being anything more than just another branch of showbiz.

The impetus to treat pop more seriously came, surprisingly, from academic quarters – from behavioural scientists and professors of literature who were interested in the sociological aspects of the developing adolescent culture. Richard

Bookends to a decade: 1961's Tops In Pops *(above) and Ralph Gleason's 1969 analysis of the SF sound (below).*

Hoggart's influential *The Uses Of Literacy* (1957) touched upon the cultural meanings of pop-song lyrics, while Mark Abrams' *The Teenage Consumer* (1959) and James Coleman's *The Adolescent Society* (1961) explored teenage leisure activities as a

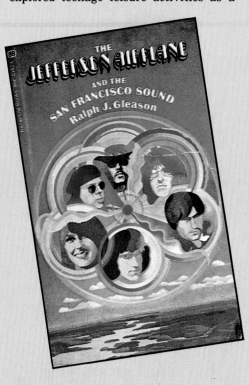

consequence of increased spending power. Books that treated pop on a musical level, as a style in its own right, were harder to come by and generally unsympathetic: Brian Bird's *Skiffle* (1958) traced the origins of skiffle in American folk and jazz, but dismissed rock'n'roll as a commercial impostor. Jazz and blues authors (who were mainly middle-class academics) took a similar line, with the exception of LeRoi Jones. In *Blues People* (1963), he strongly warned against such cultural sectarianism: 'Rock'n'roll is usually a flagrant commercialisation of rhythm and blues but the music in many cases depends on materials that are so alien to the general middle-class, middle-brow American culture as to remain interesting . . . it is still raw enough to stand dilution and in some cases, to even be made attractive by the very facts of its commercialisation.'

Paperback writers

The most obvious reason for this dismissive handling of rock was that the authors themselves were considerably older than the average pop fan and worked outside the pop industry. Even the disc jockeys who lent their names to the occasional pop book in the early Sixties were often condescending, while attempts to analyse the 'youth explosion' of the Swinging London era frequently had the air of an exposé. Charles Hamblett and Jane Deverson's *Generation X* (1964) consisted of revealing if voyeuristic interviews with young people about music, sex, drugs and lifestyles in general; *The Young Meteors* (1967), by *Evening Standard* feature writer Jonathan Aitken (then a prospective Tory MP), was an acidic account of the rapid rise of Sixties celebrities such as Twiggy, Simon Dee, David Frost, Pete Townshend, Brian Epstein and the Beatles.

The Beatles sparked off a spate of books that told their story with varying degrees of accuracy. Many were simply excuses to wrap a flimsy text around a dozen or so pictures and charge an exorbitant price for the result, but a handful stood out as excellent pieces of reportage. Michael Braun's *Love Me Do* (1964) was a straightforward record of the Beatles' first year in the limelight, written at first hand in a detached, ironic style, while Hunter Davies' *The Beatles: The Authorised Biography* (1968) was respectful but probing. Both were profiles, written by well-known reporters (Braun worked for *The New York Times*, Davies for London's *The Sunday Times*) for an interested, but not necessarily committed audience of culture-watchers and Sunday-supplement readers. Neither book contained any critical appreciation of the Beatles' music, and neither author was particularly concerned with the group's legacy to rock. Another Beatles book of the period was *A Cellarful Of Noise* (1964), Brian Epstein's inside account of the Beatles' career, ghost-written by NEMS aide Derek Taylor.

An odd mixture of picture books, socio-cultural studies and the occasional up-market biography formed the book world's chief response to the Sixties beat boom – together with enterprising one-offs such as the Hollies' *How To Run A Beat Group* (1965), which was largely the work of *Daily Mirror* columnist Anne Nightingale. It was in America after 1967 that books with a more serious approach to rock began to appear; the inspiration came partly from the 'new journalism' of writers like Tom

The Hollies' How To Run A Beat Group *(1965) was ghost-written by Anne Nightingale (below right). The 'new journalism' of writers like Tom Wolfe (below left) was in marked contrast to such uncritical pop-writing.*

Tatty glamour
If some rock books were tantamount to manifestos, depicting late-Sixties rock as something divorced from the commercial mainstream of popular music, others delved deeper into the roots of the rock sound. In the first comprehensive survey of its kind, *Rock Encyclopedia* (1969), Lillian Roxon offered punchy, often incisive summaries of the careers of everyone from the Strawberry Alarm Clock to Roosevelt Gook, from the Doors to Van Dyke Parks.

Wolfe, Richard Goldstein, Robert Christgau and Hunter S. Thompson, which found a home in newly-established 'alternative' newspapers like *Rolling Stone*. Wolfe's *The Electric Kool-Aid Acid Test* (1968) described the efforts of Ken Kesey and the Merry Pranksters to bring LSD to San Francisco, while Ralph J. Gleason (of *Rolling Stone*) summed up the optimism of the era in *The Jefferson Airplane And The San Francisco Sound* (1969), a detailed (if rather naive) appraisal of what the author called 'the new rock'.

Gleason's book mirrored the new radical, intellectual, middle-class bias in American rock, as did collections of essays like *The Age Of Rock: Sounds Of The American Cultural Revolution* (edited by Jonathan Eisen, 1969), its articles drawn from the pages of literary as well as music magazines. Established academic values were important to the new writers: Richard Goldstein's *The Poetry Of Rock* (1968) made a case for assessing rock lyrics in poetic terms, while Arnold Shaw's *The Rock Revolution* (1969) spoke approvingly of late-Sixties rock as 'the new classical music'. Meanwhile, Charles A. Reich's best-selling *The Greening Of America* (1968) presented a political strategy for overthrowing the old order, his argument laced with quotes from the Beatles and other bands. Implicit in all these books was the belief that rock *meant* something, that it provided a political rallying cry and could act as a catalyst for social change.

Jazz musician, writer and bon viveur George Melly (right) put youth obsessions under a critical microscope in his book Revolt Into Style.

Her book became the model for many of the rock encyclopedias that were to appear in the Seventies. Jerry Hopkins' *The Rock Story* (1970) was a selective, concise account of rock from its country-and-blues beginnings, including some superb penportraits of producers and rock businessmen as well as performers. Hopkins' coverage of the selling of the Monkees, the break-up of Buffalo Springfield, the groupie scene and American radio were particularly revealing.

Oddly, however, it was British journalists and authors who explored the evolution of rock with the greatest detail and flair; perhaps their detachment from the American scene inspired greater objectivity. Nik Cohn's *Pop From The Beginning* (1969, later re-published as *Awopbopaloobop*) and Charlie Gillett's *The Sound Of The City* (1970) set new standards in both the style of rock writing and the approach to content, though the two were written from completely different critical perspectives. Cohn's was a personal record of the rock scene, full of what – for 1969 – were unfashionable and controversial assertions: that pop was fundamentally trivial, its tatty glamour and innate silliness its greatest strengths; that the Beatles were 'bad for pop' because they put artistry before showmanship; and that pop belonged to teenagers, not student intellectuals. The book emphasised that rock was *fun* before it was anything else – and Cohn's snappy summaries of showmen like P. J. Proby, Little Richard and Jack Good were accurate and hilarious.

In contrast, *The Sound Of The City* had the air of a scholarly analysis – the book began, in fact, as a master's thesis. Although Gillett covered the story of rock to 1970, his main area of study was 1950-1963, in particular the birth of rock'n'roll. Taking the development of the music industry as his starting point, he showed how rock became the *cause célèbre* of the independent labels in America and declined in

Ian Whitcomb (above left) had a US Number 8 hit in 1965 with 'You Turn Me On' before writing 1972's After The Ball *(above). Charlie Gillett (above right) penned* The Sound Of The City *(below).*

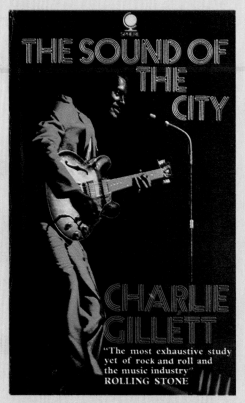

quality as the independents and majors began competing on the same level. He also looked at the growth of different styles (the evolution of R&B into soul, for example) and touched upon areas of musical, sociological and literary analysis. The book had a certain dryness of style and

clear weaknesses – the coverage of British beat music and its impact on America, for instance, was perfunctory – but it provided rock writers and historians of the Seventies with a blueprint for further research.

Other British authors produced excellent accounts of different aspects of rock history. Richard Mabey, taking a sociologist's standpoint, discussed the prevailing pop trends of the Sixties in *The Pop Process* (1969); one-time blues singer and *The Observer* arts critic George Melly took the decade apart in *Revolt Into Style* (1970), setting the youth obsession of the Sixties in a post-war context; Dave Laing wrote *The Sound Of Our Time* (1969) while attending Sussex University and suggested the critical canons to which potential students of the rock field should address themselves. His study of the life and music of *Buddy Holly* (1971) was published by Studio Vista, a small London publishing house specialising in rock and cinema titles; their series also included Gary Herman's *The Who* and Bill Millar's *The Drifters* (both 1971). In 1972, former pop singer and one-hit wonder Ian Whitcomb appeared with a spicy history of Tin Pan Alley 'from ragtime to rock', called *After The Ball*, and Granada began its own rock series with the first *Rock File*, edited by Charlie Gillett and including the first complete listing of British Top Twenty hits. Four more *Rock Files* were subsequently published, each containing a similar mixture of factual data and investigative essays.

The rock'n'roll past was the prevailing theme of early-Seventies rock books like John Broven's *Walking To New Orleans* (1974), a study of R&B in America's Deep South, and Colin Escott and Martin Hawkins' *Catalyst* (1975), a history of the legendary Sun label. Other rock biographies appeared, from Tony Scaduto's controversial *Bob Dylan* (1972), to more modest profiles of Eric Clapton, Rod Stewart, Elton John, the Grateful Dead, Janis Joplin and the Rolling Stones. Autobiography surfaced with Derek Taylor's memoirs of his Apple days, *As Time Goes By* (1976), George Martin's *All You Need Is Ears* (1977) and Mott the Hoople singer Ian Hunter's *Diary Of A Rock'n'Roll Star* (1974) – one of the few rock books to give a real insight into life on the road. Anthologies of rock criticism continued to be published, too, though collections of essays on a particular theme – like *The Soul Book* (1975) and *The Electric Muse* (1976) – tended to be more instructive and make better reading than the collected thoughts of individual rock writers. Of the latter, Robert Christgau's *Any Old Way You Choose It* (1973) and Jon Landau's *It's Too Late To Stop Now* (1972) succeeded in reflecting the changing face of rock journalism in the Seventies.

Facts and figures

The real rock publishing successes of the Seventies were 'facts'n'info' books, packed with detailed information for fans, disc jockeys, record companies and journalists alike. The *New Musical Express* commissioned its own staff (under the direction of editors Nick Logan and Bob Woffinden) to write and compile an encyclopedia of rock that was published in 1975 as *The NME Book Of Rock*; it proved to be one of the best of its kind, just nudging out Dave Laing and Phil Hardy's three-volume *Encyclopedia Of Rock* (1976) on the grounds of accuracy, writing style and presence of a discography for each artist covered. Other books presented hard facts with little or no comment: Terry Hounsome and Tim Chambre's *Rock Record* listed all the personnel on virtually every rock album released before 1978, while Clive Solomon's *Record Hits* (1978) listed every Top Fifty placing. In the same vein, but better

presented and with complete catalogue numbers of every single included, was *The Guinness Book Of Hit Singles* (1978), compiled by Paul Gambaccini, Mike Read and Jo and Tim Rice. This was the first pop book to be properly marketed, thanks partly to the presence of such 'name' authors (two disc jockeys and a composer among them); it became a best-seller, was updated and reissued in three editions, and inspired two sequels.

The success of the Guinness books marked a new phase in rock publishing in Britain. Omnibus Press, long involved in the marketing of sheet music and its repacking into song anthologies, began publishing various American titles (including Greil Marcus' *Mystery Train* and Peter Guralnick's *Feel Like Going Home*) in the late Seventies but soon specialised in its own line of rock books. These included the

Below: One of the successful Guinness-sponsored series of chart-oriented books. Bottom, from left: Authors Mike Read, Tim Rice, Jo Rice and Paul Gambaccini, whose joint credentials helped sell the volume.

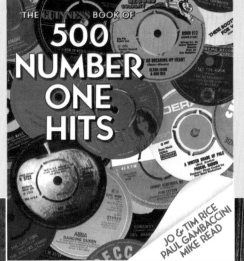

shrewdly conceived *In Their Own Words* series, which has featured collections of quotes by the Beatles, the Rolling Stones, Abba and David Bowie among others. The deaths of Elvis Presley and John Lennon inspired a mini-boom in biographical material: Jerry Hopkins' *Elvis: The Final Years* (1980) was the author's outstanding sequel to his previous *Elvis* (1971), and played down the more sensational aspects of the singer's decline – unlike Albert Goldman's *Elvis* (1981), which was little more than an exercise in character-assassination and an indictment of rock music in general. Beatles books sold steadily, the same material regurgitated in new forms, although Philip Norman's *Shout!* (1981) did attempt to defuse a few myths.

In the Eighties, rock book publishing finally became big business. Ironically, rock book sales boomed while the circulations of music papers declined. This may have been a result of changing leisure habits among teenagers or the failure of the music press to respond to the needs of their readers, but it had much to do with the entry into the publishing business of firms like Omnibus, Virgin, Proteus and Eel Pie.

By the late Eighties, however, the last three had ceased publishing or been absorbed by larger competitors. With a surfeit of impermanent chart acts, emphasis was laid on retelling old tales (eg Goldman's 1988 demolition of John Lennon) or, increasingly, on the new and more immediate medium of video.

The most active branch of rock book publishing as the Nineties beckoned was the rock encyclopedia, with most established houses unveiling variations on the theme. Rock'n'roll, it seemed, was now history.   STEPHEN BARNARD

Mirroring the Melodies

British rock weeklies: covering current issues

THE UK MUSIC PRESS has enjoyed a long, successful and generally stable history. Starting as a trade service for musicians, publishers and other sections of the industry, the papers came, in the Fifties, to be aimed at record-buyers instead – the result of changing musical trends.

Probably the most important factor behind this stability was the tradition of weekly publication. While the American music press has always been geared to monthly publication, with a consequent lack of immediacy, British readers could see reviews of the week's new singles, details of that weekend's concerts or interviews with the latest chart entrants. The key was a finger on the pulse of record-buying habits; the UK rock press established this in the Fifties, and never lost it.

Britain, too, has seen its share of monthly music magazines, mainly fan-oriented like *Elvis Monthly*, which started in the early Sixties and was still going strong in

the Eighties. There has also been a selection of publications for teenage girls that carried a high music content, from early titles like *Roxy* and *Marty*, through *Fabulous* at the height of the Mod era and *Pop Pics*. Eighties monthlies like *The Face* were the inheritors of this tradition.

Grandpa goes pop

Melody Maker has come to be regarded as the grandfather of the weekly rock press. It began in the Twenties as a musicians' monthly, and found its niche in the jazz world. In keeping with its traditional style, the paper seemed to cultivate an air of disdain for that undisciplined youth, rock 'n'roll.

By the time the big beat hit Britain, however, the *MM* had been joined by two other weeklies that tended to milk away the less jazz-oriented elements of its readership. The *New Musical Express* was relaunched under that title in 1952 after a

brief, unsuccessful run, under different ownership, as the *Musical Express*. This, too, was initially musician-oriented, but in a conscious drive to boost circulation it made a pitch for pop-oriented consumer interests and hit upon the notion of printing best-seller charts. These were initially concerned with sheet music, but the *NME* then began to reprint *Billboard*'s American record charts, and at the end of 1952 inaugurated Britain's first chart of best-selling singles. Initially a Top Twelve, it grew with the singles market to a Top Twenty in 1954 and a Top Thirty in 1956.

Record Mirror, which rolled up a couple of years after *NME*, was actually *Record And Show Mirror* for its first few years, and early coverage ranged from record features and charts to variety news and even 'show' sports like boxing. It tightened up into a pop paper with a change of ownership and name (to *New Record Mirror*) at the start of the Sixties. *NRM* rapidly be-

Above, left to right: The Melody Maker *and* NME *in the jazz age contrast with* Record Mirror *and the now-defunct* Disc *in the Sixties. Below: The Eighties weeklies (left) with their popular glossy, small-format rivals (right).*

came the enthusiasts' paper during the pre-Beatlemania years, offering a charts service completely unmatched by other weeklies, and a whole area of coverage – largely by staff writer Norman Jopling – that helped establish the record-collecting tradition in the UK.

A comparative latecomer was *Disc*, which first appeared at the beginning of 1958 when rock'n'roll was already well established. It was consumer-oriented from the start, and its coverage closely mirrored that of *NME*, although production standards seemed tighter and record reviews were more organised and authoritative. *Disc* also carried a Top Twenty

singles chart. In 1959, it found itself an important niche in the rock industry by inaugurating the 'Silver Disc' awards for records that sold 250,000 copies.

The 'big four' weekly papers ran in buoyant competition for many years, joined at intervals by short-lived rivals. *Pop Weekly*, a small-format glossy by the publisher of *Elvis Monthly*, had a brave run in the early Sixties but was never able to muscle in on the large circulations. *Music Echo* fared better in the mid Sixties; it had grown out of the regionally-oriented *Mersey Beat*, which had chronicled the Beatles and the Liverpool scene so successfully. *Music Echo* was the first consumer pop paper to compile and print a Top Hundred singles chart, which immediately endeared it to the nation's chart fanatics. Financial problems, however, were harder to overcome, and the paper was eventually sold to and absorbed into *Disc*, which became *Disc And Music Echo* for a while.

Writing on the wall

As the rock press entered the second half of the Sixties, new trends began to change the face of popular music, heralded by the increasing use of terms like 'underground' and 'progressive'. There was a parting of the ways between basic commercial pop and the more demanding forms known as rock. Previously, the music press had drawn no dividing lines between the musical styles to which they gave coverage. Frank Ifield, Andy Williams or Ken Dodd were equal grist for the mill with the Rolling Stones, the Animals or the Beatles. Slowly, as 'rock' came to specify something distinct from just 'popular music', the music press began to change too.

The first noticeable effect was an increasingly 'grown-up' approach to writing. Most music press journalism had consisted of uninquisitive and non-analytical pieces, glossing over controversies and pandering to what was felt to be an uncritical

*The changing image of the rock journalist.
Above:* Record Mirror's *Sixties ace Norman
Jopling with Elkie Brooks. Right:
Seventies* NME *personality Nick Kent.*

adolescent audience. Album reviews now
began to discuss the records in serious
musical terms.

The more serious writing first appeared
in *Melody Maker*, which had a tradition of
an in-depth approach from its jazz days.
The *MM* adopted the cause of progressive
music, and began to write about it and its
makers in musical rather than 'pop star'
terms. *Record Mirror* indulged itself similarly, covering soul music from the US as
well, while tempering the overall mixture
with more traditional pop coverage.

Disc tended to sectionalise itself, and
serious journalism therefore grew in isolated columns by writers assigned to more
progressive rock music. In the early Seventies, the *NME* changed – literally overnight – from a consciously 'pop' to a
self-consciously 'rock' paper, with a complete redesign and an influx of new writers.
A bold move, it was right for the times, and
boosted the paper's circulation. In a
natural progression from this, the *NME*
then fostered the concept of the personality
rock journalist, whose style – and ego –
became an integral part of his work.

Oi! society

There were exceptions to the trend, of
course. During the Seventies, *Record
Mirror* decided on an about-face and
started to cover teen-angled rock and pop,
championing the artists of the glitter era.
What was gone forever, though, was the
wide musical base; MOR artists, jazz and
folk musicians had no place in the rock
press (except in the specialised sections of
the *MM*). The weeklies were joined in 1970
by *Sounds*, which tried to be the most
serious of the lot. It soon started to falter in
this guise, but its presence made the
market top-heavy; the inevitable casualty
turned out to be *Disc*, which was absorbed
into *Record Mirror*. During the Seventies,
the *MM* tried to maintain a position of
being all things to all people, and slowly

lost both direction and circulation. It was
initially contemptuous of punk in 1976,
though later championed several new-
wave bands. But the paper did not
know quite where to go once the new
wave had subsided, and was still
searching for an identity (and more
readers) in the early Eighties.

The mid-Seventies new wave was
to prove a godsend to *Sounds*, which
had descended from its original
perch to ape the *NME*'s content
without its style. It now erupted
into a lurid gutter-press approach,
in pursuit of everything new,
aggressive and 'exciting'. The
graffiti-type format tightened up as
the first punk wave ebbed, but by
then *Sounds* had captured the harder
end of the street-level readership. By
administering a clever balance of
heavy metal and 'Oi', the skinhead-
engendered second phase of punk, it
kept its pot boiling healthily into the
Eighties.

Record Mirror continued to provide
the most pop-oriented approach of the
weeklies with huge charts coverage and
more than token appreciation of black
music. In the early Eighties, however,
the lower teen end of its following
started to drift away to the glossier,
simpler fortnightly *Smash Hits*. *RM*'s
answer was to adopt a booklet format
and a strikingly similar design.

The *NME* tried to create a highbrow
organ of rock criticism during the Seventies – and to a large extent succeeded,
because the *NME* at its best had style, a
sense of humour and plenty of good
writing, although an excess of journalistic ego-tripping and a sense of trendy
self-satisfaction alienated some of its
readership. The paper began to sober
up in later years, however, retaining a
sense of stylish eminence unmatched by
any of its rivals.

The success of *Q,* a magazine
launched in 1986 for the compact disc
generation, indicated a movement up the
age range and pointed the way for others to
follow in the Nineties.   JOHN HUNT

America's music press and the Creem of the crop

THE ROCK PRESS in the US has never affected musical trends or record sales as greatly or as directly as its counterpart in the UK. For one thing, there is no weekly publication in the US to compare with Britain's *New Musical Express* or *Melody Maker*, due largely to the impracticability of distributing such a publication across the nation. Radio has been the medium most responsible for 'breaking' records in the US, and has steered away from airing music that departs from the acceptable mainstream. The rock press has, therefore, held a subservient position to radio as far as affecting mass taste goes; it has existed primarily for the dissemination of information and opinion regarding non-mainstream progressive and new music (such as art rock and punk), catering largely to a minority of record-buyers whose involvement with the music goes beyond mere enjoyment.

When rock'n'roll emerged in the mid Fifties, the US music press consisted of the weekly trade publications, led by *Billboard* (published since the 1890s), and fan magazines. Both provided news and information – the trade mags concentrating on industry news and sales, the fan mags on gossip – but neither attempted to present criticism of the music. The fan mags were aimed at teenagers, especially girls, featuring such personalities as Elvis Presley, Ricky Nelson, Bobby Rydell and Fabian. The music mags shared many idols with the movie fan mags, and both simply presented their subjects in the best light, never exposing any negative traits or dark secrets.

The first major magazines to devote space to rock'n'roll were publications that had existed for years. *Song Hits* (1937) and *Hit Parader* (1942), both of which reprinted lyrics of popular songs and filled the rest of their pages with promo-like features about current stars, began to include the new stars in the Fifties when rock entered the field of popular music. The favourite teen mag was *16*, a lively monthly founded in 1957, that enjoyed its golden years under editor Gloria Stavers in the mid Sixties. *16* used – and exaggerated – the language of young teenagers, reflecting the frenzy surrounding the music.

A typical article in *16* in the Sixties might have been 'Ringo's Likes And Dislikes' or a contest to 'Win A Date With The Monkees'. The fan mags changed little subsequently – only the names are different; in the Eighties, teen idols like Rick Springfield appeared where once Frankie Avalon did. The coverage of black acts was sparse in early fan mags, although R&B did have its own publications. Other teen mags included *Tiger Beat*, *Teen Screen* and *Dig*. The increasing popularity of the genre brought an influx of free regional publications such as *Go* and *Beat*, which were distributed by local radio stations.

Do-it-yourself

An important alternative to the fan mag made its appearance in the mid Sixties in the form of the fanzine. Greg Shaw – who edited one of the first fanzines, *Mojo Navigator News*, covering the San Francisco scene – described a fanzine as 'usually the product of one person, published at his own expense and in his own house, for little or no reward above the pleasure of self-expression and writing about something he loves that is ignored in the larger press . . . read by people with the same interest'. The first fanzine was *Crawdaddy*, launched by a young student, Paul Williams. It started life as a number of mimeographed sheets stapled together, developing into a tabloid and later a slick magazine. It presented some of the best – and worst – early serious criticism of rock and survived until 1979 when it died as a magazine called *Feature*. The short-lived *Mojo* was followed in 1970 by Greg Shaw's *Who Put The Bomp?* (an influential fanzine, which later became simply *Bomp!*).

Left, from top: Magazines like Tiger Beat *(with its teen-oriented features on 'Sonny and Cher – the sweetest love story of the rock age'),* Flip *and* Datebook *were early Sixties standards. Papers like* Rolling Stone *came later in the decade.*

There have been dozens of fanzines, many using contributors to the national commercial magazines.

Values and voices
In the mid Sixties, as rock began to 'mature', daily newspaper columnists such as Ralph Gleason (*San Francisco Chronicle*) and Al Aronowitz (*New York Post*) began to take rock seriously, applying the same critical standards to the Beach Boys and the Byrds as they had previously to Miles Davis or Bob Dylan. As rock and folk crossed paths, so the folk magazines – like *Little Sandy Review* and *Sing Out!* – began to cover rock more critically. This led to the emergence of writers bringing critical evaluation of rock to weekly and monthly publications with more widespread distribution. Among the first were Richard Goldstein, with his 'Pop-Eye' column in New York's weekly *Village Voice*, and Jann Wenner, who wrote about pop in the *Sunday Ramparts* magazine. While the fan mags were still proliferating in 1966, giving birth to *Circus* (at first called *Hullabaloo*), the so-called 'underground press' (*San Francisco Oracle*, Detroit's *Fifth Estate*, New York's *East Village Other*) began associating rock with the emerging counter-culture, using rock as a means to attract attention to radical political causes.

The years 1967 and 1968 saw an explosion of 'hip' rock-oriented publications using pseudo-psychedelic graphics, among them *Eye, Cheetah* and *Fusion*. However, in November 1967, Jann Wenner's *Rolling Stone* published its first issue, and quickly established itself as *the* voice of the rock culture.

Those writers who didn't start at *Rolling Stone* probably started at *Creem*, the Detroit-based monthly established in March 1969 by the late Barry Kramer. *Creem*'s irreverent, humorous approach was a direct reaction to the *Rolling Stone*/

West Coast emphasis on eclecticism and seriousness. *Creem* preferred high-energy rock to the looser SF music, and they avoided projecting a know-it-all attitude to their readers. '*Creem* spoke to the world, not a corner of it,' said writer Dave Marsh, who helped organise and initially edited *Creem*.

The magazine's popularity rose in the mid Seventies, when its sales figures were right behind those of *Rolling Stone* and *Circus* (the latter of which covered top names only). At one time, *Creem* boasted a staff (much of which consisted of former *Stone* writers) that included Dave Marsh, Greil Marcus, Greg Shaw, Lester Bangs (who edited *Creem* from 1971-76 after Marsh left), R. Meltzer and Ed Ward. Marsh called *Creem* the magazine of 'rock as high comedy and low art, of the bizarre as normalcy'. *Creem* also supported and influenced the early new wave/punk movement in the US, and it was one of few magazines to do so.

California dreaming?
By the late Sixties there had developed three identifiable schools of rock journal-

Below left: One of Rolling Stone's *contributors Patti Smith later turned performer. Below and below right:* Fusion *and* San Francisco Oracle, *two papers of the radical underground.*

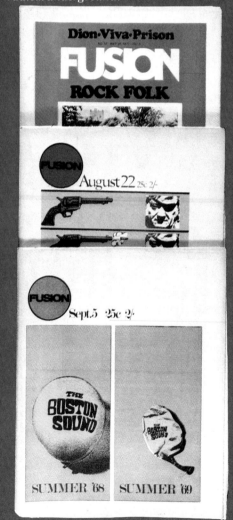

ism: the New York school (Robert Christgau, Richard Goldstein and the *Crawdaddy* writers), which used first-person journalism and saw rock as a context in which to place the writer's personal discoveries; the California school (*Rolling Stone*), which saw rock as the key to personal freedom; and the Midwestern school (*Creem*), which used a high-energy style to promote high-energy music with little emphasis at all on rock's cultural significance.

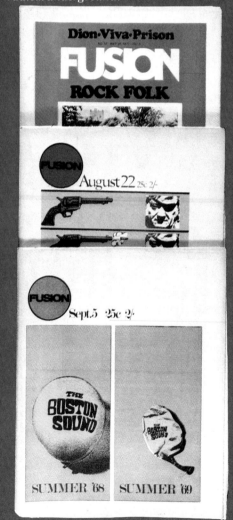

Robert Christgau, the leading proponent of the New York school, was also a member of the *Creem* staff at the same time as the aforementioned journalists. He began writing about rock in 1967 for the popular mass-market *Esquire* and in 1974 became music editor of the *Village Voice* in New York. Christgau, who has been called 'the dean of rock critics', has been responsible for some of rock journalism's most intelligent, enduring and critically sound work. The Seventies offered few revolutions in rock criticism and few major new publications entered the market. Several new entries (*Zoo World, Phonograph Record, Gig* and *Rock*, the latter of which began in the Sixties) held out for brief periods, but most were gone by the end of the decade, taking with them *Crawdaddy, Fusion* and other less important publications. In the absence of such competition, *Creem, Circus* and *Rolling Stone* became ever more predictable.

By the end of the Seventies, as rock music became fragmented, so did the rock press. Daily papers in every major city covered rock, absorbing many of the better writers. Regional and local publications (*New York Rocker* – established in 1976 by Alan Betrock and carried on by Andy Schwartz – *BAM* in California, *Boston Phoenix* and *Village Voice*) increased in importance, boosting both local and international new music, and fanzines flourished. Specialist publications, appealing to specific segments of the audience, entered the market, among them *Trouser Press* (new music and British rock), *Gold-mine* (music history and record collecting) and *Musician* (for the serious musician and listener). Mass-market general interest magazines (*Playboy, Esquire, People*) began to cover rock regularly, too.

There is no denying that the rock press in the US became somewhat isolated from mass tastes, favouring music rarely found in the charts, although the traditional commercial publications (*Circus* and *Hit Parader*) continued to feature top names only, often serving as little more than a promotional wing for the record companies. At the beginning of the Eighties, however, the rock press suffered the same financial woes as the record industry, and the outlets for the high-standard rock journalism that had been attained were sadly few and far between. JEFF TAMARKIN

Creem in their genes: Greil Marcus (left) and the late Lester Bangs (right), two influential rock critics who wrote for Creem *magazine (above).*

ROLL AWAY THE STONE

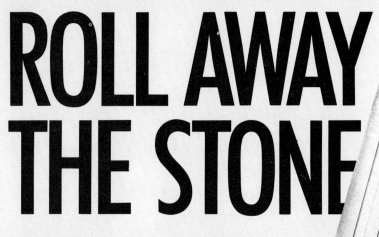

The magazine that opened a new era in rock writing

IN 1968 STREET VENDORS were arrested for selling copies of an underground magazine called *Rolling Stone*, which featured a nude picture of John and Yoko on the cover. By 1970, the street-wise journal that spoke the language of the counter-culture was nominated the Columbia Graduate School of Journalism's Magazine Of The Year.

Rolling Stone magazine grew out of a friendship between Jann Wenner and Ralph J. Gleason, who had contributed a jazz/pop column to the *San Francisco Chronicle* since the early Fifties, and also wrote for a radical magazine called *Ramparts*. Gleason encouraged Wenner, then a student at the University of California, to write for its underground offshoot, *Sunday Ramparts*. When that folded, Wenner discussed his plans for his own underground paper with Gleason.

The outcome was *Rolling Stone*, with Wenner as its editor and publisher. His initial efforts were aided by his wife Jane, while Gleason continued to provide encouragement, finance (the remainder was coaxed from Wenner's family and friends) and much practical advice. He suggested that the only feasible way of launching such a paper was to persuade the printers to give it office space; many of *Rolling Stone*'s early editions were put to bed while the presses roared deafeningly below.

A letter from home

Rolling Stone Number 1 was published on 9 November 1967 in San Francisco, where the underground movement was in full swing. The magazine's two-fold aim reflected this background: to consider rock 'n'roll as an enduring and not an ephemeral music, and to report on the sub-culture in which it was created.

Being a part of the underground, *Rolling Stone* refused to be shackled by the conventions of professional journalism. Sometimes deadlines were met, and sometimes they weren't. Nevertheless, while similar

Ralph J. Gleason (left), Jann Wenner (right) and the paper they founded (above).

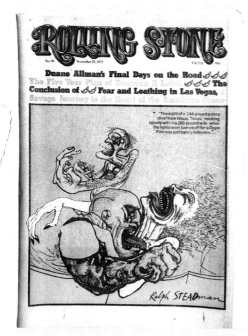

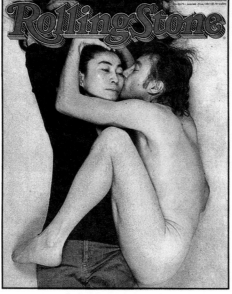

Above: Hold the front page! Four faces of Rolling Stone, *from the classic 'Fear And Loathing' series (top left) to the tragic killing of John Lennon (above right).*

periodicals were undone by a lack of application and a surfeit of drugs, *Rolling Stone*, under Wenner's helmsmanship, struck a balance between alternative lifestyles and publishing practicalities. The paper did espouse the ethics of the underground; but it was also expertly designed, intelligently written and immaculately produced.

Rolling Stone had a ready-made audience. It was, in Gleason's phrase, like a letter from home. Thousands of rock fans across America suddenly discovered that there were others who appreciated the same things they did. No comparable publication existed in the US. *Billboard*, *Cashbox* and *Record World* were all trade papers, and nothing else pitched between them and the fan magazines. *Rolling Stone* thus survived and prospered simply because there were so many who wanted to

read it. The key to its success was its assumption that the views and lifestyles of rock musicians were as interesting as those of politicians or businessmen.

All this came at a time when the music was changing, and rock musicians were taking themselves more seriously. Although the magazine did write appreciatively about such black music stars as Aretha Franklin and Sam and Dave, who regarded themselves primarily as entertainers, it is nevertheless true that its intellectual approach to rock'n'roll often encouraged a self-conscious artistry in performers of very limited abilities. Dr Hook and the Medicine Show satirised the magazine's pre-eminence in 'The Cover Of *Rolling Stone*'.

Beyond that, *Rolling Stone* succeeded simply because there had previously been virtually no informed coverage of rock music. Two aspects of this coverage were of particular significance. The first were the record reviews, which were thorough, literate and (usually) serious. The other

was the *Rolling Stone* interview. Rock music celebrities were questioned at length about all aspects of their career, as well as their overall philosophy and aesthetic values. The interviews appeared in question-and-answer form – a device that newspapers had traditionally reserved only for the most erudite subjects.

The apogee of this approach came with the John Lennon interviews, conducted by Wenner himself in New York in December 1970. Lennon took the opportunity to demolish a number of popular myths surrounding the Beatles. The interviews, which appeared in *Rolling Stone* Numbers 74 and 75, were duly turned into a book, *Lennon Remembers*. Annie Leibovitz took the pictures, and she never looked back.

Rolling Stone made headlines itself across the US in October 1975 with its Patty Hearst revelations. Meanwhile its assiduous reporters had proved of incomparable benefit to Lennon in his battle with the US Immigration authorities; likewise, the magazine remained commendably persistent in its pursuit of the case of Karen Silkwood, the nuclear worker who died in suspicious circumstances in 1974 after secretly investigating irregularities in industry.

Stone rolls east

In 1977 *Rolling Stone* moved to New York. There were fears that such an upheaval would jeopardise the magazine's unique character. While such fears have not proved justified, the magazine has long since achieved journalistic respectability, and with sales of over 800,000 has ceased to be an 'alternative' newspaper.

One of *Rolling Stone*'s abiding strengths has been its consistently impressive design, which was totally revised in January 1981. This last change was accompanied by an editorial shake-up. The music section was put into the back half of the paper, with the longer articles, interviews and political commentary occupying the front half. *Rolling Stone* thus continued its drift away from music; film stars have since been awarded cover stories more regularly than rock performers.

Critics chided *Rolling Stone* for deserting the music; it could equally be argued that the music deserted *Rolling Stone*. Although the magazine has played its part in helping to establish new acts like the Clash and Elvis Costello in the US charts, it was all too obvious that American rock lost much of its excitement in the late Seventies and after.

Rolling Stone, though, will always be criticised – precisely because it is in many ways a peerless publication. Ralph Gleason, who died in 1975 but is still affectionately remembered on the stafflist, told Wenner at the outset that the magazine could become established if someone devoted a year of his life to it. Wenner has since devoted many years of his life to it, and it is impossible to conceive of the magazine without him.

BOB WOFFINDEN

THE PRESS GANG

Newspapers' love-hate relationship with rock

THE EMERGENCE of rock'n'roll in the decade following the Second World War coincided with major developments in the technology of communication. The transistor, reliable high-power amplification systems and the tape-recorder provided the basis of an entirely new approach to sound recording. And the period saw the introduction of the lightweight, unbreakable 45 rpm single and the microgroove LP.

Rock'n'roll was a creature of new technologies and of the attendant changes in musical style, marketing strategies and the nature of performance and recording that went along with them. Arguably, it was this fact, as much as anything else, that inspired establishment loathing for the new form. Far from being a return to the 'artistic ideals of the jungle' (as the *Encyclopaedia Brittanica Yearbook* for 1956 put it), rock'n'roll was a look forward to the 'global village' described by Sixties media pundit Marshall McLuhan. Its tribalism was ultra-modern, heralding the electronic age.

Rock'n'roll riot
Not surprisingly, the traditional print-based media found rock'n'roll threatening and attempted to disarm it by holding it up to ridicule or condemning its 'savagery'. The first time that rock'n'roll hit the headlines was in 1958, when a Cleveland DJ, Alan Freed, organised a concert featuring a number of black performers. There were 10,000 seats available and some 25,000 kids turned up. The police were called in, and in the ensuing disturbances one man was stabbed and five people arrested. It was hardly a remarkable statistic except for the racial mix of Cleveland's rock'n'roll fans, which was what most interested the Ohio press. Reports of the 'riot' varied in detail, but they all drew attention to the presence of black youths in the crowd.

Racism, of course, played an important part in the press's response to rock'n'roll, but did not in itself completely explain that response. The music's apparent disregard of racial barriers was one aspect of what the press perceived as a wide-ranging threat to the traditional values. By 1956, rock'n'roll had become a phenomenon, and the opinions of the newspapers and magazines themselves were almost invariably hostile, but they seemed to attack the music's brashness and vulgarity more than its ethnic or sexual overtones. The press reaction to Elvis Presley, however, was a precise indicator of its stock attitude and under the guidance of Tom Parker, Presley's image was significantly shorn of its black associations and generally 'cleaned' up.

Inset above: The Beatles, happy to be grilled at a mid-Sixties press conference. Above: Mick Jagger in the Eighties beams for the cameras – but the intrusions of the press could still annoy (below right).

The end of the Fifties saw the American press indulge in an orgy of condemnation as the seamier side of rock'n'roll was exposed in the payola scandals of 1959 and 1960, while in Britain the music remained very much a side-show of the traditional entertainment business. With the British boasting little homegrown talent, the national press could afford to be as condescending to the young as it always had been.

Journalism with a sneer
Typical of this attitude was George Gale's coverage of Bill Haley's 1957 tour of Britain. Reporting Haley's arrival at London's Waterloo Station in the *Daily Express*, Gale watched the fans. 'You saw all around faces turned upwards, crumpled in fear by now, the ecstasy gone; angry faces trying to touch the car and see the face inside, faces bewildered like faces in the panic scenes of Russian films.' Meanwhile, the *Express* warned youthful readers, 'preparations are being made to start a new trend' to replace rock'n'roll. Quite clearly, this was journalism with a sneer on its face.

The Beatles, however, changed all that. Interestingly, the first national coverage of the group (outside of the music papers) was a *Daily Mirror* report of an incident at Paul McCartney's 21st birthday party on 20 June 1963. The party was held in Liverpool, and a drunken John Lennon had hit local Merseyside DJ Bob Wooler after the latter had insinuated that Lennon and Brian Epstein were lovers. The full details were not reported – a feature of press coverage of the Beatles that was to become increasingly familiar – but even so, the story had more than a hint of scandal.

But nobody could have predicted the extent to which the Beatles would become popular in future months. In the summer of 1963 the group were seen by the press as simply the newest in a long line of kiddies' heroes. Yet, in the heady days of the mid Sixties, they were soon being touted as messiahs of a British economic and cultural resurgence. Everybody from prime ministers to the next-door neighbour eventually hitched their wagons to the Beatles' rising star: the press were among the first and most loyal to do so.

John Lennon once commented that the group was never criticised in the early days of Beatlemania because the press corps that formed a large part of the Beatles' entourage were effectively co-opted by all the free drink, drugs and sex that went with the job. But the sycophancy actually started before the group's orgiastic tours reached their peak. It was as though there had been a sudden mass conversion to a new religion of youth. The classical music critic of *The Times* wrote an over-the-top review of the second Beatles album, while other critics went so far as to bracket them with Beethoven and Schubert.

Idol gossip
Of course, the press still sniffed eagerly for scandal, which they found in the burgeoning drug culture – but even then, for a while at least, the Beatles were exempt. The heights to which the press's traditional double standard now aspired were seen in the events that followed the *News Of The World*'s publication of a series of four articles (starting on 5 February 1967) entitled 'Pop Stars And Drugs'. In the course of their investigation, two representatives of the *News Of The World* gained a revealing interview with Brian Jones about his drug-taking habits. Unfortunately, the paper ascribed the substance of this interview to Mick Jagger, and Jagger – not surprisingly – instituted libel proceedings.

The Stones, of course, had built much of their success on an outrageous image that was seized on gleefully by the press. But the *News Of The World* had made serious allegations at a time when large-scale LSD use was attracting considerable antagonism from the authorities. However, before Jagger's libel suit could be heard, the police raided Keith Richards' home in Sussex and arrested Richards, Jagger and

art dealer Robert Fraser on drugs charges.

The ensuing court case was marked by overt hostility to the morals of the young in general and rock stars in particular. Exceptionally severe sentences were passed and it was admitted that the *News Of The World* had tipped off the police on the night of the raid. The whole affair was loudly condemned in demonstrations, by many well-known people and even in the leader column of *The Times*. The *News Of The World* came in for special criticism on account of its dealings with the police, and the sentences were substantially reduced on appeal.

Perhaps the most interesting aspect of the whole business was the attention paid to the Beatles. The original series of *News Of The World* articles – whether through ignorance or reticence – took great care to dissociate rock's demi-gods from any allegations of drug abuse. The Beatles, like royalty, were not considered proper subjects for gossip or scandal. They had become, in a few short years, part of the British way of life.

But in response to the Jagger-Richards arrests, Paul McCartney revealed to *Life* magazine that he had taken LSD. Manager Brian Epstein followed with a similar admission. Together with John Lennon's statement to the London *Evening Standard* that 'the Beatles are now more popular than Christ', the effect was to tarnish the Beatles' image irretrievably. By the late Sixties it was 'open season', and there seemed to have been little progress since the disgraceful episode in 1958 when Jerry Lee Lewis was hounded out of Britain by a ferocious press armed with the knowledge of Lewis' marriage to his 13-year-old cousin.

But in one respect things had changed; the press's schizoid moralism now dis-

guised a new awareness of rock's youthful market. There was far too much money at stake to be condescending about the music and idols of the young. It was now recognised that rock could sell papers – and it was no less understood that the papers could sell rock.

The art of hype
The result of this realisation was the development of well-regulated hype, in which the press bartered what little integrity it aspired to in return for easy access to the rock publicity machine. The practice reached a new height of absurdity in 1968 with MGM Records' attempt to promote Boston as the next Liverpool or San Francisco. Articles appeared in *Newsweek*, *Time*, *Vogue*, *Village Voice* and the *Wall Street Journal* (among the non-music press) extolling the virtues of a number of groups including the intriguing Ultimate Spinach. There was little substance in this hype and the groups concerned all sank without trace – but not before they had helped to cement an intimate relationship between the press and the record industry that thenceforth grew from strength to strength.

One of the best-known hypes of the Seventies actually made a victim of Bruce Springsteen in 1975, when CBS Records decided to re-promote the performer on the basis of rock critic Jon Landau's personal assessment, 'I have seen the rock'n'roll future and its name is Bruce Springsteen'. The campaign won Springsteen simultaneous front-covers on *Newsweek* and *Time*, but he himself found it difficult to cope with and it may have retarded his career. The great Springsteen hype demonstrated, once and for all, that the press is more interested in rock phenomena than in rock music.

In fact, the Seventies was a period in which rock phenomena seemed to exist exclusively by courtesy of the newspapers. It was almost as though the press had decided that there were to be no more Beatles unless it said so. Superstars like Rod Stewart, Alice Cooper, David Bowie and Elton John could almost have been creatures of the media, so frequently did their most private lives apear in print. The late Eighties saw 'tabloid journalism' hit a new low with vendettas such as that pursued by *The Sun* against Elton John; a concerted hate campaign that threatened to end in legal action.

Punk and possibilities

With the advent of punk in the mid Seventies, a movement existed in rock which declared itself to be specifically against the mass media and their cosy relationship with rock, establishing instead its own network of communication in a plethora of fanzines and independent labels. This was a new departure from the established relationship between the media and the music industry.

It was the challenge to orthodox corporate control of the media (whether recording or print) that was threatening about punk. In the Sex Pistols, who would insist on attacking the media on the media's ground, the press found a natural target for its freshly rediscovered bile. Through 1977 the papers hurled torrents of abuse at the Pistols, whose behaviour – variously described as 'degenerate', 'shocking' and 'revolting' – was actually less offensive than that of many more successful rock stars who were regularly mentioned with great respect in the tabloids' gossip columns.

The press's problem with punk and the Pistols was that the punks didn't care to hide their behaviour or to maintain the illusion of politeness and decency. In a word, they had no respect for the press's claim to control public opinion through its control of the content and quality of information received by the public.

In the end, the press was more powerful than the movement. After the initial shock-horror mileage of punk had been exhausted, the papers were able to promote the 'new trend' (as the *Daily Express* had once intimated that they might do) and split it into its component elements: the socially rebellious, which it has since effectively ignored, and the aesthetically experimental, which held a place of honour in the review pages of the more serious newspapers in the Eighties. The anger of punk was thereby diluted by press patronage. Meanwhile the press continues to fight against the future promised by rock'n'roll.   GARY HERMAN

Hype! The front cover of a 1975 Newsweek *declares the birth of a brilliant new rock star – Bruce Springsteen, whose career suffered as a result. Outrage! The UK tabloids took savage delight in the 'disgusting' antics of the punks.*

NASTIES

PUNK ROCK

The violence, the money and the heartbreak in th

Sex Pistols stormed in new battle

week

making

of Rock

...Alamo

...io, Texas

... the Sex Pistols latest
...with his guitar. As cans,
..., sheriffs armed with
...en the group and the

... minutes while the riot
...re high on beer and
...marijuana.

Lead singer Johnny Rotten
continued to scream a string
of four-letter words during
the fusillade, stirring the
crowd to the point of mass
frenzy.

Randy's Rodeo is just down
the road from the site of the
battle of the Alamo—and it
almost looked like it.

The fury was so menacing
that Vicious, clad in black
leather, chains and padlocks,
had to be led to the back of
the stage, because friends of
the youth he hit were trying
to reach him.

The riot was sparked when
Vicious raising his bass guitar
like an executioner about to
bring down the axe, hit 19-
year-old Brien Falpin on the
head twice.

Craziness

The teenag...
the S...

FAN FARE

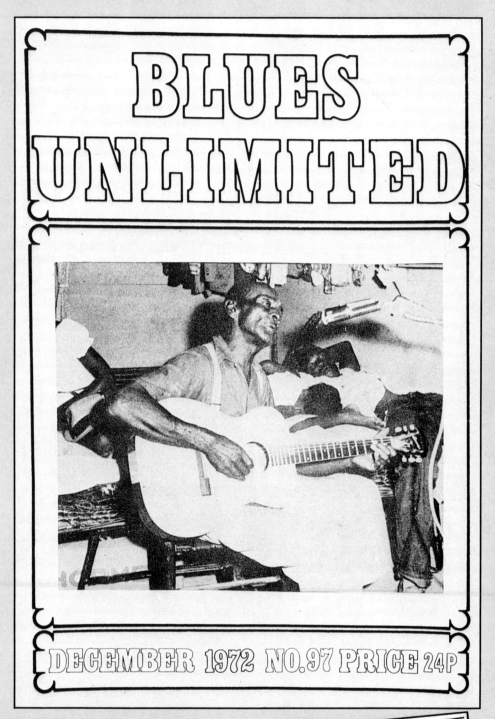

BLUES UNLIMITED

DECEMBER 1972 NO.97 PRICE 24P

The dedication of the DIY music journalists

IT ALL BEGAN, as did so much to do with rock 'n'roll, with the blues. *Blues Unlimited* appeared in April 1963, just before the British R&B boom; in comparison with other music publications, it was decidedly amateurish; but then, unlike them, it was written, published and distributed not by professionals but by fans. It was an immediate success: the first issue's 200 duplicated copies sold out at the princely price of

1s 6d each. More significantly, it was the first rock'n'roll fanzine, the first magazine written *by* as well as *for* fans.

This last feature captures the essential character of fanzines, whatever aspect of music they may be devoted to, and marks them off from fan magazines such as *Beatles Monthly* and *Elvis Monthly* on the one hand and the weekly pop papers on the other. Where the weeklies conform to market pressures – the state of the charts, the interests of their intended audience, and especially their dependence on advertising revenue – fanzines live in a completely different world. The editor may have to lick the stamps and crank the mimeograph machine, but in return he (or she, but generally he) gets to write at length about an aspect of music that is little covered in the weekly press.

The grass is greener

The Sixties blues boom was reflected by weeklies like *Melody Maker*, but it was only in the likes of *Blues Unlimited* that minor but influential figures like Juke Boy Bonner were given any serious treatment. *Blues Unlimited* and the magazines that followed – *R&B Monthly* and, most importantly, *Shout*, which dealt with the whole gamut of black music – were not just informed; they were influential far beyond their own small readership. They were read by music-press journalists who quickly popularised their ideas through specialist columns in the pop papers. This process was continued when several fanzine writers went on to pop papers themselves. Notable examples of this in Britain were Mike Leadbitter, Bill Millar and John Broven; in America the process went one stage further when fanzines transformed themselves into mainstream magazines for mass consumption.

Blues Unlimited also introduced notions of scholarship, long the preserve of jazz fans. Label and session discographies appeared with charming if alarming regularity, signalling the arrival of the 'trainspotting' mentality in the world of rock 'n'roll. Perhaps the strangest feature of *Blues Unlimited* was what might be called the 'grass is greener' syndrome. It was devoted to a music that was geographically far removed from Bexhill-on-Sea, Sussex, where the magazine was based. Subsequent fanzines tended to follow this principle; in the early Seventies, British fanzines were generally concerned with West Coast rock, while American publications dealt with British Beat. It wasn't until the arrival of punk that fanzines took account of what was happening on their own doorsteps.

In the wake of the hippie counterculture, the American fanzine explosion was fuelled by the same energy as *Rolling Stone*. With the exception of Greg Shaw, however, whose business activities quickly expanded beyond running *Who Put The Bomp!*, few of the fanzine publishers had the commercial vision, let alone the knowhow, of *Rolling Stone*'s Jann Wenner.

Founding fathers

The range was considerable. *Crawdaddy*, established in 1966, soon became a mainstream magazine, but for a few issues it was the mimeographed home of the truly bizarre rock criticism of Richard Meltzer and Sandy Pearlman, as well as the mysticism of Paul Williams. Between them they can claim to be the founding fathers of American 'intellectual' rock criticism. In complete contrast, Art Turco's *Record Exchanger* (established in 1969) was unfashionably concerned with the Fifties, especially the wonders of doo-wop, and record numbers. The most important, however, was Greg Shaw's *Who Put The Bomp!* (later abbreviated to *Bomp!*) which opened its doors in 1969. Shaw's heart was clearly in Britain – the magazine was eventually to publish an encyclopedia of British Beat over several issues – but of all the fanzine editors, Shaw was the most capable at controlling his own obsessions. Moreover, Shaw had worked on San Francisco's *Mojo Navigator* in 1966 and 1967, and had good contacts. *Bomp!* carried articles by writers of the standard of Greil Marcus and Lester Bangs, appeared fairly regularly (which few fanzines did) and introduced considerable variety into its issues. In America, it was Shaw's cheerful, unflagging enthusiasm that did more than anything else to encourage others.

As other fanzines appeared – notably *Trans-Oceanic Trouser Press* (which billed itself as 'America's only British rock magazine') and Alan Betrock's *Rock Market Place* – the discographies and wants lists tended to proliferate at the expense of quirky but likeable *and* informative oddities. An example of the latter is *Bomp*'s 'A short history of the weird world of Beatle novelties', in which Shaw's co-editor Ken Barnes reminisced about the likes of 'Treat Him Tender Maureen' (Apt 2508) by Angie and the Chiclettes, a song directed

Opposite: Two classic blues fanzines. Right: The indefatigable Greg Shaw, editor of Who Put The Bomp! *Below: A handful of American 'zines – including the newly named* Bomp!

Below: P. Frame Esq., rock genealogist and former editor of ZigZag (above left and right). Its rivals included Liquorice *(top left) and* Trouser Press *(top right).*

at Ringo Starr's newly-acquired wife.

By the mid Seventies, the revolution wrought by the American fanzines had come almost full circle. In the beginning they had existed in amiable opposition to commercial publications like *Rolling Stone* and *Creem*. Increasingly, however, the fanzines either came to be aimed at collectors (in which case strings of numbers replaced articles), or seemed no different from the mainstream magazines they still belaboured for commercialism; certainly they seemed to be written by the same people.

The Byrds in the trees

The British fanzine story is a similar but gentler version of the same story. *ZigZag*, established in 1969, carried an advert for the Record Room in its first issue, in which the shop claimed to be 'specialists in *Zig-Zag* music'. Subsequent issues quickly revealed what '*ZigZag* music' was: the Byrds, Love and Fairport Convention. Such tastes were hardly remarkable; what was new was founder Pete Frame's and his fellow chronicler Andy Childs' coverage of them. Frame's lasting contribution to rock scholarship is the group family tree, a form he made uniquely his own. *ZigZag*'s uncritical search for knowledge (the interview was the magazine's favoured format) gave its favourite artists a platform for their laid-back, mid-Seventies West Coast attitudes.

The magazine hardly changed its policy at all as it became more and more a part of the rock establishment. It continued along its own sweet path while the likes of T. Rex, Slade, David Cassidy and the Village People came and went, and it belatedly recognised the arrival of punk in 1977. Frame and Andy Childs (who graduated to editing *ZigZag* after he'd established his own fanzine, *Fat Angel*) joined the industry, and other *ZigZag* writers joined the pop press, but the magazine somehow remained untainted. In its shade there flourished a second division of British fanzines, which included *Liquorice, Bam-Balam, Hot Wacks, Dark Star* and *Omaha Rainbow* (whose hero, John Stewart, regularly dominated issues; but even that wasn't unusual – Little Richard was the sole subject of *Penniman News*).

Like their American counterparts, the British fanzines influenced record companies' re-issue policies and the opinions of other journalists, and brought less obviously commercial talents like Ry Cooder to a wider audience. Similarly, as the Eighties grew closer and the 'zines became more nostalgic, they made themselves irrelevant. With few exceptions, the most notable of which was *ZigZag* itself, they were made obsolete when punk came along. Their replacements, the punkzines – which, following the example set by Mark Perry's *Sniffin' Glue*, appeared in a great rush – served a more immediate and important purpose; but the innocence of the first generation of fanzines remains appealing.   PHIL HARDY

Single Images

Rock's introspective singer-songwriters serenaded the close of the Sixties

IF THE MEDIA were to be believed, 1969's Woodstock Festival was proof that hippie dreams of togetherness might be realised. In reality, however, those dreams had already died. The San Francisco scene had long become commercialised, the best of the psychedelic and acid-rock bands had been annexed by the industry and the naive anti-establishment protestations of the hippie mass had changed nothing. By the turn of the decade, while their younger siblings were being seduced by the apolitical hard rock of Grand Funk Railroad, Led Zeppelin and Black Sabbath, the original hippies were 'mellowing'. A mood of introspection – examination of the self rather than society at large – had taken hold of the older rock audience. It was to this that the new breed of singer-songwriter appealed.

The successful singer-songwriters of the early Seventies came from varying backgrounds. Like Bob Dylan, some – Joni Mitchell, Leonard Cohen, Carly Simon – had their musical roots in folk music; others, like Carole King, Randy Newman and Laura Nyro, had served their apprenticeship in Tin Pan Alley, while Cat Stevens had started out in straight pop. But although 'singer-songwriter' was, in effect, more a label imposed by the rock press than a genuine musical genre, the artists concerned were united by their simplicity of approach: all could perform competently as soloists, accompanying themselves on guitar or piano, and all – initially at least – used the sparest of musical accompaniment on stage and record. The words they sang assumed an equal importance to the music – and those words were, for the most part, intensely personal. They spoke not of the overthrow of society or the evils of war but of personal relationships and inner conflicts; the 'we' of the hippies had been replaced by 'I'.

Pale stars

If the words and music of the singer-songwriters were contrary to rock traditions, so were their public images. Rather than adopting the stereotyped 'fast and dangerous' rock'n'roll lifestyle, they presented themselves as sensitive and reserved figures. They shunned glamour – few possessed conventional good looks, most dressed modestly and none used overt sexuality as a selling point – and they sought privacy. Their appeal lay in their self-absorption.

It is somewhat ironic that it should have been Joni Mitchell who wrote 'Woodstock', the theme song for those 'three days of peace and love'. From the start, her preoccupations had been personal; 'Both Sides Now' (which brought her to notice when recorded by Judy Collins) was a song of mild self-criticism, while 'I Had A King', the opening track of her first album, dissected the failure of her marriage. Despite the untypical 'Woodstock' and the 1970

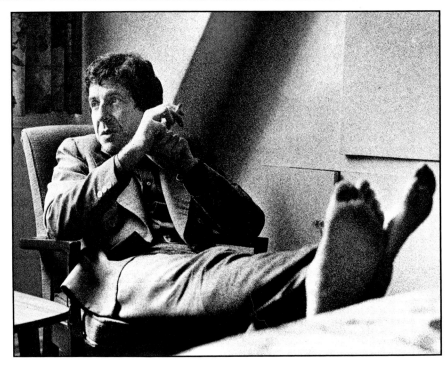

hit 'Big Yellow Taxi' – her contribution to the ecology movement – she always sounded most confident when singing about herself.

Cloaks and shadows

Leonard Cohen was another songwriter whose path to solo success was aided by Judy Collins; formerly a folk singer, Collins' own standing was based on interpretations of new or unknown writers. The antithesis of a rock star, Cohen was over 30 when he recorded his first album. His voice was nasal and monotonous, while his face – except when photographed in 'mysterious' shadows – was forgettable. But his sombre and often bitter lyrics, drawled over a minimalistic musical backdrop, revealed a rare sophistication and insight.

While both Cohen and Joni Mitchell had a gift for sometimes savage self-examination, the approach of Cat Stevens, one of the few singer-songwriters to emerge from Britain, was somewhat different. Cloaked in obscurity, his words only *hinted* at introspection; coupled with the singer's soul-searching but retiring image, they proved equally soul-stirring.

The success of Mitchell, Cohen and Stevens reflected the fact that the youth of the Sixties was growing up; conflict between generations was giving way to strivings for emotional security. As the young-adult album-buying public grew more conservative, new and more middle-of-the-road singer-songwriters, as exemplified by James Taylor, Carole King and John Denver, would arrive to take full advantage of changing musical tastes.

TOM HIBBERT

Leonard Cohen's successful transition from poet and author to million-selling singer-songwriter confirmed the growing importance of lyrics in late Sixties rock.

ROCK '70

As the Sixties drew to a close, the rebellious, anti-establishment spirit of previous years seemed to fade as a new mood of brooding and introspection took hold. Though loud rock continued to make itself heard – Grand Funk Railroad, Led Zeppelin and Black Sabbath all notched up million-selling albums – 1970 was the year in which singer-songwriters came to the fore. James Taylor (hailed by *Time* magazine as the figurehead of the post-Woodstock generation), Joni Mitchell and Leonard Cohen were among the most successful of this new breed of soul-searching rock artist who put themselves rather than society under the microscope; even John Lennon, on his *Plastic Ono Band* LP, appeared to replace his former political stance with something more personal.

The Jackson Five announced their arrival with a soul-flavoured brand of pop that brought them four US Number 1 hits, but the singles charts on both sides of the Atlantic generally revealed a dearth of teen-oriented acts. The stage was set for the emergence of glam-rock in the early Seventies to attempt an antidote to rock's overt self-consciousness.

January
6 Crosby, Stills, Nash and Young make their first appearance on English soil at London's Albert Hall.
21 *Change Of Habit*, the last film in which Elvis Presley takes an acting role, is released.
31 Singer Carl Wayne leaves the Move to pursue a career on the cabaret circuit.
Blues harp-player Slim Harpo dies of a heart attack at the age of 56.

February
11 Arlo Guthrie attends the British premiere of his film *Alice's Restaurant* at the London Pavilion.
13 Black Sabbath's eponymous debut album is released; although the group is relatively unknown, the LP soon charts on both sides of the Atlantic and goes on to sell over a million copies.
28 'Love Grows' by Edison Lighthouse tops the UK charts, while Simon and Garfunkel are Number 1 in the US with 'Bridge Over Troubled Water'.

March
6 Charles Manson, who is on trial for the murder of Sharon Tate and others, releases an album entitled *Lie*.
18 Andrew Loog Oldham's Immediate label goes into liquidation. Its roster had included such acts as the Small Faces, the Nice, Chris Farlowe and P. P. Arnold.
20 Dana wins the Eurovision Song

Mystic murderer Charles Manson (above) moved into rock with an LP called Lie, *while Fleetwood Mac guitarist Peter Green (right) left rock for the mystic life. Safely back in the mainstream, Dana (below) won the Eurovision Song Contest.*

Contest, held in Amsterdam, with 'All Kinds Of Everything'. The Irish chanteuse beats the UK entrant, Mary Hopkin, into second place.
David Bowie marries American Mary Angela Barnett in Bromley, Kent.

April
1 Drummer Spencer Dryden leaves Jefferson Airplane, to be replaced by Joey Covington.
4 Simon and Garfunkel hold the UK Number 1 position in both the singles and LP charts with 'Bridge Over Troubled

Water' and the album of the same name. The LP remains at the top for 35 weeks.
17 *McCartney*, the first solo album by Paul McCartney, is released. He simultaneously announces in a press release that the Beatles no longer exist.
19 Violence erupts when Hell's Angels run amok at a Who concert at Leicester University; Pete Townshend requires eight stitches for a gash in his head.

May
Woodstock, a triple LP set recorded at the previous year's festival, is released. Despite being the most expensive rock album set ever, it sells over a million copies within four months.
5 Simon and Garfunkel perform at London's Albert Hall before an ecstatic sellout crowd.
16 The England World Cup Squad become the first football team to top the charts when 'Back Home' shoots to Number 1.
25 In the week that Fleetwood Mac's 'The Green Manalishi' enters the UK Top Fifty, Peter Green announces his departure from the group.

June
6 Commenting on Britain's forthcoming General Election, Eric Clapton tells *Melody Maker*: 'I shall vote for B. B. King. The first thing any new MP should do is to apply the mind to producing a self-tuning electric guitar.'
13 The Beatles' 'The Long And Winding Road' reaches Number 1 in the States. It is not released as a single in the UK, however.
14 Derek and the Dominos featuring Eric Clapton make their debut appearance at London's Lyceum.

July
4 The Rattles become the first German group ever to appear in the US charts when 'The Witch' enters the Hot Hundred.
12 Janis Joplin makes her first appearance with her new group, the Full Tilt Boogie Band, in Louisville, Kentucky.

is the best-selling single of the year – the only time Presley achieves this feat.
23 Lou Reed performs with the Velvet Underground for the last time at New York's Max's Kansas City.

September
3 Al 'Blind Owl' Wilson, guitarist and harmonica player of Canned Heat, is found dead in a sleeping bag in Topanga Canyon, Los Angeles, at the age of 24.
5 The Applejacks, who have never been able to follow up the success of 'Tell Me When' (a UK Number 7 hit in 1964), finally split up.
18 Jimi Hendrix is found dead in Notting Hill Gate, London.
26 Led Zeppelin play two shows before 24,000 people at New York's Madison Square Garden.

October
1 Jimi Hendrix is buried in his hometown of Seattle, Washington.
2 *After The Goldrush*, Neil Young's third solo album, is released.
4 Janis Joplin is found dead in her Hollywood flat.
9 Donovan marries Linda Lawrence at Windsor registry office.
23 Los Angeles' largest rock auditorium, Winterland, reopens with a bill that includes Jefferson Airplane, the Grateful Dead, Hot Tuna and the New Riders of the Purple Sage.
31 'Woodstock' by Matthews Southern Comfort heads the UK singles charts, while the Jackson Five top the US Hot Hundred with 'I'll Be There'.

November
6 Jim Morrison of the Doors is released on bail of 50,000 dollars pending an appeal against his conviction for indecent exposure in Miami the previous year.
11 Bob Dylan's obscure 'novel' *Tarantula* is published in the US.
16 Grand Funk Railroad's *Live Album* is released; the double LP has advance orders totalling 750,000, and by the end of the year has sold in excess of two million copies.

December
6 *Gimme Shelter*, the film of the Rolling Stones' Altamont concert, is released on the anniversary of the event.
11 John Lennon's *Plastic Ono Band* album, on which the singer avows 'I don't believe in Beatles', is released.
12 Dave Edmunds' revival of 'I Hear You Knocking', a hit in 1955 for Gale Storm and again in 1961 for Fats Domino, is Number 1 in the UK.
20 The Who play a Christmas charity concert at the Roundhouse for the 'needy'; they are joined on stage by Elton John.

TOM HIBBERT, JENNY DAWSON

18 Arthur Brown is arrested in Palermo, Sicily, for stripping on stage.
25 Creedence Clearwater Revival's 'Lookin' Out My Back Door' is released; within five weeks the record has sold over a million copies. It becomes the group's seventh consecutive single to go gold.

August
5 Denny Laine (ex-Moody Blues), Trevor Burton (ex-Move) and drummer Alan White join forces to create short-lived Birmingham supergroup Balls.
7 The Popanalia pop festival, held near Nice, France, is abandoned after 12 hours when members of radical group Les Companions de la Route vandalise the stage and equipment.
8 'The Wonder Of You' becomes the last Elvis Presley single to reach the UK Number 1 position during his lifetime. The record, which spends five weeks at the top,

BOTH SIDES OF *Joni*

Joni Mitchell: from folk to jazz-rock fusion

OF ALL the singer-songwriters who emerged at the beginning of the Seventies, only Joni Mitchell has been able to build significantly on the music which first made her name. While many of her peers were finding it increasingly difficult to follow up their first success, Mitchell was developing from a gifted, folksy songwriter into a popular artist of unusual breadth and originality. Always innovative, Mitchell never ceased to absorb new influences. She cast the traditional rock devices aside in favour of the less-structured framework of jazz. To describe her work as jazz-rock, however, would be to do it an injustice, for whatever Mitchell turned her attention to she made her own.

She was born Roberta Joan Anderson on 7 November 1943 and brought up in the Canadian prairies of Alberta by her middle-class family. Her first instrument was the ukelele, learnt from a Pete Seeger instructional record. She discovered folk just as it was enjoying its largest revival, one which would have enormous implications for popular music. As Mitchell later put it: 'Rock'n'roll went through a really dumb vanilla period. And during that period, folk came in to fill the hole.'

After visiting the Mariposa Folk Festival in 1964, she abandoned her art-school course and began singing in the coffee bars of Toronto's Yorktown folk scene. In 1965 she married fellow folkie Chuck Mitchell, with whom she worked together for a while in a duo. But the marriage was short-lived. After moving to Detroit, from where they hoped to conquer the eastern states folk circuit, the couple went their separate ways. (In 1983 she was married again, to bassist Larry Klein.) Mitchell based herself in New York, booking her own tours and handling her own finances.

Rush for stardom

In Detroit, the Mitchells had met Tom Rush, one of the more adventurous new folk-singers. Rush tried to get Judy Collins to cover one of Joni Mitchell's songs, 'Urge For Going', in 1966. Collins demurred, so Rush recorded it himself and scored a local hit with it. Mitchell herself did not record the song until 1972.

Tom Rush's next LP, the commercially and critically successful *The Circle Game*, contained two of Mitchell's songs, including the title track. That same year, 1967, Judy Collins featured two Mitchell tunes on her LP *Wildflowers*. One was 'Michael From Mountains'; the other, 'Both Sides Now', which made the US Top Ten and established Mitchell as a major songwriter. By this time, Mitchell had got herself a record deal with Warner-Reprise. Originally Frank Sinatra's label, Reprise was in need of some hip credibility by 1967; that year, the label signed Jimi Hendrix, Randy Newman, Arlo Guthrie and Joni Mitchell herself. Elliot Roberts, who was responsible for the signing, remained Mitchell's manager into the Eighties, a role he also fulfilled for her fellow countryman Neil Young.

Joni Mitchell's self-titled debut album, produced by former Byrd David Crosby, was released in the summer of 1968. Like her songs for Rush and Collins, *Joni Mitchell* and its successor, *Clouds* (1969),

The artistic development of Joni Mitchell (above) took her from idealistic youth to confident maturity. Inset opposite: The young folk singer at Newport Folk Festival in 1967. Opposite: The assured rock star of the mid Seventies, stunning packed houses.

displayed her obvious way with words and flair for melody. But neither album suggested that Mitchell was anything more than another folksy 'poet' whose main function would be to furnish more gifted vocalists with the occasional song, and she herself was later to call *Clouds* her artistic nadir. Her phrasing was locked firmly within the folk tradition, and she sounded uncomfortably self-conscious in the recording studio. Her songs tended to be dour; her portrait of her ex-husband, 'I Had A King', was, despite its vitriol, too solemn to make the impact of, say, Dylan's epistle to rejected love, 'Positively Fourth Street'. Many of her songs indulged in fanciful imagery inspired by the natural world, a tendency that was reinforced by her move to California during the last phase of flower-power.

By this time, Mitchell had become part of the Los Angeles Laurel Canyon rock-star community, a predicament reflected in the title of her third LP, *Ladies Of The Canyon* (1970). She was also living with former Hollies star Graham Nash; in case the public didn't get the message, Nash and Mitchell wrote their respective ditties about it. CSN&Y recorded 'Our House', while the somewhat slight 'Willy' was included on *Ladies Of The Canyon*.

Not all the songs on the album were so disposable, fortunately. Mitchell was beginning to take musical chances. Piano now shared the limelight with Joni's acoustic guitar, and the feel of the music was closer to rock. Jim Horn's exuberant sax playing made a fitting coda to 'For Free'. This song introduced one of Mitchell's recurrent concerns, the paradoxes of making a living out of self-expression. As time went by, she would address herself more and more to the problem of her relationship with her audience.

Yellow and blue

Ladies Of The Canyon also included 'Big Yellow Taxi', which became her first UK hit single. A great little plug for ecology, the song was a vocal *tour de force*, delicately poised between exuberance and regret. 'The Circle Game', which Rush had recorded earlier, saw Mitchell breathing new life into the traditional folk metaphor of the seasons as a symbol for ageing. And, despite its naivety, 'Woodstock' was a landmark for Mitchell. While Crosby, Stills, Nash and Young never shook off their identification with the song – their frenzied electric arrangement appeared on their album *Déjà Vu* (1970) – Mitchell was only briefly associated with that myth, in spite of having written its theme tune.

By the end of 1970, Joni Mitchell had established herself as a recording artist in her own right. Commercial logic would have suggested a world tour to consolidate her success, but Mitchell was uncomfortable with the role of rock star. Instead, she decided to withdraw from the limelight, travelling in Europe and sailing from Jamaica to California with David Crosby and Graham Nash. It was a time of reassessment: 'Like falling to earth,' she

tended to writing telling songs about other people's experiences as well as her own, such as 'Cold Blue Steel And Sweet Fire' and her 'Beethoven' number 'Judgement Of The Moon And Stars (Ludwig's Tune)'.

Mitchell's fans had to wait until 1974 for another album. With *Court And Spark* and the live double album *Miles Of Aisles* – and an extensive tour including two visits to Britain – they were amply rewarded. Working with Tom Scott's elegant jazz-rock combo, the LA Express, Mitchell was now projecting an image closer to night-club chic than folksy hippie. Scott's bright, immaculate arrangements, deftly executed by the band, propelled Mitchell's music to new heights of expressiveness.

Richly melodic and featuring some singularly sharp songs of observation, *Court And Spark* gave Mitchell an unprecedented commercial success. She still used her songs to reveal her own inner struggles, although a kind of giddy humour now underlay some of the material. This was most noticeable on 'Twisted', an Annie Ross song – the first time Mitchell had sung a song by another writer on her albums, and proof of her increasing desire to jettison rock for jazz.

Summer sophistication
The Hissing Of Summer Lawns (1975) confirmed this change of direction. Exceptional for its dearth of confessional material, it was even more elaborately arranged than its predecessor. It touched levels of sophistication rare in pop, both musically and in terms of its subject matter, for the most part a commentary on middle-class American suburbia.

Mitchell carried off this ambitious experiment with remarkable aplomb. Unfortunately much of her trailblazing fell on deaf ears, particularly in America where the critics sharpened their knives for a ritual shredding.

Undaunted, Mitchell's next work, *Hejira* (1976) was just as adventurous. In sharp contrast to the luxuriant textures of *The Hissing Of Summer Lawns*, *Hejira* echoed the stark beauty of *Blue*, only this time Mitchell's rhythms derived from jazz and not rock. Named after Muhammad's flight from Mecca to Medina, the LP sprang out of Mitchell's own flight from a relationship. Filled with the restless imagery of travel, the songs indicated an acceptance of the impossibility of reconciling the demands of love and freedom.

In five years Mitchell had made as many great albums. She'd assimilated rock and jazz influences in a unique way. She'd written about a range of subjects and situations with an incisiveness and wit unprecedented in rock. Her more recent work

Above left: Joni Mitchell jams with B.B. King at the Bread and Roses Festival in Berkeley, California in 1980. Right: Playing at Wembley, September 1979. Far right: On stage with Tom Scott, whose LA Express backed Mitchell live and on record in the mid Seventies.

said. 'It felt almost as if I'd had my head in the clouds long enough . . . Shortly after that time, everything began to change. There were fewer adjectives in my poetry. Fewer curlicues to my drawing. Everything began to get more bold and solid in a way.'

That year's sabbatical produced the album *Blue* (1971). Where Mitchell's idealism has previously got the better of her, she now told the story from the other side, taking a wry and anti-sentimental look at both personal relationships and public affairs. 'California' saw the author of 'Woodstock' admit, 'That was just a dream some of us had'. Despite this new mood, *Blue* was an international success, and established Mitchell at quite a different level. The generation that had been told it could have everything – the world included – responded to her mood of disillusionment.

Instrumentally, too, the LP was a breakthrough. Apart from Joni Mitchell's acoustic guitar work, the contributions of Stephen Stills, James Taylor and Sneaky Pete of the Flying Burrito Brothers (on pedal steel guitar) all formed a supple and rhythmic backdrop. And, for the first time, Mitchell was using her full vocal range, singing with passion and skill.

After an extensive American and European tour, accompanied by the then-unknown Jackson Browne, she retired to Canada to contemplate her next move. The hippie in Mitchell had taken a battering on *Blue*, but she was still trying to put some of the dream into practice: 'I actually tried to move back to Canada, into the bush. My idea was to follow my advice and get back to nature.'

In contrast to the restrained arrangements of *Blue*, the subsequent *For The Roses* (1972) featured the elaborate horn and woodwind arrangements of Tom Scott, though there was still room for Mitchell's doleful piano. Much of the LP dealt with the ambiguities of exploiting one's personal history for fame and fortune. Mitchell's new maturity, however, ex-

had taken on a mystical quality as her desire for musical progress seemed to mirror an inner search.

A reckless release?

It was only on *Don Juan's Reckless Daughter* (1977) that Mitchell began to show signs of losing her sustained creative momentum. Yet there was much to applaud on the record, particularly the playing of Wayne Shorter and Jaco Pastorius from Weather Report.

In 1979, Joni Mitchell took her preoccupation with jazz to its logical conclusion, collaborating with that giant of post-war jazz, Charles Mingus. The resulting LP, *Mingus*, her most ambitious yet, proved a critical success but a commercial failure. If Mitchell was to be admired for her audacity in making the album, in truth it failed to match her previous triumphs.

Mingus was followed by a pregnant silence. In 1982 Mitchell returned with *Wild Things Run Free*, a hollowish resumé of what had gone before. For once Mitchell was not, as she had remarked in 1979, 'pushing the limits . . . or the perimeters of what entails a popular song'.

Marriage to bass player Larry Klein saw Mitchell retreat into her shell still further, releasing only *Dog Eat Dog* (1985), a patchy but more interesting album produced by synth wizard Thomas Dolby.

But 1988's *Chalk Mark In A Rainstorm* saw her finally emerge from the shadow of past glories with the help of some famous friends (Peter Gabriel, Tom Petty and Willie Nelson).   STEVE CLARKE

Joni Mitchell
Recommended Listening

Blue (Reprise K44128) (Includes: All I Want, A Case Of You, This Flight Tonight, Carey, Little Green); *Court And Spark* (Asylum SYLA8756) (Includes: Free Man In Paris, Car On A Hill, Raised On Robbery, Twisted, People's Parties).

JUDY COLLINS

An enduring talent and an influential voice

THE GREAT TRIUMVIRATE of Joan Baez, Bob Dylan and Judy Collins that led the Sixties folk revival on campuses across the US was largely responsible for putting the folk ethic across to a mass audience. By 1963 they were enjoying considerable popular success, although their brand of folk music was far removed from the commercial sound of the Kingston Trio or Peter, Paul and Mary. Since her recording debut with *A Maid Of Constant Sorrow* in 1961, Judy Collins has explored many genres. Today, it would be wrong to label her a folk-singer; her constant experimentation and growth are the reasons why she has continued to play a significant role in the ever-changing history of rock.

Born in Seattle, on 1 May 1939, Judith Marjorie Collins was the eldest of five children. Her blind father, Charles 'Chuck' Collins, was a self-taught musician and a well-known radio personality. The family moved to Los Angeles when Judy was four. There, she began piano lessons, and also appeared on her father's radio shows – singing the songs of Irving Berlin and Rodgers and Hart. On to Denver where Judy's musical gifts were further encouraged, at 10 she began studying with the distinguished pianist and conductor Dr Antonia Brico. At 13 she played a Mozart piano concerto with the Denver Businessmen's Symphony Orchestra, and she seemed destined for a career in classical music. Like so many of her peers, however, she was drawn by the sounds of the Fifties folk revival and at 16 she quit piano in favour of the guitar, teaching herself from records.

On graduating from high school, Collins took up a scholarship at MacMurray College, Illinois. Dropping out after a brief spell, she returned to Denver to marry her childhood sweetheart, Peter Taylor. It was during their first summer together, in a log cabin high in the Rockies, that Judy began to immerse herself seriously in folk music; mountain travellers would stay the night, sit around an open fire and sing the songs of their heritage, particularly the songs of Woody Guthrie. (Collins later recalled this period of her life in 'Song For Martin'.)

Judy began her professional singing career in Boulder in early 1959, following the birth of son Clark. Summer 1960 was spent at Chicago's famed Gate of Horn, where Lord Buckley would do the late show. Jac Holzman of Elektra Records heard her in New York in early 1961, singing at Gerde's Folk City. Immediately, he signed her up and *A Maid Of Constant Sorrow* – featuring traditional material – was released that October. *Golden Apples Of The Sun* followed in July 1962 and *Time* praised her as 'a major contender for the female folk crown' – a view that was confirmed by her debut at Carnegie Hall later that year. But the closing months of 1962 also brought traumas: emotionally

Three faces of Judy Collins: the young singer's poppy 'English' look, with dyed hair and heavy eyeliner (left) gave way to a more serious, folky image (above). She latterly presented herself as a sophisticated entertainer (below left).

drained from the break-up of her marriage and physically exhausted from all the touring, Judy Collins contracted tuberculosis and was hospitalised for six months.

Talent spotting
By the time Judy returned to Greenwich Village in 1963, the folk revival had spread beyond the campuses and the new generation of poet/singer-songwriters represented by *Broadside* magazine – notably Bob Dylan – was very much in the ascendant. *Judy Collins No 3* (1963) reflected all the trends, as did *Concert* and *Fifth Album* in 1964 and 1965 respectively.

With *In My Life*, recorded in London in 1966, and *Wildflowers* (1967), Collins emerged as something of a musical visionary. Not only was she now a foremost interpreter of contemporary talent, she was also responsible for bringing Leonard Cohen, Joni Mitchell and Randy Newman to the attention of the public. She drew from the theatre, using songs from Peter Brook's Aldwych Theatre production of Peter Weiss' *The Marat/Sade*, as well as from Jacques Brel, Dylan, Donovan and Lennon and McCartney.

Throughout the late Sixties and early Seventies, Judy Collins continued to diversify. The 1968 album *Who Knows Where The Time Goes* featured her own backing band, which included Stephen Stills on guitar. In 1972 she used the sound of whales calling to each other on the LP *Whales And Nightingales*, an album that produced a second American and British hit single (following her moving version of Joni Mitchell's 'Both Sides Now') with her arrangement of the traditional hymn 'Amazing Grace'. While continuing to present her interpretations of other people's

songs, Judy Collins' own songwriting talents came to the fore on her later albums. *True Stories And Other Dreams* (1973) presented some emotive and stylised originals – notably, 'Che' (Guevara) and 'Song For Martin'. There was then a two-year hiatus before *Judith* (1975) and *Bread And Roses* (1976). 'Send In The Clowns' – a big hit on both sides of the Atlantic – was culled from the former and was the first of several Stephen Sondheim numbers to be afforded the Collins treatment.

Peace moves
Not surprisingly, music remains at the heart of Judy Collins' life and experience, though it is by no means *all* she lives for. She is also a talented painter and writer; in 1969, she spent a summer season acting opposite Stacy Keach in Ibsen's *Peer Gynt*; and in 1973-74, she directed a well-received film documentary, *Antonia: A Portrait Of The Woman*, about her former piano teacher. These talents she sees as 'all part of the same creative drive'. She has remained politically active throughout, although she has never allowed her politics to dictate to her musical career.

Like so many of her Sixties colleagues, Judy Collins has since all too frequently been regarded as old-fashioned. However, she never set out to compete in the charts and, in many ways, has always been something of a musician's musician. As an interpreter of contemporary song she is first rank; as a discoverer of raw talent, she is unsurpassed. She was a key figure in the development of folk-rock into a serious art form – a fact that is perhaps best exemplified by her own sophisticated songwriting.

ELIZABETH M THOMSON

Songs from a ROOM

The inside story of Leonard Cohen

It was in 1956 that the work of Leonard Cohen first appeared before the general public in book form, an event that marked his transformation from unofficial poet laureate of McGill University to fully-fledged writer. While Anthony Eden grappled with the problems of Suez, the Soviets faced the war of the Hungarian Revolution and General Eisenhower began his last presidential term, the protest era was being cautiously ushered in by the Beat Generation. Although Leonard Cohen was essentially a child of the Fifties, he has come to be regarded as a figure of the Sixties when the poet/singer-songwriter became a new type of idol.

Poetic licence
Cohen was born in Montreal on 21 September 1934, the son of middle-class Jewish parents. On graduating from high school, he studied English Literature at McGill and Columbia Universities. It was at McGill that Cohen's poetic gift was discovered, and his work was chosen to inaugurate the McGill Poetry Series, a collection of books designed to bring to public notice the work of the university's more outstanding students.

Referring to his anthology *Let Us Compare Mythologies*, written during his teenage years and published in 1956, Cohen has since commented: 'A lot (of the poems) are as good, if not better, than anything I'm doing today in that field.' Reviewing the collection in *The Fiddlehead*, Allan Donaldson noted that Cohen's 'handling of the character and problems of his people strikes one particularly for its imaginativeness and honesty'. His observation is a key to almost all of Cohen's work, including his best-known novel *Beautiful Losers*, published in 1966.

The early Sixties anthology entitled *Parasites of Heaven* assumes a particular historical importance, since it contained five of Cohen's poems that were later to become songs: 'Suzanne', 'Teachers', 'Master Song', 'Avalanche' and 'Fingerprints'. It was a mid-Sixties performance by Judy Collins that had inspired Cohen to write songs. Her renditions of 'Suzanne' and 'Dress Rehearsal Rag' (on her 1966 album *In My Life*) brought Cohen international recognition as a songwriter, turning artistic acclaim into popular success.

Collins continued to champion Cohen's talent in the years that followed, recording a number of his songs. In 1967 she brought him on stage at a concert in New York's Central Park. The poet was almost too frightened to sing, and the late Lillian Roxon wrote that he looked 'diffident, handsome and very vulnerable'. A couple of months later, he debuted in his own right at the Newport Folk Festival. In 1959, the Newport showcase had brought a young Joan Baez into the spotlight; in 1963, Bob Dylan had emerged as 'crown

Good guys don't wear white: Leonard Cohen (opposite and above), sardonic singer of sentiment and cynicism.

prince'; and in 1967 Leonard Cohen and Joni Mitchell – fellow Canadians – triumphed there. Both owed their success to Judy Collins, who was on the festival's board of directors.

Finally, in 1968, an album appeared: *Songs Of Leonard Cohen*. Within a few months, a Cohen cult of considerable magnitude had grown up, and it became a cliché to spend a night alone with a bottle of burgundy and a Leonard Cohen LP, basking in acute romantic agony. *Songs Of Leonard Cohen* was a powerful first record, including 'Suzanne', 'The Stranger Song', 'Sisters Of Mercy', 'So Long, Marianne' and 'Hey, That's No Way To Say Goodbye'. To quote Lillian Roxon again: 'His thin and diffident voice made for a realism that seemed to bring him right into the room with the listener . . . there is a hypnotic repetitiousness that makes the album a calm antidote for loneliness . . .'

Cohen's emergence as a singer-songwriter at a time when he was a *cause célèbre* of the world's literary establishment did not owe entirely to inspiration, however; it was also an economic necessity. As he later commented: 'I couldn't pay the grocery bills . . . [but] anyone who leaves writing to try to make a living as a singer would have to be a fool. If there's anything chancier than writing, it's singing.'

In 1956, a poet could not have existed in the music scene, for anything beyond three minutes of moon/June rhymes about boy-meets-girl, falls in love and lives happily ever after was considered far too heavy for popular consumption. Bob Dylan made it possible to be a poet *and* a rock star, but even he was well-established before he began to employ the rich allusive imagery that characterised his *Highway 61 Revisited* and *Blonde On Blonde* period. Dylan's achievement enabled Cohen to enter the music scene as a poet first and foremost. Cohen saw no anomaly in his being both a poet and a singer-songwriter. He has said: 'I was always a musician, so I always had a feeling of the closeness between the written lyric and the lyric that is

sung. Indeed, they were the same at one point, and they've always been the same for me. Narrative song, lyric expression migrate easily from music to the page.'

Songs Of Leonard Cohen was a runaway best-seller – much to the surprise of the DJs, who hadn't given it needletime. 1969's *Songs From A Room* was similarly successful, although a less consistent album than its predecessor. Attempting to place contemporary despair and violence in relation to the European holocaust, the album's high point was 'Bird On The Wire'. *Songs Of Love And Hate* appeared in 1971, and was a more remarkable opus, containing three of Cohen's best songs: 'Dress Rehearsal Rag', 'Joan Of Arc' and 'Famous Blue Raincoat' – exquisite expressions of anguish, detached objectivity and resignation, respectively. Cohen had also begun to tour and, in 1972, Tony Palmer filmed a *cinéma-vérité*-style movie of his European jaunt, entitled *Bird On A Wire*. An album, *Live Songs*, appeared the following year.

In 1974, with *New Skin For The Old Ceremony*, Cohen leaned heavily toward cabaret-style soft rock and a much fuller sound, with the help of producer/arranger John Lissauer. Cohen's work had always contained a good deal of sardonic self-parody; now the humour was more manifest, as in lines such as 'You were the sensitive woman, I was the Very Reverend Freud/You were the manual orgasm/I was the dirty little poet' (from 'Is This What You Wanted?').

Lost words
1977 saw Cohen in the studio with the legendary Phil Spector to produce *Death Of A Ladies' Man*. The album showed Spector at his most extravagant – as Cohen put it, 'in his Wagnerian phase'. Cohen was far from happy with the end product, although he by no means disavowed the content: 'The songs are very, very good and there are some of my best lyrics on that album . . . (but) the words got lost in the mix, from which I was excluded by both secrecy and armed bodyguards.'

Recent Songs, his 1979 release, was very much a return to the spirit of his early albums, although musically it was much more sophisticated, using some fine instrumental touches – including a Mariachi band and a gypsy violinist. Cohesive, thematic and replete with richly ornate, symbolic imagery and allegorical reflections, it is a fully-fledged romantic album which once again mixes sex with religion – here with a droll sense of the absurd. Cohen's ironic delivery ideally suits the ambiguous emotions expressed in the lyrics.

To call Leonard Cohen a folk-singer is an inaccurate pigeonholing of his talent, for his melodies bear little relation to traditional Anglo-American ballads. He remains an intellectual poet, working mainly on the stage, rather than the page, fusing poetry and music in a very exacting manner. His lyrics are meticulously chosen and, with his scholarly linguistic precision, Cohen has brought to rock music an awareness of the classical themes and formal disciplines of poetry. His word-weaving and imagery can hypnotise, and Cohen punctuates the trance by the juxtaposition of everyday speech and elaborate metaphor.

Raincoats and reunions

A six-year silence followed *Recent Songs* before Cohen returned with a volume—*Book Of Mercy,* which won the Canadian Authors' Association literary prize in 1985—and an album, the wryly titled *Various Positions.* Former backing singer Jennifer Warnes received plaudits for her album of Cohen songs *Famous Blue Raincoat* (1986), and the man himself broke cover two years later with *I'm Your Man,* his best album in years.

Cynics and detractors might say that Cohen appeals only to the professionally depressed and self-consciously tormented aficionados of gloom. True, he can be self-pitying and indulgent, lacing his songs with seconal, razor blades and consuming fires, but to denigrate his talent is to denigrate rock itself. Far from being simply a doom-mongering writer singing in a gloom-laden monotone, Cohen's voice is one of the most intimately expressive sounds in contemporary music.

ELIZABETH M THOMSON

Right: Poet-balladeer Cohen strums his guitar. Inset above: On stage in France, 1972.

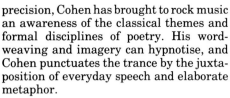

Leonard Cohen
Recommended Listening

Songs Of Leonard Cohen (CBS63241) (Includes: Suzanne, Sisters Of Mercy, Master Song, Teachers, The Stranger Song, So Long Marianne); *Songs From A Room* (CBS32074) (Includes: Tonight Will Be Fine, The Butcher, Story Of Isaac, Lady Midnight, The Partisan, Bird On The Wire).

DAY OF THE CAT

CAT STEVENS' instantly identifiable voice – a sort of honeyed whine, sometimes harsh, usually gentle, always uplifting – and his highly melodic songs were very popular in the early Seventies. Some levelled the criticism at Stevens that he was little more than a 'bedsit balladeer', providing solace for the lonely and unloved, but much of this sensitive singer-songwriter's music had a genuine emotional urgency or rare mystic beauty, as well as a timeless quality all its own.

The son of a Greek restaurateur and his Swedish wife, Cat Stevens was born Steven Georgiou in London's Soho on 21

Cat Stevens' persuasive pop philosophies

July 1947. Leaving school in 1965, he enrolled at Hammersmith College, and it was at this unlikely venue that his part-time songwriting and folk-styled singing attracted the attention of record producer Mike Hurst. Formerly a performer himself as one third of the Springfields, Hurst had achieved little success in two years of producing, and had actually booked an air ticket to try his luck in the States when he suddenly heard the sound of potential hit

talent. He organised and produced a session to record Cat's own song, 'I Love My Dog', which was then taken to Decca. On the strength of this, the singer was signed as one of the artists to launch the company's brand-new Deram label, to be devoted to the development of progressive young British talent.

Aided by strong pirate radio airplay and goodly exposure in the music press, which capitalised on Cat's darkly Mediterranean

Below: The bearded Cat Stevens of 'bedsit balladeer' days searches for an elusive minor chord.

good looks, 'I Love My Dog' entered the UK charts in October 1966 and climbed steadily to peak at Number 28. Simultaneously, the word was being spread that this newcomer also had a fund of his own quality songs with strong commercial appeal, and was writing more. Labels and managers in search of material for their artists began to take an interest.

Pulling the strings

The first week of 1967 saw the release of Cat's follow-up single, 'Matthew And Son'. With a clever lyric about the drudgery of office life, this song also boasted an exciting string arrangement; the combination captured the nation's imagination and helped shoot the record rapidly to Number 2 in the chart. Only the phenomenal success of the Monkees with 'I'm A Believer' kept Cat from the Number 1 position. At the same time, cover versions of his songs

first began to appear in the charts; the Tremeloes led the way with their version of 'Here Comes My Baby', which went to Number 4.

'I'm Gonna Get Me A Gun', Cat's next single, was released during March and moved swiftly to Number 6, again demonstrating the effective combination of intriguing lyric and sparkling string arrangement. At the same time came an entirely self-penned debut album, *Matthew And Son*. In May of 1967, the Immediate label issued former Ikette P. P. Arnold's version of a dramatic ballad by Stevens, 'First Cut Is The Deepest', which reached Number 18 in the UK charts. This song established itself with 'Matthew And Son' as the most enduring of Cat's early compositions; ten years later, Rod Stewart was to take the song to Number 1 with a virtually identical arrangement to the original.

Cat made little secret of the fact that he disliked the glamour-boy pop star image that the sudden flush of commercial success brought; he was more interested in developing the scope of his songwriting and experimenting with subtler and more adventurous arrangements. Evidence of this showed on his next two singles; his major sacrifice, inevitably, was the commercial immediacy of his previous work, and sales reflected this – 'A Bad Night', released in the summer of 1967, just reached Number 20, and in December 'Kitty' could only manage one week in the Top Fifty.

Further singles – 'Lovely City', 'Here Comes My Wife' and 'Where Are You' – were generally ignored, and although Cat's second album, *New Masters*, was well-reviewed (and contained his own version of 'First Cut Is The Deepest'), it sold considerably less well than *Matthew*

And Son. However, the artist himself was not available for promotion of much of this material. During 1968 he became seriously ill with tuberculosis and his long hospitalisation and subsequent recuperation led to him dropping out of the public eye completely; his early following moved on to other idols and his contract with Deram ran out.

Cat up the ladder

Phase two of the Stevens career effectively began during his long recovery from illness. Slowly and carefully, he crafted a set of songs in a quieter, folkier, simpler vein

Inset below left: The young dandy of an early publicity shot, an image Stevens was later to reject. Below: The successful singer-songwriter of the Seventies. Inset below: Stevens shorn for a sober maturity away from the pop world.

than anything he had previously offered. They were recorded without a trace of the earlier elaborate production, using only a guitar, bass and drums accompaniment. Picked up by Island Records, these songs were collected as the *Mona Bone Jakon* album, and the delicate 'Lady D'Arbanville' (dedicated to former girlfriend Patti D'Arbanville) was released as a single. After a slowish climb, this finally re-established Cat in the UK charts in August 1970, when it reached Number 8. Island united him with producer (and former Yardbird) Paul Samwell-Smith, and over the next few years the singer-producer combination put out a series of albums that made Cat Stevens one of the most consistent LP-sellers on both sides of the Atlantic.

Sales of 1971's *Tea For The Tillerman* were helped by the impact of the single 'Wild World', which became Stevens' first US hit single when it reached Number 11. Not issued as a single in Britain by Cat, this song was successfully covered by reggae artist Jimmy Cliff, with Stevens himself producing. The next album, *Teaser And The Firecat*, was even stronger song-wise – and still more successful commercially – than its predecessor. A further development of the by now familiar acoustic, melodic Stevens style, it also turned out to be packed with hit singles, spawning 'Moon Shadow', 'Peace Train' and an appealingly straightforward rendition of Eleanor Farjeon's well-known children's hymn 'Morning Has Broken'. The latter featured Rick Wakeman on piano as sole accompaniment to Stevens' plaintive vocal.

In international sales terms, *Teaser* was probably Cat's most successful recording project ever; all the singles bar 'Peace Train' (which was not released in the UK) were transatlantic Top Thirty hits. As each year of the early Seventies produced one successful Cat Stevens album apiece, his work within them grew more complex, although not in the earlier commercial vein. The essential simplicity of the music and lyrics took a turn for the philosophical, then the metaphysical, and finally the religious as the singer became absorbed in Eastern faiths.

Catch Bull At Four topped the US album charts in 1972 – and deservedly so, for it saw Stevens broaden his range of instrumentation. His arrangements had latterly relied heavily on frantically-strummed acoustic guitars on uptempo tracks and a single instrument – piano or guitar – for ballads. Here, the formula varied slightly: Cat himself played synthesiser to effect on such atmospheric tracks as 'Angelsea' and 'Ruins', while his backing musicians – drummer Gerry Conway, bassist Alan James, pianist Jean Roussel and guitarist Alun Davies – played with an assured unity throughout. Unusually, too, the album included a song with lyrics in Latin: 'O Caritas'.

Foreigner was released in 1973 and also sold well, but this period saw Cat's singles

releases in the UK dwindle suddenly as the Island label concentrated on making Cat one of their best-selling album artists; 'Can't Keep It In' sold well, reaching Number 13, but 'The Hurt' in mid 1973 failed to chart at all. By this time Cat had adopted the lifestyle of a recluse; personal appearances were fewer, and he seldom gave interviews. A lot of his private hours, in fact, were spent in his religious studies, and *Foreigner* displayed this intensely philosophical approach in its long, complex and lyrically profound 'Foreigner Suite' which occupied one side of the album. Stevens also became a 'foreigner' himself for a year or so; as a tax-exile he left the UK and went to live in South America.

1974 and 1975 saw two new albums, *Buddha And The Chocolate Box* and the heavy, complex *Numbers*, plus the compilation *Cat Stevens' Greatest Hits*. An isolated British hit single was an unpretentious revival of Sam Cooke's 'Another Saturday Night', which reached Number 19. A long period of silence then ensued until the spring of 1977, when the *Izitso* album appeared; it sold much less successfully then most of its predecessors – particularly in the UK, where it only scraped into the bottom of the Top Twenty. In the UK the single '(Remember The Days Of The) Old School Yard' reached Number 44 that July.

Back to basics

Towards the end of 1978 came Stevens' last album for Island. It was followed by what has amounted to a complete retirement from the music scene and public life. The album was titled *Back To Earth*, which some critics interpreted as meaning 'back to basics' – presumably hoping to find the seeds of a new pop revivalist Cat Stevens contained therein. In fact, if it heralded any kind of rebirth during this period it was of Cat Stevens the private individual: he underwent a full conversion to the Moslem faith and changed his name accordingly to Yusuf Islam.

Little was heard of Cat Stevens at all thereafter as he immersed himself increasingly in his faith. Stevens' commercial success as a performer and a songwriter had seemingly failed to satisfy him; however, a devotion to a private, spiritual life has obviously provided his ever-philosophical frame of mind with the goal it required. He very briefly made a headline again in 1979 when, on 9 September, he was married to Fouzia Ali at Kensington Mosque in London; but in terms of music it now looks as if Cat's 12 years of recordings will remain his total legacy.   BARRY LAZELL

**Cat Stevens
Recommended Listening**

Teaser And The Firecat (Island ILPS9154) (Includes: Rubylove, Changes IV, How Can I Tell You, Moonshadow, Peace Train, Morning Has Broken); *Catch Bull At Four* (Island ILPS9206) (Includes: Can't Keep It In, Sitting, Freezing Steel, Angelsea, O Caritas).

WAXING LYRICAL

The everyday poetry of rock words

BY THE MID FIFTIES, being a teenager was something to sing about. And no one sang about it better than Chuck Berry, with his tales of fast cars, flighty women and the magic of rock'n'roll. It was a time when teenagers were emerging as a new social group; while many pop songs paid only lip service to their needs, others – like Berry's – helped define this strange new existence.

Berry was the best rock'n'roll lyricist of that decade because, semi-literate though his songs often were, they provided vivid glimpses of an ideal teenage lifestyle – the first teenage American Dream. His images worked well, partly as a result of his own enthusiasm, being a black man looking at white consumer society on something approaching equal terms.

Berry's lyrics – and those of other contemporary rock'n'rollers – drew as much from blues and country as did the music itself. If the musical influences weren't always clear-cut – on 'Maybellene', Berry played fast country runs in a blues-picking style while other records of the time feature blues-based rock'n'roll with a country feel – neither were the lyrical factors, especially as blues and country had been modifying each other for 50 years. But certain elements that predominated in each tradition were absorbed almost wholesale by rock'n'roll.

Generation gap

The blues, dating from the American Civil War, was mainly a migratory music sung by men in search of work, sex and self respect. Such themes displayed an obvious appeal for the embryonic Beat generation, avidly reading Jack Kerouac's *On The Road* and searching for an identity and a freer way of life. The blues-singing negro may have been making the transition from slavery to individual independence in his songs but that, in a much more comfortable way, was what many teenagers saw themselves as doing in the Fifties and early Sixties – breaking away from the commands of adults who didn't understand and a society that didn't care: a tension between the generations neatly summed up

Above left: Chuck Berry, whose flashy, aggressive lyrics espoused the American teen dream. Far left: Leaving desolation row behind – Bob Dylan, rock's most influential writer, in 1968. Left: Darts perform Yakety Yak! *the stage show, 1982.*

in Leiber and Stoller's 'Yakety Yak':

Take out the papers and the trash
Or you don't get no spending cash
If you don't scrub that kitchen floor
You ain't gonna rock'n'roll no more
Yakety yak (Don't talk back).

The dialogue gives the song the dramatic quality of a small play – a technique that, in time, developed into the gallery of characters portrayed by Dylan and the Beatles, rock operas and concept albums.

Country music, on the other hand, offered strong storylines and weighty melodramatic themes – murder, hardship, unrequited love – that were easily adapted to fascinate teenagers and their adolescent emotions. This sense of melodrama quickly became a central part of rock lyrics. It was apparent in the Shangri-Las' 'Walking In The Sand' or the teen-death songs of the early Sixties, and was still present in 1967 in the Doors' 'The End'. This melodramatic ingredient helps explain the ease with which the early deaths among pop stars gained mystique and became a vital element in the mythology of rock.

By the end of the Fifties rock'n'roll was in decline, leaving the way clear for the golden age of American songwriting teams. All of them – Leiber and Stoller, Goffin and King, Pomus and Shuman, Mann and Weil, Greenfield and Sedaka – introduced a high standard of craftsmanship to pop-writing, but the results were essentially lightweight, centred around what were considered teenage affairs. Barry Mann and Cynthia Weil attempted the odd protest song like 'Uptown' and 'We Gotta Get Out Of This Place' but, on the whole, most of these compositions dealt with an unreal world of painless, safe emotion where sex rarely raised its head. The titles alone tell the story: 'Teenager In Love', 'This Magic Moment', 'Lucky Lips', 'Crying In The Rain'.

Such songs cushioned the traumas of the teenager, offering fairytale expectations and encouraging them to wallow melodramatically in their unrequited love. This was an over-simplification of the fears and anxieties adolescents face, and no doubt ignored or glossed over the more serious problems. The first significant expression of adolescent angst in the Sixties came in 1965 with the Who's anthem for disaffected youth 'My Generation', peaked in the mid Seventies with the sentiments of punk, and subsequently survived in the more coherent observations of bands like the Clash and the Jam, offering the teenager lyrics he could identify with.

Misrepresentation of a particular section of society applies to women, as well as youth. In rock music – as in Western culture generally – there were only two images of women: the unobtainable woman and the earthy good-time girl – the Donnas and the Lucilles. An equally intrinsic part of the blues' sexual attitudes has always been the boastful male, the lyrics becoming the vehicle for the rock star to give voice to his own inflated ego, as in the Rolling Stones' 'Under My Thumb' or the Who's 'Anyway, Anyhow, Anywhere' with its cocky chorus: 'I can do anything (Without you)/I can go anywhere (Without you . . .)'.

The early Who were also influenced by soul music – a genre to which rock owes more than is probably recognised. Firstly, black music was never shamefaced about sex, and the gradual emergence in rock songs of women who enjoyed their sexuality (around the time teenagers themselves were becoming more sexually active) represents an acceptance of black songwriting images in white music. But soul's main contribution – apart from items like call-and-response choruses – was to widen the emotional range of rock songs. The cracked voice and stuttered phrases formed an essential part of many soul cuts like James Brown's 'Please, Please, Please', a song that turned up on the Who's first album, alongside the stuttering 'My Generation'. Among all this macho rock, it was becoming increasingly acceptable to express feelings of frustration – even if they were sexist.

Shotgun marriage
Adultery was a subject that had always been commonplace in the blues: 'Well I saw Uncle John/With Long Tall Sally/He saw Aunt Mary comin'/And he ducked back in the alley.' But its first guilt-free appearance in a rock song occurred as late as 1965 in Lennon's 'Norwegian Wood'. The singer/songwriters of the early Seventies discussed their personal relationships *ad infinitum* and adultery had, by then, become a regular ingredient. But Lennon had probably been wise to keep the lyrics fairly obscure, as songs about sex and drugs were frequently banned from the airwaves – a fact he discovered a couple of years later with the line 'Boy, you been a naughty girl, you let your knickers down' on 'I Am The Walrus'. Lennon gained much of his lyrical honesty from Dylan, and there is no doubt that Dylan's shotgun marriage of folk and rock'n'roll in the mid Sixties was the biggest single influence on rock lyrics.

Certainly they needed each other – folk lacked excitement and rock'n'roll lacked intelligence. The political situation in the States – the Cuban missile crisis of October 1962 and the murder of civil rights workers in the Deep South – was already responsible for the protest boom on which political folk singers like Dylan and Tom Paxton had been riding high; and others soon followed suit – Peter, Paul and Mary,

Barry McGuire, even Donovan chipped in with 'Universal Soldier'. But these protests needed a more anarchic voice than folk could ever provide, and by combining the rebellious spirit of rock'n'roll with the moral urgency of folk, Dylan kitted out rock with its first real sense of values.

Getting personal
From the songwriter's point of view, however, there were all kinds of technical problems to be solved, like finding a satisfactory way of writing about social and political situations within a pop format. One of Dylan's devices, which he took from the folk tradition of Woody Guthrie, was to make political statements from a personal viewpoint, building up a picture of a corrupt, alienated society through brief glimpses of one of its citizens: 'You've got a lot of nerve, to say you are my friend/When I was down, you just stood there grinnin''.

In early pop songs, imagery had always been used simply as superficial colouring. Buddy Holly compared the rain in his

Top: Socially-aware lyrics about London abound in the songs of Ian Dury (left) and the Kinks' Ray Davies (right), whose wistful mid-Sixties 'Waterloo Sunset' inspired a BBC-TV play in 1979. Above: Scathing lyrics on the sleeve of a Sex Pistols single.

the singer-songwriters. These included Joni Mitchell, Neil Young, Leonard Cohen and James Taylor; they didn't have a great deal in common, although the oft-recurring themes of lost dreams, loneliness and wasted time give the general flavour of their lyrics. They represented a retreat into personal relationships at a point when, politically, the going was getting pretty tough.

All the same, their transitory songs about leaving, breaking up with lovers and making new discoveries were a genuine part of that trend towards individual freedom and identity that had started with the blues and, in the Fifties, attempted to assert teenage independence. Ten years on, that battle won, lyricists were searching for individual independence – and self-exploration was at the heart of many of these songs. Joni Mitchell expressed her feelings thus: 'Acid, booze and ass/Needles, guns and grass/Everybody's saying/That hell's the hippest way to go/Well, I don't think so/But I'm gonna take a look around it though.'

The long way down

Despite such fairly brash examples, many of these confessional lyrics would have been considered fairly flimsy by early rock 'n'rollers. But the realisation was gradually dawning on rock composers that life might perhaps be a *problem*, possibly with no way out. 'It's come to this', sighs Leonard Cohen on 'Dress Rehearsal Rag', 'And wasn't it a long way down?' The Fifties lyricists had dealt with teenage troubles which, by definition, would automatically depart with adolescence. But these new writers expanded a suspicion hinted at with Dylan's 'Mr Jones': that there might be something of a rather greater magnitude to concern them. Song lyrics were beginning to assume such an unprecedented importance that album sleeves looked naked without them, even when the sentiments voiced were unbelievably trite.

These plaintive lyrics demanded – and got – a simple conversational style that played around with techniques that a few years earlier would have been confined to page poetry. Joni Mitchell, for instance, at times wrote almost in a free verse style, and there was sharp vivid imagery which shared its stark efficiency with the blues. These singer-songwriters firmly established rock lyrics as a vehicle for wide-ranging emotional exploration.

With his lyrical sophistication and tight analytical vision of America, Paul Simon stood slightly apart from this group. But the sense of disappointment at the heart of his best work – most explicitly expressed by 'Everything Put Together Falls Apart' – throws the singer-songwriters' collective personal anxieties into wider political and social relief. Simon's innocent distrust of the world and its ways articulated the social roots of this group's problems clearly and, in his later work at least, more honestly. He seemed to have grown up

heart with the sun in the sky and Donovan saw his true love as shelter for the time when 'the rain has hung the leaves with tears'. But the rain in the lyrics of 'Desolation Row' was making a moral comment on a gloomy human situation. One of Dylan's claims to be considered a poet is that all his imagery works cohesively to produce a consistent emotional response in the listener. Other writers picked up on this technique – the Mamas and the Papas' 'California Dreamin'', for example, sees the winter's day as a symbol of spiritual desolation. The device also led to a whole new mode of obscurity and endless guessing-games about what songs actually meant.

To accompany the injection of poetic imagery and political statements into pop records a new tone of voice had to be found. Dylan came up with scorn and disbelief, tones of voice never heard in the medium before. He was also the first rock lyricist to think in paragraphs rather than four-line verses. This device gave weight to the increasingly complex political ideas that were forcing their way into rock songs and, by extension, even punk's nihilistic sloganising – given its political orientation – might not have been possible without Dylan's precedent.

The result was that not only did artists begin to write their own material but were also free to deal with more or less any topic they wished. Ray Davies was free to plug away at his delicate social commentaries, Cat Stevens came up with a Top Ten hit about going to work – a subject Tin Pan Alley had claimed would kill a song – and the Moody Blues managed to pass off many a lightweight lyric as being philosophically meaningful. Dylan's breakthrough not only made it easier to write more seriously within a rock format, but ensured that such work was taken seriously by the rest of the world.

Eventually, as a flood of self-compositions hit the rock world in the late Sixties, a number of artists emerged from the folk/rock tradition to become known simply as unable to understand why the quality of life was in reality much thinner than he'd been led to believe. There's an air of bewilderment in his work as he looks around for the American Dream, only to find carloads of sensation-seekers bumper-to-bumper along the New Jersey Turnpike where once Chuck Berry cruised his Cadillac.

The disco decade

By the Seventies, with rock firmly established on the arts pages of serious newspapers, all manner of pretentious nonsense was being produced by both lyricists and critics alike. Inevitably, a reaction set in. The decade saw a move away from lyrical complexity to an emphasis on both the appearance of performers – David Bowie's self-referring images and the new romantics he inspired – and their sound. The advent of disco relegated lyrics (and, indeed, melody) to relative insignificance

in favour of the pervasive four-four beat, while rapping – which appeared in the early Eighties as a development of reggae's DJ talkover – gave more emphasis to the rhythm of the lyrics than to their meaning.

Punk, meanwhile, may have shared the same rebellious air of protest that has always surrounded rock but that didn't stop it raising two dirty fingers to the whole idea of well-crafted lyrics and setting a new vogue in bad taste with items like 'Gary Gilmore's Eyes'.

Below: The moody singer-songwriter mentality was often captured in the lyrics of Joni Mitchell (left), Joan Baez (centre) and Leonard Cohen (hands in pockets), pictured backstage at the Newport Festival in 1967. Inset: James Taylor and Carole King, here depicted in the book Rock Dreams, *refined the style with great commercial success in the early Seventies.*

Among the writers of social eloquence who emerged from the new wave movement both Ian Dury and Elvis Costello adopted a belligerent stance towards the world. Dury's tales of East End life took ideas into the Top Ten which had never been there before, while Costello had more in common with the singer-song-writers of the early Seventies, although in his case the retreat was not so much away from public problems into personal affairs as a matter of being trapped by both.

A study of the history of rock lyrics seems to show poetry returning to the medium of song, and rock lyricists being sufficiently engaged by the political and personal struggles of their times to stretch the form to what they consider are its limits. And, since rock is, arguably, the most influential of the modern performing arts, that is a responsibility that can never be carried lightly.   COLIN SHEARMAN

Hard Times

Stripping rock down to the basics produced a durable new style

As THE SENSE OF SOLIDARITY of the hippie era faded with the Sixties, the rock audience split into separate – and often strongly opposed – factions. Many of the older listeners acquired a taste for the mellower sounds of the singer-songwriters, the early teens went for the bright pop of T. Rex or the Sweet, while the group in-between opted for heavy rock. This hard and sometimes aggressive music was a million miles away from the acoustic whimsy of flower-power or progressive rock's lyrical intellectualism.

Cream and Jimi Hendrix had shown the way, forcing simple blues scales through a barrage of feedback over pounding bass guitar and drums to create a new, powerful blues based on electric sound. The blues boom of the Sixties, which had produced bands like Ten Years After, had ensured that there were thousands of young guitarists accomplished in white urban blues throughout Britain and America. (Not that they confined themselves to playing 12-bar blues, but their music *was* firmly based on the traditional blues scales with flattened thirds and sevenths.)

One such guitarist was Jimmy Page, a precocious young session musician who had filled the departing Jeff Beck's shoes in the Yardbirds. Out of the ashes of that group, he formed Led Zeppelin, one of the bands which was to dominate the Seventies with their powerful brand of riff-based blues-rock and moody, mythical folk.

Black magic was one of the regular trappings of heavy metal. If Page was genuinely obsessed by it, purchasing Aleister Crowley's Scottish castle, Black Sabbath exploited it more fully as a theatrical device, donning crucifixes to complement their sinister, brooding music and general air of malevolent mysticism. Deep Purple, too, dabbled with occult imagery in songs like 'Mandrake Root' and Devil's Eye'.

Metal magic

Led Zeppelin, with their technical sophistication and their lingering identification with hippie preoccupations like drugs and the Orient, appealed to a massive and varied audience on both sides of the Atlantic. But they had one foot firmly planted in what was to become the heavy-metal subculture – a large if isolated community of music fans, who also provided Black Sabbath and Deep Purple with Top Ten hits and a very comfortable living. (Zeppelin, true to the 'progressive rock' ethos, refused to release singles in the UK.)

This massive tribe, clad for the most part in bedraggled denim, was mainly young and male. For the machismo of singers like Ian Gillan and Ozzy Osbourne seemed to appeal more to their own sex – as a model to aspire to – than to women. The ideals of the Sixties freaks were, to a large extent, the preserve of a middle-class intelligentsia, and seemed far removed from the experience of the young of the early Seventies. Ozzy Osbourne's cheerful pessimism and celebration of manhood mocked the peace and love optimism of the hippies. That optimism was now *establishment*, and since rock identifies with the rebel not the cause, it had become redundant.

NEVILLE WIGGINS

Above left: Deep Purple guitarist Ritchie Blackmore. In many ways an archetypal heavy-rock guitarist, Blackmore went on to form his own band Rainbow.

PRECIOUS METAL

How Led Zeppelin turned heavy riffs to gold discs

LED ZEPPELIN were one of the most successful bands of the Seventies – or indeed of any rock era. Their powerful blend of post-Cream, post-Hendrix heavy metal and acoustic-folk mysticism provided a heady soundtrack for the decline and fall of the hippie dream.

As the remnants of the associated counter-culture drifted away from politics towards a Tolkien-inspired romanticism, Led Zeppelin conjured a vision of mist-shrouded towers and a (conveniently mythical) search for the One Truth: 'And it's whispered that soon/If we all call the tune/Then the piper will lead us to reason/And a new day will dawn/For those who stand long/And the forests will echo with laughter' ('Stairway To Heaven').

Led Zeppelin (left) transformed rock economics. Their phenomenally successful music and the business acumen of manager Peter Grant (below, celebrating with his boys) turned all their records gold.

The brainchild of a seasoned session man and a hard-headed showbiz hustler, Led Zeppelin were run with an icy, and at times ruthless professionalism. Others may have exerted a greater influence on the development of rock music, but when it came to business Led Zeppelin rewrote the rule book. When they signed to Atlantic Records, the band not only acquired the largest advance ever given to a new act – without the label even having seen them perform – they got total control over everything from record production to merchandise marketing.

Zeppelin successfully capitalised on the underground, FM-radio-oriented circuit that had built up around progressive rock in the late Sixties, and were the first to exploit its commercial potential to the full. They pioneered the route to success through constant touring and word of mouth, which has since become almost standard for heavy-rock bands. Before Led Zeppelin, it was generally assumed that bands needed hit singles to make big money. Zeppelin had only one Top Ten single in the States, and never released a single in the UK. When Atlantic pleaded

with them to put out 'Whole Lotta Love' in the UK, Zeppelin refused and watched the album sell like a single instead. And, by forming their own production and publishing companies and using their position to dictate terms to concert promoters, Led Zeppelin managed to keep a large proportion of the money they generated for themselves.

The professionals
The break-up of the Yardbirds in July 1968 had left guitarist Jimmy Page and manager Peter Grant with the defunct band's name and little else. James Patrick Page (born 9 January 1944 at Heston, Middlesex) had been one of the Sixties' top young session players. A former art student, he was well-versed in the early rock classics, having learned studiously from Scotty Moore's guitar breaks on Elvis Presley's early recordings and from James Burton's solos on Ricky Nelson records. Page played sessions for many rock groups, including the Who, the Kinks (his guitar-work being prominent on 'You Really Got

Me'), Jeff Beck, the Rolling Stones and even top MOR artists like Tom Jones. He was also an experienced producer, arranger and composer, having fulfilled all these roles at Andrew Loog Oldham's Immediate label with artists like Nico, Fleur de Lys and even John Mayall and Eric Clapton (who, like Page, had passed through the ranks of the Yardbirds).

Grant was equally seasoned. A former sheet-metal worker, bit-part actor and bouncer, he had been a tour manager for Little Eva, Chuck Berry and Gene Vincent, and manager for the Animals and the Nashville Teens before taking hold of the Yardbirds' business affairs.

The Yardbirds and Page enjoyed some cult status in the US but at the time of their break-up meant little in the UK, where they had not had a hit for over two years. Undeterred by this, Page wasted little time in putting a new line-up together. His first recruit was John Paul Jones (born John Baldwin, 3 January 1946), a bassist, organist and arranger whom Page knew from his session days.

Page's first choices for vocalist and drummer, Terry Reid and B. J. Wilson, were both unavailable. Reid suggested a young singer called Robert Plant (born 20 August 1948), who had spent his teens scuffling around the Midlands with various blues and R&B outfits and had come down to London looking for a break. Page and Grant caught up with him at a teacher-training-college dance, where he was appearing in a group called Hobbstweedle before a small, uninterested audience. Both guitarist and manager were, however, suitably impressed.

The final piece of the jigsaw came at Plant's recommendation. His earlier bands had included the Crawling King Snakes and the Band of Joy, both of which boasted the talents of John Bonham (born 31 May 1949), a drummer whose volume and aggression had earned him a considerable reputation with Midlands club-goers. Bonham was enjoying lucrative session work for the first time and was initially reluctant to join, but agreed after considerable persuasion.

interest in the UK was hardly overwhelming. It was as much as Grant could do to get them occasional club, pub or small college dates, and even then they were usually billed as 'ex-Yardbirds'.

Success came first in the States. Led Zeppelin made their US debut in Denver on Boxing Day 1968, and went on to support Vanilla Fudge and Iron Butterfly, America's top hard-rock bands. Both these outfits were, to use the phrase of the day, 'blown off the stage' by Zeppelin. Peter Grant's experience in the States with the Yardbirds and the Animals had enabled him to plan the tour for maximum impact, taking in those cities and venues with the highest media profile and the best audiences. By the time Led Zeppelin flew home at the end of February, they were a headline attraction and their LP was racing up the US charts.

Recorded in the autumn of 1968 for a mere £1782 before their Atlantic deal had been finalised, the album *Led Zeppelin* went on to gross over £3½ million by 1975. Produced by Jimmy Page (as were all their subsequent albums), it welded electric blues, acoustic folk and fuzzed, feedback-drenched heavy rock into a startling whole. Musically, it set the format for most of Led Zeppelin's subsequent output. Another precedent it introduced, however, was its wholesale use of time-honoured riffs and lyrics, previously used by blues artists like Howlin' Wolf and Albert King, in songs credited to Page and Plant alone.

The album wasn't released in the UK until the end of March, when the band were halfway through a nationwide tour. At the time, they were playing tiny clubs

Left: Led Zeppelin's powerful sound was ideally suited to the vast outdoor venues of the US circuit. Below: At Knebworth, 1979, large video screens projected the band's movements and expressions.

on this tour for as little as £60 a night. Nevertheless, word of their American triumphs was filtering back and, helped by a batch of rave reviews in the UK rock press, the album was in the Top Ten when the tour finished in mid-April.

Having cracked it on both sides of the Atlantic in record time, Zeppelin spent the next year consolidating that position. In those 12 months they visited the US no fewer than four times, culminating in a prestige date at New York's Carnegie Hall, and did two tours of major British halls, plus a one-off appearance at London's Lyceum Ballroom.

Amid this intense activity, the second album was being written in hotel rooms and recorded in various studios over a period of several months. The result was *Led Zeppelin II*, a frenetic burst of heavy rock. 'Whole Lotta Love' (another uncredited reworking, this time of Willie Dixon's 'You Need Love'), edited down to a single in the US, was a smash hit and became a heavy-metal classic. Released in October 1969, the album topped the charts in both the UK and US: it displaced the Beatles' *Abbey Road* as Number 1 and stayed in the *Billboard* Top Two Hundred for 18 months.

Back to nature
May 1970 saw the band take a break from their relentless touring. Page and Plant went off to a cottage in the Welsh mountains for a holiday, where they composed a number of new, rurally-inspired songs. Page's interest in folk came to the fore on this set, as did Robert Plant's love of laid-back, West Coast music. Although it contained a few heavy rockers, like the crashing 'Immigrant Song', *Led Zeppelin III* disappointed both critics and fans with its emphasis on acoustic material. Despite huge advance orders, it ended up selling less well than its predecessors.

Zeppelin lifts off
Rehearsals began in September at Page's London flat. Legend claims that the first number they ever played was 'Train Kept A-Rollin'', a Yardbirds number that became a regular stage favourite. The rest of the repertoire consisted of new material that Page had been writing, together with old blues and R&B tunes. According to Plant: 'You just couldn't walk away and forget it. The sound was so great.'

Within three weeks the band were off on a 10-day Scandinavian tour, fulfilling contractual obligations as the New Yardbirds. They also did a few early UK dates under this name, the last being at Liverpool University on 19 October 1968, before renaming themselves Led Zeppelin. The name had been thought up by Keith Moon and John Entwistle when they were thinking of leaving the Who. It had originally been spelled Lead Zeppelin, but Grant realised that this might be mispronounced.

At first, the name-change proved a liability. Even after they had recorded their first album and signed with Atlantic,

The band's response was to sever their already tenuous ties with the press almost completely. Compared with other acts of the same commercial stature, Led Zeppelin had always been relatively unknown outside the world of rock music. Even among their fans, the individual band members remained virtual enigmas. Robert Plant's love of home life on his Worcestershire farm; Bonham's fondness for alcohol and fast cars; Page's interest in the occult – these were the snippets with which fans had to content themselves.

Whether by accident or design, this created a mystique which did Zeppelin's career prospects no harm at all. From 1970 through to the end of 1973, regular tours round Britain and across North America sold out with a minimum of promotion, as did visits to new venues in Europe, Australasia and the Far East. Each year, members of the band topped popularity polls in the world's music journals, both collectively and individually, while their increasingly infrequent album releases continued to be landmarks in the rock calendar.

Climbing the Stairway

In November 1971 their fourth album – officially untitled but commonly known as 'Led Zeppelin IV' – confirmed the broader musical direction of the previous album. It was to become the band's most consistent seller around the world, thanks largely to the inclusion of 'Stairway To Heaven', the song that – building from a gentle acoustic ballad to a blazing hard-rock finale – brought mass acceptance for the softer aspects of Zeppelin's music and replaced 'Whole Lotta Love' as their anthem.

The next album gave Zeppelin's critics a stationary target to aim at. Released in March 1973, *Houses Of The Holy* contained little of the heavy blues-rock on which Zeppelin had been founded, and a couple of tongue-in-cheek spoofs. Even some of their staunchest supporters had doubts about it, though it followed the other Zeppelin albums to the top of the world's charts. As if to refute their detractors, Zeppelin made that summer's American jaunt their biggest yet. Stretching from the first week in May to the end of July, it broke attendance records from the very first date, when over 50,000 people filled the Atlanta Braves Stadium, and grossed Zeppelin over 4½ million dollars.

Some of the proceeds from the tour were spent filming a few of the later concerts for a planned Led Zeppelin movie. Work continued on their return from the States, with all four band members plus Peter Grant shooting individual fantasy sequences intended to symbolise each man's character. All the footage had been shot by the end of 1973, but three more years were to pass before the public had a chance to see the film. This was to be indicative of Zeppelin's pace of working from this point onwards.

1974 saw a dearth of live concerts and record releases. Instead of playing and re-cording, Zeppelin were laying the foundations of Swan Song, the record label they formed when their Atlantic contract expired. This included launching the label with lavish parties in New York, Los Angeles and Chislehurst Caves; getting involved with their new signings, who included Bad Company (initially in the US only), Maggie Bell and the Pretty Things; and recording their first Swan Song album, to be distributed by Atlantic.

This album, in typical Zeppelin style, was delayed for several months while final mixing and sleeve artwork were perfected, finally coming out in March 1975 at the end of the band's tenth American tour. The tour demonstrated that the band had lost none of their popularity during the 18-month lay-off, while the album, *Physical Graffiti*, proved to be well worth the wait.

A double album, combining recordings from the previous year with half-a-dozen songs left over from previous albums, *Physical Graffiti* was an impressive indication of how far Zeppelin had developed in their six years together. There was plenty of the hard rock that some fans felt had been missing from Zeppelin's later work. Frantic rockers like 'Night Flight' and 'Custard Pie' rubbed shoulders with gentle acoustic excursions like 'Bron-Y-Aur' or the post-psychedelic grandeur of 'Kashmir'; both critics and fans approved, while the tour pulled all six Led Zeppelin albums into the American charts simultaneously.

Crash landing

From then on, however, things started to take a turn for the worse. That August, Robert Plant and his wife were seriously injured in a car crash on the Greek island of Rhodes, forcing the band to cancel their planned US tour. During Plant's recuperation, a new album was recorded at Munich's Musicland Studios, but its release was held up, with the artwork once again the source of delay. Prior to its appearance in April 1976, Page and Plant had both gone out of their way to make clear in interviews just how much the coming LP meant to Zeppelin, so there was some disappointment when *Presence* turned out to be a generally uninspired, if thoroughly competent effort. It boasted one classic, the driving 10-minute rocker 'Achilles Last Stand'. UK sales hinted that Zeppelin's popularity might be starting to wane, but no such question arose in the States, where *Presence* became the first album ever to go platinum on advance orders alone.

In October 1976 the long-awaited movie finally got its premiere, accompanied by a

Right: James Patrick Page Esq., gentleman landowner, dabbler in the black arts of the occult and a fantastically influential guitar stylist. He has maintained a presence that is as enigmatic off-stage as flamboyant on-stage. Inset above right: Robert Plant, R&B screamer extraordinaire. Inset right: The phantom of the opera – John Paul Jones, shrouded in dry ice, at the organ.

double album of the soundtrack. Described by Peter Grant as 'the most expensive home-movie ever made', *The Song Remains The Same* was decidedly amateurish as a piece of film-making and didn't even catch the band in particularly inspired live form. But it did at least give people the chance to see Zeppelin in action, and was a predictable success, grossing over 200,000 dollars in its first week alone in the States.

Back in action
The band embarked on a massive American tour in April 1977, an enterprise originally planned for February but postponed because Plant had had tonsillitis. Stretching through to mid August, it was to take in 51 dates and reach an audience of over 1,300,000 fans. For nearly four months, everything went well; the concerts were a great success, the band were apparently enjoying being back in action, and the spectacular effects – smoke bombs,

video screens and synchronised lasers – worked perfectly. Then, within the space of five days, the whole thing collapsed.

At a concert in Oakland, Bonham, Grant and two of the Led Zeppelin entourage were arrested after they beat up two of tour promoter Bill Graham's staff, one of whom was hospitalised. They were bailed out (and later found guilty and given fines and suspended prison sentences) and proceeded to New Orleans, where worse news reached them. On 26 July, Robert Plant's five-year-old son Karac fell ill with a stomach complaint and died on his way to hospital the next day. Plant flew home immediately and the rest of the tour was cancelled.

Below: John Bonham was for many people the heavy-rock drummer. Crashing his way around an enormous kit, which even included orchestral timpani, he made his mark in numbers like 'Moby Dick' and 'Four Sticks'.

Rumours circulated about the band's future, and it was widely held that Jimmy Page's dabblings in the occult were responsible for their troubles. Page gave a series of interviews denying the rumours. Apart from some rehearsals at Clearwell Castle in the Forest of Dean in May 1978, however, Led Zeppelin did not work together again until the end of that year when they went into Abba's Stockholm studio to cut a new album. The result was *In Through The Out Door*, which appeared in August 1979.

The out door
During those two years of silence, the UK music scene had been almost totally revolutionised by the arrival of punk, and Led Zeppelin, with their guitar solos, tax-exile lifestyle and massive tours (with attendant hotel-wrecking, wild parties and groupie scene), had come to symbolise everything that the punks said was wrong with the old rock. The two concerts Led Zeppelin played at Knebworth in August 1979 sold well enough, but poorly in comparison to the band's days of glory. *In Through The Out Door* reached Number 1 in the LP charts, but had dropped out of the Top Twenty by the end of October. It was a different story in the States, where the album stayed at the top of the charts for a record seven weeks and went on to sell over four million copies, despite Zeppelin's absence from their shores.

A short, low-key tour of Europe in June 1980 went well enough to persuade the band to embark on another US tour. But, during rehearsals at Jimmy Page's home in Windsor, John Bonham was found dead in his bed after a lengthy drinking session. A subsequent inquest recorded a verdict of accidental death. The tributes from fellow musicians poured in, and the rumours of a possible replacement abounded, but on 4 December, Swan Song issued a short statement announcing that Led Zeppelin would not be continuing.

Robert Plant made a solo album, *Pictures At Eleven*, which did well, especially in America, while Jimmy Page composed the soundtrack for the film *Death Wish II*. John Paul Jones, meanwhile, managed to reduce his once-low profile to the point of invisibility. Despite the finality of the title of *Coda,* an album of unreleased songs issued in 1982, Zeppelin reformed twice; once for Live Aid and once in 1988 for an Atlantic Records anniversary party.

PAUL KENDALL

LED ZEPPELIN
Discography

Albums
Led Zeppelin (Atlantic 588171, 1969); *Led Zeppelin II* (Atlantic 588198, 1969); *Led Zeppelin III* (Atlantic 2401 002, 1970); *Led Zeppelin IV* (Atlantic 2401 012, 1971); *Houses Of The Holy* (Atlantic K 50014, 1973); *Physical Graffiti* (Swan Song SSK 89400, 1975); *Presence* (Swan Song SSK 59402, 1976); *The Song Remains The Same* (Swan Song SSK 89402, 1976); *In Through The Out Door* (Swan Song SSK 59410, 1979); *Coda* (Swan Song A 0051, 1982).

Black Sabbath: idols of an occult following?

BLACK SABBATH are the archetypal heavy metal band, the blueprint for countless imitators that sprang up in the late Seventies. While Deep Purple had pseudo-classical pretensions and Led Zeppelin indulged in post-hippie mysticism, Sabbath blended down-to-earth heavy rock with highly theatrical occult imagery. Their menacing presence, aided and abetted on stage by the manic leaps of singer Ozzy Osbourne, provided an aggressive contrast to late Sixties flower-power. It also established a musical formula, which would, with time, come to seem restrictive, and lead to serious disagreements within the band.

The four original members – guitarist Tony Iommi (born 19 February 1948), drummer Bill Ward (born 5 May 1948), bassist Geezer Butler (born 17 July 1949) and singer Ozzy Osbourne (born 3 December 1948) – left the same Birmingham school together in 1968 to form a group called Earth. Playing a jazz-blues fusion, they gigged continuously in Birmingham and Hamburg, where they broke the Beatles' house record at the Star Club. Despite their cult following, they became frustrated by their lack of international success. Under the guidance of their first manager Jim Simpson, they changed their name in 1969 to Black Sabbath (the title of one of their early songs), increased the volume and adopted a suitably macabre image.

Paranoid and paranormal

They continued touring the club circuit in Britain and Germany, and released a one-off single on Fontana. The same cut – 'Evil Woman' – became their first single on Vertigo Records in March 1970. Their first LP, *Black Sabbath*, was released simultaneously. Recorded in two days at a cost of £600, it reflected their adherence to rock basics, although overdubbed sound effects – pattering rain, doom-laden church bells – added the required 'occult' flavour. Heavily promoted for its association with the paranormal, tenuous as it was, the album achieved a three-month stay in the UK charts.

Maintaining their momentum, the band returned to the studio to record what was to become their classic single, 'Paranoid', and the album of the same name. Released together in September 1970, these records confirmed the band's domestic popularity. 'Paranoid' reached Number 4 in the UK chart and also won interest for the band in the US. Embarking on a university tour there in the autumn of 1970, Ozzy and the band consolidated the strong impression they had made on American hard-rock fans. The quick success of both LP and

'Finished with my woman/'Cos she couldn't help me/With my mind': Ozzy strangles the microphone (below) while Geezer pounds out the bass riff (above).

single surprised both the band and their record company, with the album eventually clocking up a 65-week stay in the *Billboard* chart.

Sabbath under strain

Sabbath went on to extend their popularity by maintaining a gruelling worldwide touring schedule throughout the early Seventies. Their behaviour on the road and in hotels conformed to heavy rock traditions – room-wrecking, groupie and drinking binges, and so on. Ozzy in particular appeared to be interested only in alcohol and hectic rock music, drawing his energy from the rapport he created with his increasingly dedicated following. The *Master Of Reality* LP (1971) and *Black Sabbath 4* (1972) earned Black Sabbath worldwide

recognition, but it was *Sabbath Bloody Sabbath* (1973) that finally achieved an ideal fusion of the band's live energy and the crushing, oppressive weight of their doomy songs.

Success brought its problems for Black Sabbath. They had parted company from their original manager Jim Simpson, replacing him first with Patrick Meehan and then with Don Arden. Now they found themselves on the receiving end of accusations of contract-breaking from Simpson, and Ozzy Osbourne was handed a subpoena as he walked on stage at an American date in 1975.

As a result of these wrangles, Black Sabbath attempted to manage themselves. Since they were then writing and recording an album a year and undertaking a punishing tour schedule – including their debut at New York's prestigious Madison Square Gardens in July 1975 – the strain began to tell. Ozzy was drinking heavily, and personality conflicts were developing within the band.

Ozzy's insistence that the band live up to his hard-drinking, hard-living image was beginning to concern the other members, while on a musical level, Tony Iommi's increasing interest in more complex arrangements was alienating Ozzy, who preferred a basic approach. *Sabotage*, released in September 1975, adhered to the basic heavy-rock formula, but the sessions for *Technical Ecstasy* the following year saw Iommi experimenting with overdubbing and even, in Ozzy's absence, a horn section. Ozzy drew away from the other members of the band, and in 1977 he left Black Sabbath, only to rejoin a year later, ousting his temporary replacement, former Savoy Brown singer Dave Walker. Ozzy and Black Sabbath cut one more album together, *Never Say Die*, in 1979, but the ill-feeling remained and Ozzy departed in a flurry of insults to launch his solo project, Blizzard of Oz.

Ozzy goes bats

Ozzy's departure deprived the band of their front man, one who went on to develop even higher peaks of the macabre, appearing covered in fake blood, in only a loincloth and reputedly biting the heads off live bats. He took with him a sizeable portion of Black Sabbath's audience, for whom he had always been the focal point. His albums *Blizzard Of Oz* (1980) and *Diary Of A Madman* (1982) were remarkably successful, particularly in the States, where the latter remained on the *Billboard* charts for over a year.

The remaining members of Black Sabbath, meanwhile, recruited former Rainbow vocalist Ronnie James Dio. Bill Ward retired for health reasons, to be replaced behind the drumkit by Vinnie Appice, younger brother of former Vanilla Fudge drummer Carmine Appice. (Geezer Butler also left briefly but returned to the fold soon afterwards.) Dio resisted the temptation to imitate Ozzy's style, stamping his own personality on the two studio LPs,

Heaven And Hell (1980) and *Mob Rules* (1981). Acrimony persisted between Ozzy and the band, especially after the release in 1980 of *Sabbath, Live At Last*, which featured recordings made before the split. (Ozzy still laid claim to much of the Sabbath catalogue, using the old numbers in his act and on a live album.)

Tension was developing between Dio and the other members of Black Sabbath over his dominant role in the group, with Iommi alleging that Dio had tampered with the mixes of *Live Evil* (1982) to make his vocals more prominent. In November 1982 they split with Dio, who took drummer Vinnie Appice with him to form a new band, entitled Dio. At the same time Butler and Iommi, dissatisfied with the efforts of Sandy Pearlman, who had become their manager, signed a deal with their old boss Don Arden.

The group continued through the Eighties with varying personnel, Tony Iommi the only surviving founder member.

Below: The classic Black Sabbath line-up in action, from left Ozzy Osbourne, Geezer Butler, Tony Iommi and Bill Ward. Right: Ronnie Dio, who replaced the outrageous Ozzy as vocalist.

But his group had already left its mark. For several years, Black Sabbath were *the* heavy metal band, and 'Paranoid' was *the* heavy metal anthem; their ponderous, doomy rock and sinister visual image was a crucial influence on new heavy-metal bands like Samson, Iron Maiden and Saxon.

LUKE CRAMPTON

Black Sabbath
Recommended Listening

We Sold Our Souls For Rock'n'Roll (NEMS NELD 101) (Includes: Paranoid, War Pigs, Children Of The Grave, Snowblind, Sabbath Bloody Sabbath, The Wizard).

Rock's fatal fascination with black magic

SYMPATHY FOR The Devil

IN THE SPRING of 1982 Jaz, a member of the apocalyptic post-punk group Killing Joke, was unexpectedly absent from a scheduled television appearance. He had suddenly decided to visit Iceland. Not, so it was reported, because he had been seized with an uncontrollable urge to see the volcanic plains and boiling geysers of that barren and thinly populated island. But because his researches into psychic and occult prophecies had convinced him that some great catastrophe was about to strike the earth. Iceland, for mysterious and unexplained reasons, was likely to escape the worst effects of the coming disaster. The expected calamity did not, of course, take place (the only upheaval occurring within the ranks of Killing Joke). Nevertheless, Jaz's belief in the truth of at least *some* occult prophecies remained unshaken. Clearly, at least one rock musician has an unshakeable faith in things psychic and their value as a guide to everyday activity.

Hex appeal

Such a concern with the supernatural and its interaction with the world in which we carry on our ordinary lives is a continuation of a long-established tradition. There have always been musicians – rock and otherwise – who have been influenced by and concerned with unorthodox fringe religions: the occult, the spells and charms of ritual magic, and even voodoo.

Both Bob Marley and Jimi Hendrix were influenced by Akonidi Hini – sometimes inaccurately referred to as 'high priestess of voodoo'. She is a Ghanaian occultist and president of the African Psychic and Traditional Healers Association, who usually carries out her religious and magical rites in her private temple, a ramshackle building situated beside her homeland's River Zribi. Hendrix was sufficiently impressed with Akonidi's occult powers to dedicate his 'Voodoo Chile' to her, and she believed her 'magic' to be partly responsible for his success.

Akonidi continues to take an interest in all types of black music and, if a record particularly appeals to her, will carry out rituals designed to achieve its commercial success. In 1982, for example, she underwent a 'three-day spiritual fast' to bless Eddy Grant's UK chart-topping single 'I Don't Wanna Dance'.

During the decade from 1965 to 1975 there was much experimentation by musicians with allegedly consciousness-expanding drugs – from laboratory-made LSD and STP to such traditional Amerindian 'spirit medicines' as peyote and magic mushrooms. Many of the rock stars who experimented with these and similar substances did so purely for kicks. But others were genuinely seeking mystical experiences.

While some musicians were carrying out drug experiments designed to 'loosen the girders of the soul', that is, to force their way into the world of the psychic (or into the depths of their own unconscious minds) by chemical short-cuts, others were using more traditional methods to achieve the same results. They spent long hours in meditation, practised yoga, studied astrology and other traditional symbol systems, and even experimented with ritual magic. This last technique always invites a bad press. Horror films, Dennis Wheatley novels and Sunday newspaper exposures of occult eccentrics have given the impression that all practitioners of

Below, left to right: Killing Joke, Black Widow and Arthur Brown. All have projected an 'occult' image, as did US hard-rockers Blue Öyster Cult (right).

ritual magic spend their time sacrificing virgins in honour of imaginary and meaningless gods. Believers contend that authentic ritual magic is the 'yoga of the West', a combination of mental and physical techniques designed to produce deep and beneficial changes in the minds and bodies of those who practise it (whatever else it does to others).

It is not surprising that many rock musicians have been concerned with the supernatural, for occult elements were present in many of rock's musical ancestors and some of those who pre-dated contemporary rock associated themselves with the world of demons, devils and other denizens of hell. Blues singer 'Peetie Wheatstraw' (William Bunch) boasted of his close relationship to Satan, calling himself 'The Devil's Son-in-Law and High Sheriff of Hell', while Robert Johnson, the brilliant blues guitarist and singer, believed that the Devil was ever-active in the modern world and sang convincingly of 'the Hell Hound on my trail'. The R&B songs of Willy Dixon, meanwhile, are directly concerned with occult spells, charms and magic plants – such as 'High John the Conqueror'.

The use of 'High John' seems to have originated in Louisiana but, curiously enough, the artist who has most referred to it in his work is white – Mac Rebennack, a former session musician better known as Dr John the Night Tripper. The references in many of Dr John's lyrics to 'goofer dust' and 'drawing powder' are only understandable in the context of New Orleans voodoo-witchcraft. 'Goofer dust' is earth taken from a freshly dug grave, and it is

believed that some occultists know secret methods of using it by which they can kill or injure their enemies. 'Drawing powder' is more innocent, usually consisting of powdered lodestone or magnetised iron filings that have been subjected to magical processes believed to confer the power of 'drawing' love, money or good luck to its owner. It is difficult to know how seriously Dr John took the voodoo of which he sang. Possibly he just used occult concepts to provide structural frameworks for the remarkable albums he released.

Tongue-in-cheek use of the supernatural for theatrical effect has been quite common. It is, for example, difficult to believe in the seriousness of either Arthur Brown – 'I am the God of Hellfire' – or Screamin' Jay Hawkins, who, juggling with a skull like some demented Hamlet, was accustomed to have himself carried on stage in a blazing coffin.

A similar doubt surrounds the motives of Black Widow, the rock group which in 1970 recorded *Sacrifice*, once described as 'the purest Satanic rock album'. Certainly Satanism is predominant – the listener is told of 'a way to power', urged to come to the Witches' Sabbat, and given much information about the 'Secret Art'. And yet the impression made on most of those who have listened to the album is of a self-conscious stage performance – the soundtrack of a Hammer horror film rather than the authentic voice of devil worship.

Sabbath rites

Two famous British heavy-metal bands have been associated with the black arts. In the earlier part of their career Black Sabbath displayed a seemingly genuine, and certainly chilling concern with Satan and his works. They began each concert with an eerie and sometimes long drawn-out occult ceremony, which seems to have been derived from a *grimoire*, one of the many textbooks of ritual magic circulated among the occultists of the Middle Ages and the Renaissance. So authentic-seeming was this rite that the group was approached by Alex Sanders, 'the King of the Witches', at the time chief of a whole network of occult societies, who warned them that they were in danger of raising forces beyond their power to control.

Whether Black Sabbath took Sanders' advice seriously or not, there is no doubt that they subsequently played down the Satanic aspect of their music. Indeed, it has been argued that the band's vision of Satanism was *cautionary*. As Andrew Weiner commented in 'Doom Patrol' (an article in *Rock File 2*): '. . . they took a stand *against* black magic. Their songs warned against it. They used to wear those crucifixes to fend off evil spirits.'

The rock musician who has made the deepest study of the occult in general, and of ritual magic in particular, is undoubtedly Jimmy Page of Led Zeppelin. Page became fascinated by the life and occult teachings of Aleister Crowley, the self-styled 'Beast 666'. Crowley believed

that he was the prophet of a new age of 'Force and Fire', in which Christianity would be replaced by 'Crowleyanity', a religion of his own devising. Whether Page believed in this strange magical religion is uncertain; certainly he was sufficiently impressed by Crowley's faith to make a profound study of his occult teachings and to buy Boleskine House, once Crowley's home. When a series of tragedies befell the members of Led Zeppelin in the late Seventies and early Eighties – including the deaths of drummer John Bonham and one of Page's friends at one of his other houses – the wisdom of the guitarist's occultist interests were seriously questioned.

It would be foolish, however, to make any sinister inferences about the fatalities. Rather, it is more realistic to view the flirtation of rock stars like Page with the occult as one of the taboo indulgences made available by the rock lifestyle, much like excessive drug-taking and drinking (the latter of which was the cause of Bonham's death). Meanwhile, the occult has offered the type of evil imagery and theatrical possibilities that rock audiences, especially those of heavy-metal bands, have always found fascinating (sword-and-sorcery mythology has a similar appeal) and which, for the most part, provide little more than harmless escapism.   FRANCIS KING

TEN YEARS AFTER

TEN YEARS AFTER
TEN YEARS AFTER
TEN YEARS AFTER
TEN YEARS AFTER

High-octane rock from Alvin Lee and the boys

FORMED IN 1967, Ten Years After emerged as part of the late-Sixties British blues boom, becoming a big-selling album act and premier live attraction – particularly on the emergent American stadium circuit – before their break-up in 1974. The star of their act was singer/guitarist Alvin Lee, probably the flashiest blues/rock guitarist of the lot.

Jaybirds of a feather
Lee, born in Nottingham on 19 December 1944, grew up in a musical environment – both his parents played guitar. After taking lessons for a year, he joined his first local group at the age of 13. A couple of years later he paired up with bassist Leo Lyons (born 30 November 1944) and they played together in various line-ups, one of which took them to Hamburg in Germany, before meeting drummer Ric Lee (born 20 October 1945). The three of them formed the nucleus of a band called the Jaybirds. Chick Churchill (born 2 January 1946) was initially given a job as road manager of this outfit, but soon began to make a more direct contribution as organist.

In 1967 the group decided on a change of name to Ten Years After, and swiftly established a strong reputation in the London clubs – most notably at the Marquee, where they held down a residency. At this point, they met Chris Wright, who became their manager (and later, with Terry Ellis, formed Chrysalis Records). With Wright's help, they secured a contract with Decca Records who, perceiving the band's underground as opposed to commercial appeal, assigned them to their new progressive label Deram and allowed them to release an album, *Ten Years After*, without the customary requirement of a hit single. The album sold reasonably well and during the rest of the year Ten Years After played as many gigs as they possibly could, further establishing their grass-roots following in Britain.

General Lee

In 1968, Deram released a second album, *Undead*, recorded live at London's Klook's Kleek club. American promoter Bill Graham, impressed with the album, telegrammed Chris Wright inviting Ten Years After to play at the prestigious Fillmore West, and the band departed for what was to be the first of numerous Stateside tours.

Although the two 1969 albums, *Stonedhenge* (on which Lee's guitar work was uncharacteristically subdued) and *Ssssh* (a heavier, more fully produced effort), established them in the British charts, it was *Undead* that conveyed most accurately what the band was about – high-energy, high-velocity performance rock, as raw and unsubtle as it comes. Despite the fact that Ric Lee, Leo Lyons and Chick

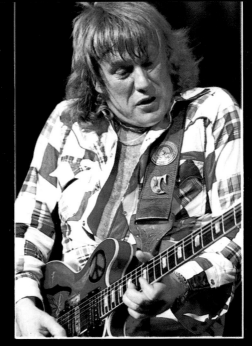

Alvin Lee (above and below left), lead guitarist with Ten Years After (left), was an early example of the rock 'axe hero'.

Churchill were all extremely capable musicians, each having had more formal training than Alvin Lee, it was very much the guitarist's show.

Alvin Lee sang, wrote nearly all the songs and produced the albums. On stage he was always the centre of attention. A tall, well-built figure, with scowling face and thick blond hair, he quickly became renowned for the incredible speed with which he played his familiar sticker-festooned red Gibson 335. His guitar playing came to dominate proceedings to such an extent that Churchill would often leave his keyboards – which were drowned by the guitar – to stand on a stack at the back of the stage and clap his hands impotently in the air. For a while audiences loved Ten Years After's show, particularly in America, but the critical response was less favourable.

The situation crystallised with Ten Years After's appearance at the Woodstock Festival in 1969 and subsequent inclusion in the film of the event, which became a worldwide box-office success in 1970. *Woodstock* featured the band storming, stomping and wailing their way through an Alvin Lee song called 'I'm Going Home' – an extended shuffle/boogie 12-bar that tended towards indulgence when taken out of context with the rest of the show. But the effect of that appearance was dramatic – the band was suddenly hoisted into a position of international superstar status. In Britain they were rewarded in June of 1970 with their only hit single, an edited version of 'Love Like A Man', but Lee didn't care for the number and refused to play it on 'Top Of The Pops'. Meanwhile *Cricklewood Green* (1970) and *Watt* (1971) both reached the Top Five in the album charts.

Ironically, Woodstock also heralded the start of Ten Years After's decline. 'It was a big break, but it was the start of the end

too,' said Alvin Lee. They found themselves in an artistic strait-jacket, hedged in on the one side by audiences demanding nothing but the formula of 'I'm Going Home' and 'Good Morning Little Schoolgirl', and on the other by critics lambasting their lack of finesse and paucity of imagination. Moreover, the band suffered from a work schedule that left them little time to draw breath, let alone write new songs and develop in any new directions. Alvin Lee commented: 'We just kept working and working and working . . . and the fun went out of it. We didn't feel we were achieving anything particularly, it was just what I call the travelling jukebox syndrome. Get on stage, plug in, and away you go – do the same as you did last night.' It has been reliably documented that Ten Years After undertook as many as 28 American tours, as well as appearing all over Europe.

Bad vibrations

The band's last new album, *Positive Vibrations*, was released in the spring of 1974, but Ten Years After had already split, having played their last British gig at London's Rainbow earlier that year. They did, however, undertake a final American tour in 1975, and got together briefly in the studio in early 1977, though no recordings were ever released from these sessions.

Alvin Lee embarked on a solo career with mixed results. He worked initially with Mylon LeFevre, producing the country-rock-flavoured *On The Road To Freedom* (1973), and then set up a nine-piece touring band – casting himself in a more 'tasteful', laid-back role. But his new image suited neither his audience nor himself, and it wasn't too long before he was back in the heavy-rock fold. In late 1977 he formed Ten Years Later in response to record company pressures, but after two lacklustre albums they split, and since then he has again worked solo, using a three-piece Alvin Lee Band – with bassist Fuzzy Samuels and drummer Tom Compton for touring.

Leo Lyons became a producer, working most notably on a trio of UFO albums, and eventually setting up a studio in Oxfordshire. Ric Lee did a spell with Stan Webb's Chicken Shack before moving into management, while Chick Churchill recorded a solo album, *You And Me* (1973), before joining Chrysalis Publishing.

Perhaps Ten Years After failed to take a firm enough stand against the many pressures that boxed them in, and perhaps they should have established a stronger musical identity as a band, rather than as a vehicle for Lee's greased-lightning guitar. But whatever their detractors may say, they worked long and hard, and gave many an audience one hell of a buzz.

DAVID SINCLAIR

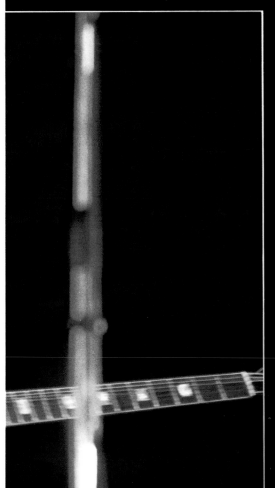

POWER
TO THE
PURPLE

Classic hard rock in shades of Deep Purple

'DEEP PURPLE came into being in February 1968, and they promptly moved into the wilds of Hertfordshire, wisely choosing to isolate themselves for two months while they argued out their musical policy and knocked the musical splinters from the surface of their act.

'Basically Jon Lord and Ritchie Blackmore were responsible for Deep Purple's existence. They roped in drummer Ian Paice and later added Ian Gillan and Roger Glover as replacements for their departing singer and bassist.'

Thus reads the official record of the first 18 months in the career of Deep Purple. The quote comes from a press release sent out at the end of 1969 to mark the group's first excursion into 'serious' music, Jon Lord's 'Concerto For Group And Orchestra'. Formed at the end of the Sixties and contemporaries of Led Zeppelin and Black Sabbath, Deep Purple must be bracketed with those bands as among the most successful and influential of the Seventies.

The events surrounding the band's formation were, however, somewhat more complicated than that press release had indicated. Chris Curtis, formerly drummer with the Searchers, had forsaken the drumkit for the microphone and wished to put together a group to back his vocal talents. Around the end of 1967 he persuaded two London businessman, Tony Edwards and John Coletta, to provide him with the financial backing. Only two musicians – keyboard-player Jon Lord and bassist Nicky Simper – had been recruited when the eccentric Curtis dropped out of the project in the spring of 1968, but

Coletta and Edwards remained keen to invest in the music business and encouraged Lord and Simper to form a band of their own.

Beneath the covers

Lord, born in Leicester on 9 June 1941, was a classically trained keyboard-player. He had turned his back on music for three years to train as an actor at drama school before returning to music to 'save himself from complete starvation', as another early press release succinctly put it. In the

Above: The original Deep Purple, from left Ritchie Blackmore, Rod Evans, Ian Paice, Jon Lord and Nicky Simper. Below: The line-up after Ian Gillan (far right) and Roger Glover (right) joined. They were replaced by Glenn Hughes and David Coverdale (left), who entered the Purple fold in 1973.

early Sixties, he played with various jazz outfits before switching to beat and R&B with the Artwoods – the band set up by Ron Wood's brother Art – and, subsequently, the Riot Squad.

Simper, meanwhile, had served a spell as bass-player with Johnny Kidd and the Pirates – he was injured in the car crash that killed Kidd in October 1966 – before turning to session work. It was at a session in the summer of 1967, for the Flowerpot Men's 'Let's Go To San Francisco', that he met Jon Lord.

The first recruit for the duo's new group was Ritchie Blackmore. Born in Weston-Super-Mare on 14 April 1945, he had been a session guitarist since his mid-teens and had played with Nero and the Gladiators and Screaming Lord Sutch and the Savages among others. Drummer Ian Paice (born Hounslow, London, 29 June 1948) and vocalist Rod Evans were found through advertising in the music press.

Signed to EMI's Parlophone label, this first incarnation of Deep Purple was an instant success in the United States, where their records appeared on the Tetragrammaton label. 'Hush', a version of the Joe South song replete with Lord's churning organ and Blackmore's stinging guitar fills, was released on 21 June 1968 and reached Number 4 in the Hot Hundred three months later. Further singles successes followed with covers of Neil Diamond's 'Kentucky Woman' and Phil Spector's 'River Deep Mountain High', while the first three albums, *Shades Of Deep Purple* (1968), *The Book Of Taliesyn* and *Deep Purple* (both 1969) also sold well.

However, while US sales were good enough, the group's direction left much to be desired. The albums had been over-reliant on cover versions – 'Hey Joe', the Beatles' 'Help' and 'We Can Work It Out' and Donovan's 'Lalena' included – and, although Blackmore's impressively flamboyant style and Lord's churchy organ dominated proceedings, the overall sound

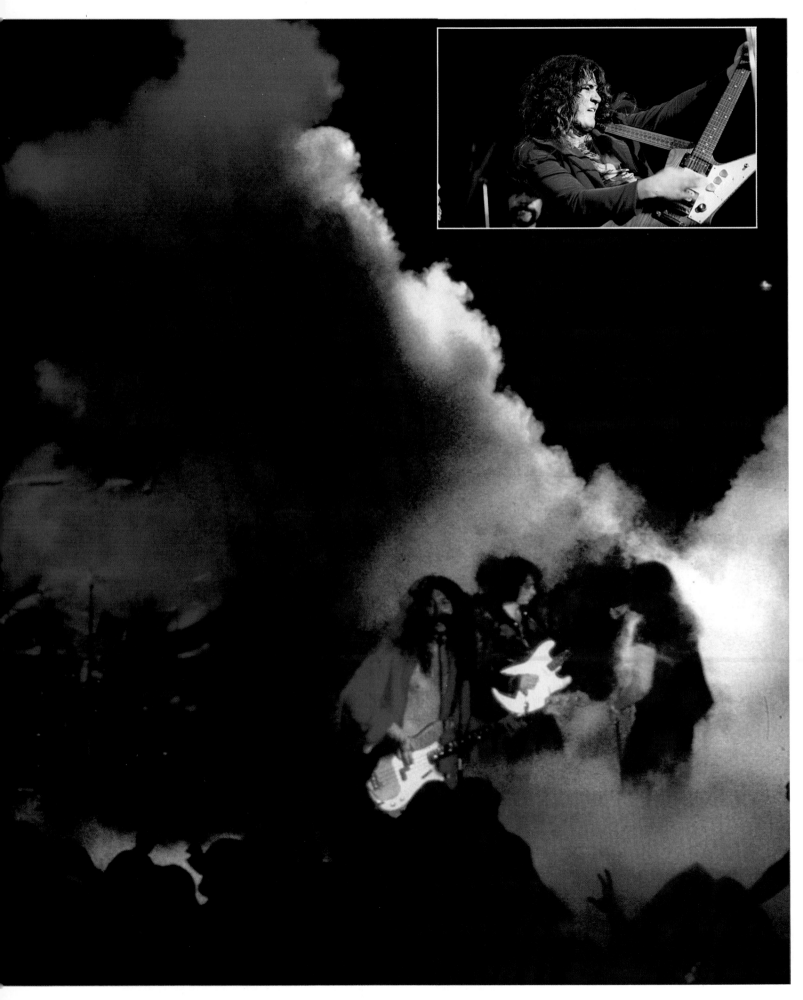

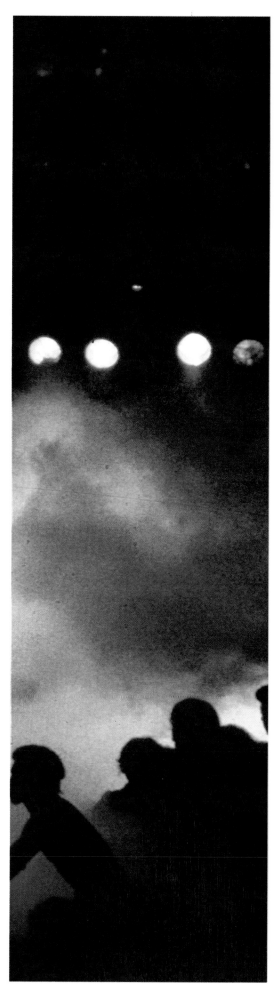

of the band was at times embarrassingly weak. In the States Deep Purple were considered to be little more than a pop group, reasonably strong at doing cover versions but none too original, while they made minimal impact in their native Britain.

A re-structuring of the band was thought necessary, and Simper and Evans were sacked in the spring of 1969 – much to founder member Simper's annoyance. Speaking in 1975, he revealed his dissatisfaction: 'Evans and myself were just as important as the other three 'superstars' which explains why the band's career slumped to an all-time low in the US on our departure. Without Rod Evans and myself, Deep Purple would probably never have been and without those early hits they would certainly never have survived.' Nonetheless, the decision to oust the two seems valid in retrospect, for with the addition of vocalist Ian Gillan and bassist Roger Glover the band began to assume a heavier rock identity.

The rock machine

Gillan, born in Hounslow on 19 August 1945, and Glover, born in Brecon on 30 November 1945, had been through a variety of obscure semi-pro bands before finally linking in a pop outfit called Episode Six, from which they were recruited to Deep Purple. Gillan proved to be an inspired choice because of his remarkably powerful and distinctive voice, while Glover's imaginative bass-lines and sheer precision helped to move Purple into harder rock territory. The breakthrough in Britain came with Lord's concerto, which received its public debut at the Royal Albert Hall in London on 24 September 1969. The orchestra was the Royal Philharmonic and the conductor Malcolm Arnold.

The concerto turned out to be something of a mixed bag – pleasant, classically derived themes intertwined with heavy riffs – but its Albert Hall debut was received with rapture.

In 1970, the band released *Deep Purple In Rock*, an album that established the Deep Purple formula – wailing, shrieking vocal work and extended instrumental pyrotechnics built around simple but rock-hard riffs. The album rapidly sold a million copies, while the band also assailed the pop charts with the commercial heavy metal of 'Black Night', which rose to Number 2 in the UK in late September.

For the next couple of years Purple followed a gruelling work schedule. They were tied to a recording contract that demanded two albums a year and, at the same time, were gigging constantly all over the world.

At the same time rumours were flying thick and fast about the impending dissolution of the band, with the mercurial and short-tempered Ritchie Blackmore as the

Left: Armageddon in Purple – the band hit Paris. Inset: Tommy Bolin, Blackmore's replacement, died tragically young.

prime contender for departure. He openly lashed the band's next album *Fireball* (1971) and midway through 1972, with *Machine Head* at the top of the LP charts, he was predicting that Purple would do one more album and then fold up.

At the time, he said 'I think there's room for more excitement in today's music and I want to do something about it. I think I can do something more exciting than Deep Purple. Although we are all good musicians in Purple we are limited to certain things. It's hard to write hard riffs all the time. I don't think we can get much bigger than we are at the moment and it's a nice position to be in but it can't last forever.'

Surprisingly, however, it was the new boys, Gillan and Glover, who decided to leave midway through 1973. Gillan had actually handed in his notice in 1972, but was persuaded to remain for a spell because of the band's enormous success in the States. When he actually made his decision public – after the music press had erroneously 'revealed' that Blackmore and Ian Paice were to leave – three of the band's albums, *Machine Head, Made In Japan* (1972) and *Who Do We Think We Are?* (1973), had become million-sellers in America.

A combination of Gillan's own business interests and heightening differences of opinion about musical direction – plus personality clashes between Gillan and Blackmore – had led the singer to quit. He had purchased a recording studio with the profits made from his (pre-Purple) participation in the *Jesus Christ Superstar* album, which had become an enormous success, and intended to concentrate on this new venture.

Within a few weeks of Gillan's departure from Purple – and press speculation of ex-Free vocalist Paul Rodgers coming in on vocals – Roger Glover quit to become head of A&R for Purple Records, the band's own label. He continued to record his own material, however, including 1974's *Butterfly Ball*, a terrible mish-mash of an album which had been inspired by the drawings of Alan Aldridge. Glover's replacement in Deep Purple was Glenn Hughes, a comparative youngster who had been with the highly-talented trio Trapeze for the previous three years. The replacement for Gillan was much more surprising – the totally unknown David Coverdale.

'I was working in a clothes shop in Redcar and I was playing in semi-pro bands at nights – world-famous bands like the Fabulosa Brothers,' Coverdale recalled in a later interview. 'I heard that Purple wanted a new singer so I was conceited enough to think I might stand a chance. I sent a tape and I was astonished when I got the message that they wanted to see me. When I actually got the job I couldn't speak.'

One of Coverdale's first professional dates with the band was at the California Jam in 1973, where the band headlined in front of some three-quarters of a million people. With Blackmore revealing his infamous temper by trashing a highly expensive TV camera and with a stunt involving exploding amps going so wrong that the stage was set ablaze, it was very much a baptism of fire for Coverdale.

During 1974 and the first half of the following year the third Deep Purple line-up recorded two further albums, *Burn* and *Stormbringer*. Then in mid 1975 Blackmore finally left to form Rainbow. For a while it appeared that his departure would signal the end of Deep Purple. However, Coverdale and Hughes persuaded the somewhat reluctant Lord and Paice to keep the band going and introduced a new guitarist in American Tommy Bolin, formerly of the James Gang. Bolin made an immediate impression by composing much of the material for a new album, *Come Taste The Band* (1975).

All played out
The new LP saw the group departing somewhat from the formula of the last six years. Songs were shorter than on previous albums, while the music was less dependent on heavy riffs and instrumental dexterity, leaning more towards the R&B traditions of American hard rock than the bombastic ones of British heavy metal. But worthy though *Come Taste The Band* was, it proved to be the last gasp of a spent force.

In the middle of July 1976, it was announced that Deep Purple had folded. 'Having had so many personnel changes in the past eight years we felt that rather than rearrange yet again it would be better to stop while the going was good,' manager Rob Cooksey told the press. 'David resigned a couple of months ago and we decided that rather than chase every penny while the band was going downhill

DEEP PURPLE
Discography

Singles
Hush/One More Rainy Day (Parlophone 5708, 1968); Kentucky Woman/Wring That Neck (Parlophone 5754, 1968); Emmaretta/Wring That Neck (Parlophone 5763, 1969); Hallelujah/April Part One (Harvest HAR 5006, 1969); Black Night/Speed King (Harvest HAR 5020, 1970); Strange Kind Of Woman/I'm Alone (Harvest HAR 5033, 1971); Fireball/Demon's Eye (Harvest HAR 5054, 1971); Never Before/When A Blind Man Cries (Purple PUR 102, 1972); Might Just Take Your Life/Coronarias Redig (Purple PUR 117, 1974); You Keep On Moving/Love Child (Purple PUR 130, 1976); Smoke On The Water/Child In Time/Woman From Tokyo (Purple PUR 132, 1977).

Albums (selective)
Shades Of Deep Purple (Parlophone PCS 7055, 1968); *The Book Of Taliesyn* (Harvest SHVL 751, 1969); *Deep Purple* (Harvest SHVL 759, 1969); *Concerto For Group And Orchestra* (Harvest SHVL 767, 1970); *In Rock* (Harvest SHVL 777, 1970); *Fireball* (Harvest SHVL 793, 1971); *Machine Head* (Purple Records TPSA 7504, 1972); *Made In Japan* (Purple Records TPS 351, 1972); *Who Do We Think We Are?* (Purple Records TPSA 7508, 1973); *Burn* (Purple Records TPS 3505, 1974); *Stormbringer* (Purple Records TPS 3508, 1974); *Come Taste The Band* (Purple Records TPSA 7515, 1975); *Deepest Purple* (Harvest EMTV 25, 1980); *In Concert 1970-72* (Harvest SHDW 412, 1980).

it would be better to call a halt.'

Glenn Hughes made his own solo album, *Play Me Out* (1977), disappeared into obscurity for some years, but resurfaced in 1982 with a new band called Hughes-Thrall. Paice and Lord teamed up with ex-Family keyboard-player Tony Ashton, guitarist Bernie Marsden from Babe Ruth and bass player Paul Martinez to form Paice, Ashton and Lord; they recorded one patchy album called *Malice In Wonderland* (1977) before splitting.

Coverdale recorded two solo albums, *Whitesnake* (1977) and *Northwinds* (1978), before setting up his own band, Whitesnake, which Jon Lord and Ian Paice joined in 1978. Tommy Bolin, meanwhile, had died of a drug overdose in Miami just six months after the end of Purple, cutting short a potentially dazzling solo career.

Eight years is not a particularly long career for a hard-rock band, and the number of upheavals and personnel changes that Purple suffered tends to obscure their collective significance. In their last three years they were the biggest rock band in the world – record sales testify to that fact – and at their peak they were a dynamic stage force and a remarkably talented band.

The fact that the members of Deep Purple spawned so many offshoots, did so many solo projects while still in the band and were mostly still active in the Eighties was a testament in itself to their thirst to make music and the depth of their musical ability.

Blackmore, Gillan, Glover, Lord and Paice finally succumbed to press speculation and reformed the group in 1984. UK Top Ten albums in *Perfect Strangers* and 1987's *House Of Blue Light* kept the legend alive.   BRIAN HARRIGAN

Above left: Lord of the keyboards. Below: Ritchie Blackmore's temper was notorious, often exploding on stage.

Turn on, Tune in, Drop Out

Politics, rock and fashion fuelled the West's new young consumers

THE EARLY SIXTIES saw two or three years of spectacular economic growth in the West. In particular, the increase in world trade at the beginning of the decade was unprecedented in modern times, more than matching the increase which marked the great days of Empire in the first dozen years of the twentieth century.

Inevitably, the mood of the period reflected the changed circumstance of economic expansion. A new liberalism spread across Europe and America as more money, more leisure time and a greater variety of goods and services became available to people. The relatively narrow horizons encouraged by austerity and Cold War paranoia in the Fifties broadened under the influence of cheap travel, new and powerful communications technologies and the pressure of industries seeking new markets.

In Britain, the satire boom, the Profumo affair, the popularity of the Beatles and a revolution in fashion, spreading from small boutiques in Carnaby Street and the King's Road, all heralded profound changes in mass society. Old attitudes and stale traditions were being swept aside as rampant consumerism encouraged a sense of experimentation and freedom in sexual morality, clothes, hairstyles, music, art and politics.

In the United States – where conditions were significantly different – the changing mood of the early Sixties was evidenced by the growth of folk-protest music, the increasing acceptance of 'beatnik' ideals, the burgeoning appeal of modern or 'cool' jazz and the birth of the radical student movement. Towering above all these, perhaps, was the fact of John F. Kennedy's election to the presidency in 1960.

In the president's steps

Kennedy was young, good-looking, apparently liberal and – a first for the US presidency – a Catholic. As many commentators have noted, Kennedy's assassination in 1963 provides at least a partial explanation of the Beatles' subsequent success with younger generations in America – they stepped into the vacuum Kennedy left and came to symbolise everything that the president had once symbolised: youthfulness, success, good-humour, good looks, playful boyishness, innocence combined with native cunning, hope for the future and a crucial unconventionality. And if it's argued that the Beatles were a group, then Kennedy had his family, his brother Robert, his elegant wife Jackie, his courtiers and his Camelot.

With Kennedy and the Beatles, the line between politics and showbiz became all but invisible. Both seemed to represent a new and popular urge to democracy and the overthrow of restrictive national boundaries. And rock – accepted as the form of showbiz for the young – was the perfect vehicle for the aspirations of

those who were beginning to see themselves as the first settlers in a Brave New World. The possibilities were seemingly endless.

Indeed, rock music's role in the changing mood of the Sixties can hardly be overestimated. The new electronic technologies that shaped rock and grew up on its back helped create new patterns of consumption and new styles of music. Fifties rock'n'roll was relatively unsophisticated in its aspirations, but, by the time Phil Spector was producing his 'little symphonies for kids' with the Ronettes and the Crystals, rock had developed a sense of its own artistic potential. Developments in broadcasting, recording and amplification technology would help fulfil this potential, while the widespread availability of cheap hi-fi (also made possible by rock's enormous popularity) gave rock artistic credibility by enabling the private consumption of crafted work.

High-school autograph hounds surround John F. Kennedy in Milwaukee, 1960. Kennedy's election to the presidency that year seemed to symbolise the changing, youthful and optimistic mood of the times.

Perhaps even more significant was the way that rock tied in with radical politics, becoming an instrument for stirring the consciences of the young. Consumerism created its own contradictions. In making ideas and technologies widely available for the sake of profit alone, it was unable to discourage more radical ideas and the use of technologies in a struggle against the profit-system.

The key figure in this process in the early Sixties was undeniably Bob Dylan, who had renounced rock'n'roll at the end of the previous decade to pursue a more 'committed' kind of music. Dylan's involvement in the early Sixties' movement for black civil rights made him a political figure. But that movement – like the anti-Vietnam War movement that followed it – was essentially a part of the same general process of liberalisation that lay behind Sixties consumerism.

World of hope?

One of the crucial aspects of this liberalisation was that it confirmed the end of imperialism. From the beginning of the Sixties, Third World cultures were no longer reviled as alien, inferior and merely exploitable. On the contrary, they were promoted (at least, in public) as exotic, interesting, future partners in the worldwide adventure of industrialisation. On a more superficial level, the East was famed as the source of spicy foods, colourful clothes, profound ideas and fascinating art – all of which, in one form or another, could be gainfully exchanged for dollars and pounds.

Although overt imperialism was at an end, this did not deter Western nations continuing to exploit and oppress former colonies and colonised peoples. The American blacks were such a people, and the Civil Rights movement was seen as an essentially anti-imperialist struggle. Blacks became 'Afro-Americans', some converted to Islam and many argued for a future independent of – even separate from – white America. The Vietnam War, too, was seen as an anti-imperialist struggle; as the Sixties progressed, supporters of the struggles of such colonial peoples – whose ideas had been allowed free range in the liberal atmosphere of an expansionary West – began to see that very expansionary West as an ogre.

Dylan and many of his contemporaries turned that message into song. They promoted their vision of a better world in terms that pitted the values of industrial, urbanised societies against the 'more human' values of (a probably imaginary) Third World and rural peasantry. Folk music, country blues, marijuana, Tibetan bells, Indian incense, Islam and Buddhism all became fashionable, as did many other products of Third World and rural societies. These were the overt symbols of opposition to the oppressive technocracy of the West.

Dylan – who turned the Beatles on to marijuana in 1964 and thereby opened at least one set of floodgates – was canny enough to understand technology's contradictory nature. His going electric in 1965 seemed a sell-out to many radicals and folk musicians, but it was, for Dylan, a route to vaster audiences than any traditional folk musicians could previously have dreamed of.

Top: Dr. Timothy Leary (centre) holds forth while Yippie activists Abbie Hoffman (left) and Jerry Rubin tune in. Above: Oz magazine, launched in London in February 1967 by Australian Richard Neville, was a colourful (and often illegible) mixture of radical politics, hippie philosophy, music, cartoons, graphics and pornography. Along with IT, the paper helped give a united voice to the London underground scene until it ceased publication in the early Seventies.

Into this ferment of new music, political radicalism, colourful clothes and unconventional lifestyles stepped LSD – the most powerful hallucinogenic drug known. Through the patronage of people like the novelist Aldous Huxley and the philosopher of religion Alan Watts – as well as a number of experimentally-inclined psychiatrists and psychologists – LSD had already gained something of reputation as a wonder drug. Huxley and Watts promoted a quasi-religious view of LSD, linking it to mysticism and the ancient ritual use of other hallucinogens such as the psilocybin ('magic') mushroom, mescaline and hashish. Others had investigated the drug's use in more mundane problem-solving or therapeutic contexts. Those who had come across LSD by the onset of the Sixties were inevitably convinced of its potential for changing human awareness on an individual level.

The single most important thing about LSD, however, was that it was a synthetic substance – a technological product which seemed to have profoundly humanising effects. Here was the acute contradiction of Sixties economic expansion embodied and resolved in an odourless, colourless, tasteless liquid: LSD was a mass-produced commodity in the exclusive service of the spiritual and creative lives of human beings.

The drug's messiah, psychologist Timothy Leary, was sacked from Harvard University in 1962 for spreading the LSD gospel. Travelling through California, Mexico and New York, he propounded his philosophy of 'the psychedelic revolution' (the term psychedelic – literally, 'mind manifesting' – was coined by an early LSD-experimenter to describe the drug's effects). Leary left a trail of converts whose attitudes to LSD's 'consciousness-expanding' possibilities varied from the playful to the deadly earnest. Almost everybody who came in touch with LSD in those days did take one of Leary's messages at face value: 'turn on, tune in and drop out' became the slogan of the age.

A common effect of the drug was to heighten the senses and break down the barriers to perception. Colours would glow, sounds would linger and resonate; sometimes one stimulus would provoke quite an unexpected response so

that music would become translated into
imagined visions. Rock music – loud, simple,
often repetitive and highly rhythmic – became
the favoured soundtrack for the LSD 'trip'. New
performers emerged in the 'Acid Tests', 'Trips
Festivals', 'Be-Ins' and 'Freak-Outs' that
started in the mid Sixties as anarchic events to
occupy the sensation-hungry tripper through
an eight to twelve-hour experience. These
performers – notably the Grateful Dead in
America and Pink Floyd in Britain – cultivated
a style which depended on simple chord struc-
tures, massive amplification and much repetitive improvisation. Their performances were
often accompanied by light shows using slides,
spotlights and bits of film, and audiences were
encouraged to dance, wear make-up and flowing clothes and generally pursue as many different stimuli as possible.

By 1967, LSD itself had been made almost
universally illegal. Yet the psychedelic lifestyle was in full swing, a rendered-down liquor
strained off from the casserole of economic expansion, the resurgence of rock and LSD itself.
Indeed, psychedelia was most significant as a
popular fashion towards the end of the Sixties,
when beads, bells, paisley shirts, cut-rate
Eastern religions and flower-power pop finally
found their niche in the expanded market-
place.   GARY HERMAN

GENERATION LANDSLIDE

WHO LISTENS TO ROCK – and why? Such general questions are difficult to answer in specific or useful terms, and yet the answers are essential to an understanding of how the music has developed. Almost any generalisation can be refuted by concrete examples. Was the Fifties audience for rock'n'roll essentially working class? If so, how to explain the boys at boarding schools religiously hoarding Jerry Lee Lewis records? Is rock's essential appeal connected to youthful rebellion? Then why were the Beatles cleaned up and rendered acceptable to everyone before they hit the top?

Both social and psychological generalisations about the rock audience are fraught with pitfalls. But there can be no doubt that, however indefinable, a rock audience can be perceived. Between the early years of rock'n'roll in Britain – 1956 and 1957 – and the heyday of progressive rock in the years around 1970, there undoubtedly took place a major change in the numbers of people who listened to rock, and in the social acceptability of the music. During that time the rock audience grew from being a relatively small part of the population – teenaged and essentially working-class or lower-middle class – into being a very large and wide-ranging part of the population.

UK's teenage wasteland became common ground

This broadening of the audience has a complex relationship to the development of the music. At one level, the audience's response to the music was passive, if often unpredictable – few involved in the early bouts of Beatlemania could have anticipated that the response would be so overwhelming. On another level, the audience defined and directed the music. Groups that did not appeal to a mass audience inevitably did less well. The audience was a breeding ground for new artists, and many of the constantly emerging groups started out as fans. Thus the relation between audience and artists was often reciprocal.

The rock tribes
Certain aspects of the rock audience stayed the same, of course, from 1956 to 1970. Probably the most important of these was that rock provided an excellent method of

Above: Sampling the latest sounds in the local record shop became an obligatory part of the teenager's Saturday afternoon – but the Sixties were to see the jazzy decors of the disc emporia left behind by the progressive rock revolution.

group identification for various sections of youth – as did clothing, slang, and even certain patterns of violence. The three most obvious of these groups were the Teddy Boys, the Mods, and the Skinheads.

It is usually assumed that the Teds were a product of rock'n'roll, but their arrival on the streets of London's working-class areas like the Elephant and Castle pre-dated the rock'n'roll explosion by a few years. The Teds were teenage and male, and they affected a style calculated to reflect their instinctive rejection of established authority. They dressed sharp, in flamboyant Edwardian styles geared to transcend their class origins, and which later became stylised in a tribal uniform: drape jacket, tight 'drainpipe' trousers, thick-soled crepe shoes, string ties and long hair greased to pile up at the front.

The Teds were raw and physical in a way that frightened the middle-aged and the middle-class. They were portrayed as an anarchic threat to society, but they were not concerned with revolution, merely a fulsome embrace of the traditional way of having a good time – getting drunk and having a few fights. They fought dirty, in packs, with flick-knives, coshes and bicycle chains, against anyone foolish enough to cross them, against rival gangs, and against West Indians. They were fuelled

by images that crept across from America, where a similar subculture had arisen, identifying with the inarticulate rebellion expressed on screen by Marlon Brando in *The Wild One* (1953) and James Dean in *Rebel Without A Cause* (1955). As a movement, the Teds at first lacked a rallying cry, but they soon found it in rock'n'roll. In 1955 a film melodrama about the problems faced by teachers in tough American inner-city schools, *The Blackboard Jungle*, boasted as its theme Bill Haley's 'Rock Around The Clock'. When it played in British cinemas, the theme alone was reported to drive audiences wild. When Haley made the film *Rock Around The Clock* (1956) the Teds exploded.

The Mods came from a similar background to the Teds, but were of a different age. They hailed from the suburbs of London, and were mainly working, or, at least, lower-middle-class, but their emergence as a group coincided with a boom in the economy. Money was freer, and the Mods took the opportunity it offered them to bring fashion right down into the teenage market. The Mods were cool and sharp and clothes conscious, admiring the trend-setting of their self-elected heroes, the so-called 'faces'. They sported sharp Italian-style suits, styled hair, coloured shirts, American-army parkas and rode neat, light motor-scooters. They had their own clubs and an egalitarian approach that spawned a rash of their own bands, the greatest of which was the Who. The Mods flirted with the effects of amphetamines and toyed with the decorative delights afforded by make-up – on both boys and girls. By 1965 the Mods

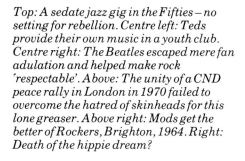

Top: A sedate jazz gig in the Fifties – no setting for rebellion. Centre left: Teds provide their own music in a youth club. Centre right: The Beatles escaped mere fan adulation and helped make rock 'respectable'. Above: The unity of a CND peace rally in London in 1970 failed to overcome the hatred of skinheads for this lone greaser. Above right: Mods get the better of Rockers, Brighton, 1964. Right: Death of the hippie dream?

were becoming the tribe most in sympathy with the time. They set London Swinging with their boutiques, boasted their own TV show, 'Ready, Steady, Go!' and claimed a uniqueness implicit in their great anthem, the Who's 'My Generation'.

Among the old style of rock'n'roll fans, Mods inspired loathing. Many of the former Teds were now getting on a bit, and their successors were a young breed who clung to the purity of rock. Dubbed Rockers, they pushed the anti-social qualities of wearing their hair long and untidy and riding solid, powerful motor-bikes in an aggressive, masculine celebration of rock'n'roll's original rawness. They were the antithesis of the Mods – one group stylish, forward-looking, prepared to experiment with apparently feminine styles, the other retrospective, deliberately untidy and swaggeringly macho. Not surprisingly, when the two collided, as they did at several seaside resorts in the mid Sixties, the result was apt to be bloody. It was perhaps inevitable that the atavistic rockers would not thrive, but the values they championed paved the way for the emergence of the 'hard-rock' or 'heavy-metal' styles of the early Seventies.

Enter the boot boys
By the end of the Sixties, another instantly recognisable tribe was emerging. While on the one hand ordinary working-class kids bought bright, new, manufactured commercial sounds regardless of trend or tribe, and on the other hand students, sixth-formers and old Mods, many now pursuing fashion into the realms of hippydom, advocated increasingly high-flown and intellectual musical ideals, a party emerged that cried 'A plague on all your houses!'

The skinheads, once again, originated in the city suburbs and were working-class. They despised the long-haired excesses of the intellectual school, and listened instead to the seductive rhythms of West Indian reggae and ska. They were austerely plebeian in their fashion, cropping their hair brutally short, wearing straight jeans turned up at the bottoms to reveal provocative 'bovver boots'. Violence was their creed, and they attacked anyone bearing the tell-tale badge of long-hair, rival football supporters, and their own pet hate, Pakistanis. Despite the difference in their dress, their attitudes were reminiscent of the early Teds – a curiously full circle.

As far as rock is concerned, these tribal groups are most illuminating when one considers what they were reacting against – what they most disliked. The Teds hated the sounds of trad jazz, modern jazz and folk music. Partly, no doubt, this was based on class envy towards a dominant culture. Skinheads, too, felt an acute class antagonism towards certain kinds of music – but the music they disliked included much of what was regarded the mainstream of rock.

This change from rock as a minority music to being the majority music involved many interacting processes; but perhaps the two most important were the growth of middle-class interest in rock and the association of rock with large-scale social changes – the thousands who streamed to the Isle of Wight festival in 1970 had little in common with the defensive, violent Teds and Skinheads.

Rock goes to college
Although it would be an exaggeration to say that the middle-classes 'took over' rock in the mid Sixties, there is no doubt that the middle-class influx was the most obvious change in the audience. College students who in 1958 would have listened to trad jazz, or perhaps skiffle or modern jazz, had condemned such sounds to the

Above: Widening the generation gap – middle-aged officials appear nonplussed as excited Rolling Stones fans take the stage in Holland around 1965. Left: Girl pop fans tend to be less tribalistic than boys, but they know what they like – David Cassidy fans express appreciation, London, 1974.

dustbin of history by 1968. Jimmy Porter, the hero of John Osborne's 1956 play 'Look Back In Anger' – the original angry young man – played jazz trumpet. By the mid Sixties, playing the trumpet would have seemed distinctly unromantic. It was scarcely possible to use the styles of New Orleans jazz to express angst or sexuality in the age of Bob Dylan and the Rolling Stones – the guitar had become the instrument of those youthful preoccupations. One of Dave Brubeck's recordings of the Fifties was *Jazz Goes To College*. By 1970, the emphasis was firmly on rock at college, and the campus social secretary was part of the national network of rock booking.

To a large extent, this middle-class interest in rock was sparked off by changes in the music itself. The vacuous candy-floss

pop of the early Sixties had certainly been replaced by something much tougher, and generally more interesting by 1965. The R&B and blues influences that Alexis Korner and others had been championing for a decade found its way into mainstream popular music – so musicians like Eric Clapton began to come to the fore, and both performers and audience could see scope for expression – and progression.

On a social level, rock performers were alerted to major concerns – and their lyrics reflected it. The folk boom of the early Sixties would probably have penetrated mainstream rock anyway, but Bob Dylan's 'conversion' to rock set an example to performers who felt they had something political, personal or universal to say – and who subsequently said it with rock music. Even if much of what came out was bogus, false or misdirected, the fact that they did it gave rock the same appeal, or rather the same justification, that had earlier been the province of ethnic, or folk music. Rock became respectable – the Beatles could be compared to Schubert, Mick Jagger could recite Shelley to an audience of thousands.

So, from one angle, it is clear that the rock audience changed; it became more broadly based, more ambitious in its tastes. But this in itself is merely part of rock's close relationship with radical social upheaval, and the assumption that rock was the true music of progress, the music that was the natural accompaniment to growing up.

Years of upheaval

During the Sixties, the confines of Fifties society began to crumble. There had been social change in the Fifties, of course; young people had become politicised enough to form the backbone of the Campaign for Nuclear Disarmament, and beatniks, folkniks, skiffle clubs and coffee bars had all been part of the growing youth culture. Such phenomena were dwarfed by what happened in the Sixties, however. From student political agitation leading to riots outside the American Embassy in London in 1968 to a revolution in women's underwear, from the widespread use of illegal drugs to the opening up of higher education, from the sexual freedom en-

couraged by the pill to the lowering of the age of majority to 18 years – the life of Britain's youth underwent a social revolution. And rock was intimately associated with this revolution, was part of it. Rock stars provided the images that young people wanted to copy; rock music was the inevitable soundtrack of adolescence.

This can partly be explained by the mass media's response to changes in society, and its recruitment of a new generation of writers, broadcasters and personalities interested in rock and dedicated to spreading their ideas. They saw rock as the music that accompanied their rise – and let everyone know it. Then there were those who pushed rock because it was profitable and because the teenage market was expanding furiously; these included a wide range of entrepreneurs and businessmen (as well as dealers and hustlers) both inside and outside the rock industry.

Additionally, musicians themselves felt that they were part of a new world; they identified with it in a way that had been impossible for the likes of Elvis or Jerry Lee Lewis in the Fifties. The Beatles, leaders of popular music and a constantly progressing group (not just an isolated totem as Elvis had become), took their social position seriously, and *wanted* to be part of the general changes that were taking place. They, and bands like them, identified with their audience and felt that they embodied its aspirations. Accordingly, rock was at the forefront of a rampant new culture, and Swinging London – its centre – was an example to the world. In San Francisco, too, in the period 1966-69, rock music trends and youth culture became synonymous.

When you're young

These developments were, perhaps, the expression of something deeper. Painting and light shows were an integral part of San Franciscan culture, but they did not take over the world like the music of the Grateful Dead or Jefferson Airplane did. Ultimately, the mass-acceptance of rock in the Sixties resulted from the development of a style, or rather many variations on a common style, around 1962-65, which suited perfectly the vast majority of young people. This audience listened to rock because it expressed emotions with which they could identify strongly; that it was rock that answered this need may have been just a cultural accident, the fortuitous outcome of artists like the Beatles, the Rolling Stones and Bob Dylan being in the right place at the right time.

By 1970, the rock audience comprised almost anyone who was young, excepting those small minorities that were captivated by other forms of music. Not all of this audience was necessarily very knowledgeable about rock, or particularly fanatical about its likes or dislikes. But, indisputably, when the young listened to music, in dance hall or hall of residence, in public bar or public school, the music it listened to was rock.   IAN J KNIGHT

Psychedelic Wallflowers

Poster power: the art of graphic rebellion

UNTIL THE ARRIVAL of psychedelia in the mid Sixties, rock posters were purely informative. Visually, they were very dull; the headline artist appeared at the top in the largest lettering, the opening act at the bottom in the smallest. The type was uniform, usually black on white, with maybe a dash of red for good measure. Such posters have no artistic value, and any interest in them is either in the names of the artists or the venues at which they played.

By 1964 there was some attempt to make the rock poster look less like an estate agent's auction list, but it was usually restricted to the use of dark-coloured paper and white ink. In the UK, one or two clubs started to experiment with lettering – notably the Crawdaddy, which adopted similar lettering to the famous Yardbirds logo.

Acid art
The rock poster as an art form dates from the beginning of the 'acid days' and comes, not surprisingly, from San Francisco. The first poster in the new style advertised a

now-famous gig – the Charlatans at the Red Dog Saloon in Nevada in the summer of 1965. The Charlatans drew their style of dress from a combination of Wild West cowboys and Mississippi gamblers, and they felt that an appropriate poster was required to reflect their image. Band members George Hunter and Michael Ferguson therefore came up with a marvellously dense design, full of different lettering, caricature drawings of the band members and all manner of little eye-catching devices. Like the band's image, it combined the consciously archaic with the boldly original and fresh. Aspects of this

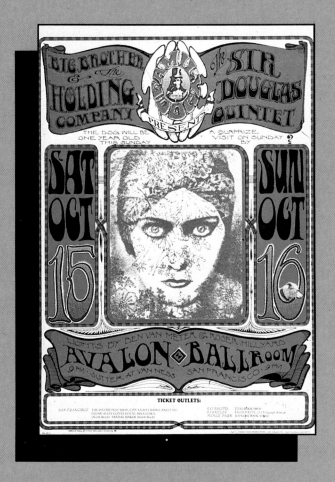

Above, left to right: George Hunter and Michael Ferguson's eclectic pioneering poster for the Charlatans; swirling acid-trip colours from Wes Wilson; movie, Americana and flower-power images boldly used in a poster from the Mouse Studios; sex and Dayglo mysticism make a brilliant effect in one of Victor Moscoso's posters.

poster influenced the San Francisco artists who became famous in the following year.

By early 1966, when the Family Dog and Bill Graham's organisation were running weekly dances at the Fillmore, the idea of having an exotic poster to advertise the gigs and reflect the nature of the music had taken hold. The first regular artist they employed was Wes Wilson, who became well-known for his original style. His work rapidly became stylised, however – he generally used only two heavily contrasting colours in a central design, surrounded by the group's name in standard lettering.

When the Family Dog moved to the Avalon, Chet Helms started to employ a variety of artists, notably Stanley 'Mouse' Miller and Alton Kelley of Mouse Studios. Their work combined Mouse's undeniable draughtsmanship with Kelley's predilec-tion for collage, and both artists would, as Mouse puts it, 'raid the image bank', get-ting their inspiration for a central image from books on art and photography.

Towards the end of 1966, the Avalon added another name to the list – Victor Moscoso, a highly accomplished SF artist. He specialised in the hypnotic effects created by weird colour combinations, which made his posters difficult to read but stunning to look at. Moscoso's series for the Matrix Club in early 1967 are among the highspots of the era. Another artist who was commissioned by Avalon was Rick Griffin, who is perhaps best known for the

cover of the Grateful Dead's *Aoxomoxoa*, originally an Avalon poster. Less prolific than the others, he was arguably the most talented and witty.

In July 1967 an exhibition by Mouse, Kelley, Griffin and Moscoso was held at a gallery in San Francisco; the posters were no longer merely a by-product of rock, they had become works of art in their own right. In the next three years, these four artists and others almost equally talented, including Randy Tuten and Bob Fried, produced many hundreds of posters for the Avalon Ballroom, the Fillmore and dozens of other smaller venues and one-off benefits; a high proportion of these subsequently became collectors' items. Although they became increasingly sophisticated, they never lost the earthy yet mind-bending quality of the early designs.

San Francisco posters disappeared with the passing of the hippie era. They were intrinsically connected with it and inseparable from groups whose names conjured up psychedelic images, such as Country Joe and the Fish or Kaleidoscope. Mouse and Kelley continued to work closely with the Grateful Dead, the group most evocative of the era, but like the music itself, the style of these posters is a thing of the past.

Other artists in different parts of the United States took their inspiration from the posters produced in San Francisco. In Detroit, Gary Grimshaw produced an excellent set of posters for the Grande and Aragon Ballrooms to rival the best work of Mouse or Griffin. Los Angeles, too, produced some good examples, notably a set of nearly 30 round posters by various artists for the Kaleidoscope Club. In Texas Jim Franklin and Fabulous Furry Freak Bros.

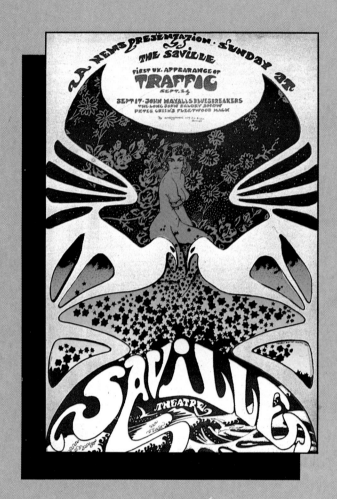

Above, left to right: Resplendent lettering and surreal creatures in a Rick Griffin poster; self-conscious psychedelia from Bob Fried; simpler images and starker colours dramatically employed by Randy Tuten; flowing lines, bird-like images, flowers, stars and a nude poetically combined by Michael English and Nigel Weymouth.

artist Gilbert Shelton designed fine posters for the Vulcan Gas Company venue.

Some of the best of the era came from Britain, from Hapshash and the Coloured Coat, the collective name of artists Michael English and Nigel Weymouth. They produced a series of beautiful silkscreen posters for UFO and the Savile Theatre, as well as promotion material for various bands. Their style was generally more lyrical than that of their American counterparts, but at times maybe just a little too fey and sentimental. Martin Sharp was another truly original British designer, whose swirling Dayglo images also enlivened many early covers of *Oz* magazine, as well as Cream's *Disraeli Gears* and *Wheels Of Fire* album sleeves.

Psychedelic posters vanished even faster in England than in America, largely because the media-inspired 'flower-power' image had become a national joke by the autumn of 1967. Michael English moved on to advertising, and his development parallels the road that rock art took in the early Seventies; posters became slick, sophisticated and very glossy.

Like so much that was good about the mid Sixties, poster art was a naive blend of imagination and talent. The talent may still be there, but the naivety and imagination seem, on the whole, long gone.

JOHN PLATT

Revolutions in Sound

The chaotic development of audio technology

THE WORLD'S FIRST RECORDING was an acappella rendition of 'Mary Had A Little Lamb' by Thomas Edison in December 1877. His device, the phonograph, used a wax cylinder and, despite some serious technical shortcomings, it became the dominant means of recording for the next 20 years. Emile Berliner patented the fore-runner of the modern gramophone disc as early as 1887 and immediately plunged the new industry into an often-to-be-repeated situation: two systems, incompatible with each other, were competing for the public's acceptance. The flat, easily-stored gramophone had an intrinsic advantage over the clumsy cylinder and, by the early Twenties, even Edison had lost interest in his original invention.

Turning to the gramophone, he refined the machine's ability to follow grooves and devised a disc that could play back more than a few minutes of music. In 1926 he patented the first 'long-player' (LP); this was 12 inches in diameter, half an inch thick and a hefty two pounds in weight. The disc could be played on one side only and any extended recording required a set or album of records.

Top: Peter Goldmark of CBS who, in 1948, revolutionised the record business with his development of the long-playing 33⅓ rpm disc. Above: An early, disc-playing wind-up phonograph.

Despite these developments, the record industry was still rather insignificant. It is generally agreed that, until the late Forties, record sales represented only a small percentage of the public's entertainment budget. The conservatism of the music industry was one of the major obstacles to the growth of record sales. Songwriters, composers and agents made their money on the sales of sheet music – and record sales threatened to destroy that market. One of the most important factors which changed this situation, and was critical to the development of rock in particular, occurred in 1948.

LP versus 45
In that year Peter Goldmark, working for CBS in the US, solved a major problem for classical music lovers. By slowing down a disc to 33⅓ revolutions per minute (rpm) and taking advantage of new techniques in cutting records, Goldmark crammed up to 25 minutes of music onto a side. Instead of a set of records, the album became a single disc that could play an entire symphony. The modern LP had arrived.

RCA's president, David Sarnoff, who led the competition to Goldmark's parent company, Columbia, refused to accept the LP and responded by developing a separate system. In 1949 he released the '45'. Seven inches in diameter and playing at 45 rpm, it was claimed by RCA to be superior in sound quality to its competitor. Of course, the two systems were incompatible, not only with each other but with all current gramophone players that operated at 78 rpm. While the two companies began a heated battle to win the public over to their respective system, several outside influences began to shape the course of events.

In the US, television was quickly becoming common in most homes. Non-musical radio shows such as 'Gunsmoke', 'Superman', 'Our Miss Brooks' and 'The Phil Silvers Show' switched over to the new medium and radio began to broadcast more music. The widespread opposition of the music industry to the playing of records on the air collapsed: it was at last apparent that massive record sales were possible if a song got played enough and became a 'hit'. Dwindling sheet music sales no longer mattered.

The widespread purchase of televisions was just one aspect of a growing American economy that allowed the average family to purchase new leisure products. This new prosperity also provided the younger members of the family with a 'weekly allowance' – and, for the first time anywhere, teenage money represented a large purchasing power in itself. Whether anyone really understood these factors as they happened is questionable but unimportant. What is important to the development of rock is that at this crucial stage, when teenagers had money in their pockets, CBS and RCA decided to cooperate by combining both the 33⅓ rpm (LP) and 45 rpm functions into a single record player.

The stereo revolution

Throughout the Fifties and early Sixties, the primary medium for rock music remained the single, which was well within the average teenager's budget. Albums were expensive, 'adult' and all too often nothing but a batch of old standards surrounding the artist's current hit. A record collection meant a pile of 45s stacked on top of each other, usually with the paper covers long since discarded. Such ill-treatment didn't really matter because the record player and its little speaker didn't exactly give the best aural reproduction anyway.

But change was coming as the new electronics industry began to develop the two sides of a record groove to recreate two separate channels of sound. Stereo had, in fact, been invented by EMI in the UK in 1931, but it was not until GIs returned from Japan with cheap and attractively packaged stereo components that its popularity began to catch on. By placing two speakers some distance apart, the audio fan could thrill as a train passed from the left side of his room to the right or listen to a conversation bounce realistically back and forth. For music lovers, stereo meant that the position of individual instruments could be detected, giving the illusion of greater realism.

The music industry was able to react quickly to public enthusiasm and began making stereo recordings readily available. Some popular releases, such as

Top: An Edwardian family delight in the sound of an Edison wax-cylinder phonograph. Above: An Adam Faith interview is recorded on a small portable reel-to-reel. Below: Leslie Ash, in 1979's Quadrophenia, *re-enacts the ill-treatment of 45s by Sixties teens.*

Tommy Edwards' 'It's All In The Game' and the Coasters' 'Yakety Yak' (both 1958), had actually been mixed in stereo long before stereo players were being marketed. Rock was gradually moving towards a marriage with stereo when an unforeseen cultural upheaval suddenly and irrevocably bound them together.

Beatles for sale

One of the most exciting and astonishing things about the Beatles when they burst onto the music scene in the early Sixties was the fact that they wrote their own material. Not only did they write excellent songs, they wrote them in greater quantity than could be released as singles. Right from the start, it seemed as necessary to collect their albums as well as their single releases. As early as the release of *Rubber Soul* in December 1965, the Beatles were producing thematic albums that needed to be heard in their entirety. Other groups followed their example and the American teen market began shifting its emphasis from singles to albums.

There were a few initial problems as much of the best rock music in the mid Sixties was by British bands recording music that was mixed in mono in the UK. Master tapes would be sent to the US to be remixed in stereo, and the results were

often diabolical; Capitol released the Beatles' early material with all the vocals on one side and the instruments on the other, while Reprise mixed the Kinks so that one channel was a slightly delayed echo of the other. At this time some albums were recorded in both mono and stereo, often with considerable differences between the two recordings.

By the end of the Sixties, 'hi-fis' – stereo record players with the turntable, amplifier and speakers boxed separately, with facilities to add tape decks and FM radio tuners – were displacing the old radiograms in many homes. And, since cheap – if unreliable – models were soon available, they also became a fixture in many a student bedsit. As the music abandoned dance for art, the equipment changed, too, from the sturdy mono Dansette to the forbidding cost and high technology of the Bang and Olufsen.

Unlike the gramophone, which was invented and refined by individuals such as Edison and Berliner, the tape deck was developed largely through the work of corporation research teams. Home tapes had made some inroads in the Forties and Fifties when mylar tape replaced the paper tape developed by the Germans during the Second World War. The mylar system was based on a reel-to-reel machine which was expensive and a little too cumbersome for domestic use. Tapes were largely reserved for the studio, where the ease with which they could be edited and mixed made them a natural choice for recording.

Efforts to produce a tape format acceptable to the public date back to the early Fifties. The 3M Corporation had developed a large cassette which was miniaturised by Philips (in Holland), who also slowed the tape speed down to 1⅞ inches per second. Philips made their system available to other manufacturers in 1963, and it has continued essentially unchanged into the Eighties. Meanwhile, US manufacturers were experimenting with a loop of tape wrapped around a single spool – this was the 8-track, and once again the public was presented with two incompatible systems. But the 8-track never really caught on – despite the fact that Ford selected this system for their cars – because of its annoying habit of interrupting tracks in the middle when they exceeded the length of the tape loop.

Quadrophonic sound

Despite the vast improvement over mono, stereo sound is still unnatural to the ear and can seem flat in comparison to live music. The Japanese tried to improve on it by developing quadrophonic sound in which, by using four separate channels of information, they intended to achieve greater realism in sound reproduction. Despite the efforts of the industry to promote quad from 1970 onwards, the concept had flopped by 1974. The expense and inconvenience of two additional speakers and an additional amplifier proved unpopular, while the industry complicated

Opposite: Home tapes in the late Fifties and early Sixties called for the use of a bulky reel-to-reel (inset left). By the Eighties, portable sound systems had become more compact (inset right). Above: Compact audio disc with laser turntable.

matters still further by producing three competing systems.

With the growth of the home sound system, it was not surprising that the public came to demand quality in-car entertainment. The miniaturising of separate audio components means that in the Eighties any car can be fitted with a megawatt system. The portable sound system has also become more compact, and it is no longer necessary to walk around carrying a 15-pound stereo pack. Instead, everyone can be 'wired for sound' to a miniature personal stereo without disturbing those around them.

Remote control

The average stereo system in the early Eighties embodies many refinements of sound reproduction that have radically changed the way the rock audience listens to music. Radio tuners memorise favourite stations, and with a remote selector the listener need not cross the room to tune to any one of these. The tuner's computer locks in on the station's strongest signal and flashes this selection on the digital display. Tape cassette decks often boast more controls than the cockpit of a Second World War fighter; digital display, memory banks, Dolby b and c and dbx noise-reduction systems, auto-reverse, bias adjustment and track selection are all standard. Turntables may be lateral-tracking, direct-drive and quartz-controlled; at the very least a moving-coil cartridge is included. The amplifier's

digital indicators with switchable scale reveal how much power is being put into what set of loudspeakers. These may boast heil-motion tweeters, direct/reflective speakers, passive radiators or any number of other arrangements, while the sound they broadcast may have been passed through a pre-amp, graphic equaliser or sound processor.

The biggest revolution in music listening habits since the 45rpm single came in the mid Eighties with the emergence of the compact disc. Like the cassette, the fact that it was initially produced in a standardised (five-inch diameter) format was undoubtedly instrumental in its fast-growing popularity. Storing sound digitally on a plastic, metallised disc, over 70 minutes of music—often two album's length—could be reproduced. From 1988, CD singles were marketed in 3-inch form, with special 'disc-men' made to play these alone.

The next revolution seemed likely to be CDV or compact disc video. Offering perfect stereo sound plus a TV image (often the track's promotional video) these were marketed by Philips at a competitive price but could not be played on existing CD equipment.

DAT or Digital Audio Tape was also tipped as an alternative to the CD, with one big advantage—the ability to tape your own music. But the possibilities of creating perfect pirate tapes from master-quality CD's held up mass commercial marketing as record companies argued in favour of a copy-prevention mechanism.

By the late Eighties, almost all new pop product was being offered in a choice of analogue (vinyl and tape) and digital (CD) form, with DAT in the wings.   ED HANEL

THE INNER LIGHT?

'IF YOU APPRECIATE the tuning so much, I hope you'll enjoy the playing more,' said Ravi Shankar at the 1971 Concert for Bangladesh when ○ the audience burst into applause after a couple of minutes warm-up from his Indian band. The incident typified the benign misunderstanding that greeted Eastern music and religion during its excursion to the West in the late Sixties and early Seventies. At the time, however, its influence seemed all-pervading – Eastern concepts like *karma* and *yin/yang* found their way into everyday language. Sitars suddenly appeared on many rock singles, notably the Rolling Stones' 'Paint It Black'. DJ John Peel, sitting in a cramped ship's cabin off the south coast of England, read late night extracts from *The Perfumed Garden* to Radio London listeners. Many young people, particularly at pop festivals, wore colourful, Eastern-influenced clothes, and a group of Hindus, under the name Radha Krishna Temple, took a Hare Krishna chant into the UK Top Twenty.

In retrospect these influences may seem superficial, but in terms of contemporary

On the Sixties trail to Eastern enlightenment

lifestyle they were revolutionary. Eastern culture, along with hallucinogenic drugs and rock music, became part of a movement that questioned the work ethic, competition and – in rock music – the Top Twenty mentality. It was genuinely believed that it would only be a matter of time before changes in individuals' personalities fostered by this new lifestyle would transform Western capitalist society beyond recognition.

The hippie trail
Travelling, well within the reach of increasingly affluent Western youth, became important, too – not only to get away from a hostile capitalist society but because travelling seemed an important concept in Eastern religion: gurus pointed out that answers often lay in the journey itself rather than in reaching a destination. Young 'seekers after truth' failed to appreciate the metaphorical nature of such

pronouncements, and, by the time MP Philip Goodhart pointed out in May 1968 that 'hippies are now, of course, the major British contribution to the Afghan scene', virtually everyone under the age of 25 seemed to be spending part of the year hitching further and further east from Morocco through Istanbul, Ankara and India to Katmandu.

These journeys weren't without difficulties, especially with cash dwindling rapidly on the way back ('And half the blasted idiots are stuck in Yugoslavia/with hardly a dina . . .' chortled Roy Harper on 'Nobody's Got Any Money In The Summer'). Many of the countries concerned, frightened that their tourist industries would be threatened by these scruffy itinerants, began to impose vindictive 30-year jail sentences for trivial drug offences. The travellers pressed on, however, and the further East they went, the greater the resulting influence of Eastern mysticism on Western ideas, music and fashion.

Young Westerners who were unhappy in their own countries tried to settle in Marrakesh, Morocco, wherever took their fancy. A hippy commune in the crumbling villas surrounding Tangier became like Ladbroke Grove in exile, with house-to-house visiting, picking up supplies of locally-grown hashish and taking odd jobs when money was needed. In return, gangs of saffron-robed Hindus came to Europe and danced up and down the city streets chanting and begging, selling religious books and records to the gullible. Neither group of exiles, in the West or the East, ever made much sense to the native population and, with their blithe disregard of local custom and feeling, seemed often to reinforce George Harrison's perspective in 'The Inner Light' that 'the farther one travels, the less one really knows . . .'

Eastern echoes

Harrison, of course, introduced the sitar to rock; it is difficult to realise just how bewildering it first sounded back in 1965 on the Beatles' 'Norwegian Wood' when most people had never even heard of the instrument. Although at this stage Harrison merely strummed the sitar, before long he and other rock musicians were explor-

The hippies (opposite) favoured Eastern thought and were hostile to Western materialism, but this was not without its contradictions. After the Beatles discovered the Maharishi (right), George Harrison had his fireplace decorated in oriental style (below).

ing its possibilities further and studying under Indian musicians like Ravi Shankar. Unlike Western music, where the scale forms the basis of both melody and harmony, Indian music is based on the idea of the *raga*. Each *raga* is a brief, modal melody that forms the basis for improvisation over a continuous drone. As a result, Indian classical pieces tend to be fairly long, and since they are devoid of the chord changes that provide tension and climax in much Western music, this has to be achieved by increasingly intricate solo patterns. The rhythmic unit – or *tal* – on which an Indian piece is based is often long and complex, resembling the 7/4 and 13/8 time signatures that had been employed in some jazz and classical music, and which were about to infiltrate rock.

Under this influence, progressive Western records became so long that Radio One DJ John Peel, whose show used to go out live on Saturday afternoons, was able to slip out to listen to the football results

and still be back at his turntable before the track he was playing had ended. Gone were the 8-bar guitar solos in the middle of conventionally-structured pop songs. Instead, lead guitar pieces – often improvised – were like long, stoned meditations that assumed an importance all their own. On tracks like the Grateful Dead's 'Dark Star', the listener was supposedly being offered an apparently spontaneous outpouring of guitarist Jerry Garcia's feelings, and the idea consequently arose that, depending on the 'vibes' from the audience or the guitarist's chemical state, no two performances of a piece were ever quite the same.

Since self-expression was now so important, tuning-up on stage became very fashionable – depending on how stoned the musician was, this could sometimes take longer than the song itself – and celebratory jam sessions, as on Harrison's *All Things Must Pass* album, also became common. At the other end of the scale,

repetition became a preoccupation of some composers. Soft Machine performed a particularly repetitious piece entitled 'We Did It Again', which deliberately set out to be boring because, according to organist Mike Ratledge: 'If you find something boring, a basic Zen concept, then in the end you find it interesting. If you listen to something repeated in the same way your mind changes the structure of it each time.' This idea was taken up by Mike Oldfield in the repetitive layers of *Tubular Bells*, while John Lennon had used it in a more accessible way with the loop tapes on 'I Want You (She's So Heavy)'. It wasn't always easy to tell just how serious musicians took this, however; Ratledge admitted that 'We Did It Again' was a piece Soft Machine saved especially for when they wanted to annoy their audience.

Lyrically, terms of reference were set by the Beatles' flower-power anthem 'All You Need Is Love'. Its underlying sentiment – that anything is possible for the individual – was somewhat at odds with the self-effacing lifestyle extolled by Eastern religion, but the emphasis, in both Buddhism and

Hinduism, on intuition had an obvious appeal for a generation that rejected Western rationalism and regarded the entire educational system as misguided. 'We can miss off school', suggested Steve Marriott in the drug-oriented lyrics of 'Itchycoo Park' (1967), 'Why go to learn the words of fools?' There had always been a rebellious streak in rock, but in the late Sixties it began to flirt with a structured, philosophical view of the world.

The Beatles may have set the general parameters – and popularised the East at a stroke with their trip to India to visit the Maharishi Mahesh Yogi – but others gave lyrics a more specific direction. Despite their antiquity and basic passivity, Eastern ideas seemed in tune with a

decade that sought instant salvation, in the same way that, a few years earlier, a demand for instant art in Swinging London had made photography fashionable. *Be Here Now*, the title of a book which became a hippie primer, was also an idea that cropped up constantly alongside lyrics that dealt with the psychedelic experience, colours, the illusion of the real world and the knowledge that all truth is within.

Partly due to Indian influences, styles of writing changed too: images were piled up one on top of another in an attempt to express states of mind rather than creating a flowing narrative. This technique was by no means confined to overtly religious lyrics. King Crimson, for instance, offered 'Pictures Of A City': 'Concrete dream flesh

broken skull/Lost soul lost trance lost in hell'. Lennon's 'Across The Universe', the lyrics of which forced their way into his head in the middle of the night, was equally typical of the trend.

The dream-like quality captured in many of the songs at this time was often linked to an underlying principle of the Universe. Robin Williamson of the Incredible String Band, describing his writing technique to *Oz* magazine in 1969,

Below: Ravi Shankar was the musician most responsible for popularising Indian classical music in the West. Inset below left: Quintessence emerged from Notting Hill's hippie community to adopt Hindu names and chant mantras.

observed: 'A year ago I'd have said I was in touch with the spirit that wrote all the songs. I would have said I wasn't responsible for their existence, it was just the music. But now I'm starting to take responsibility for actually creating them.' People actually based their lives around such ideas; Quintessence dressed in robes and sandals, adopted Indian names and chanted mantras that they recorded for their albums. Lead vocalist Shiva said: 'What we are trying to put across in the music is that it is within the grasp of everyone to attain infinite knowledge, love and peace.'

Seeing the light

Many aspects of Eastern religion, however, were ignored – like the proscription of sex and drugs – if they were considered inconvenient. The fundamental doctrines of Hinduism were never really followed. In brief, they hold that all phenomena are manifestations of a divine ground and that the only aim in life should be to reach a full, intuitive knowledge of this divine ground and become one with it. Hindus believe that human beings can penetrate to this divine reality by intuition ('You can penetrate any place you go', sang John Lennon on 'Dig A Pony') and that man has a double nature: a phenomenal ego, which should be disregarded, and an eternal self.

These philosophies led to a vaguely benign outlook that fostered ideas about such concepts as communal living. The belief that the human species is one with all nature tended to manifest itself in a fascination for the children's stories of A. A. Milne (*Winnie The Pooh*) and Kenneth Grahame (*The Wind In The Willows*), as well as fostering a vague interest in UFOs and space travellers. Such fantasy – quite the opposite of a Hindu search for a divine *reality* – became entangled with a general worship of the past (Eastern beliefs were ancient as well as distant) that had little significance apart from heavily subsidising the old-age pension of J. R. R. Tolkien, author of *The Hobbit* and *The Lord of the Rings*.

Denial of the personality, in practice, often amounted to self-indulgence: rock stars pretended to be gurus and gurus passed themselves off as rock stars (the Maharishi Mahesh Yogi actually went on a bill-topping tour with the Beach Boys) and people wandered around with a dramatic sense of their own importance. Much importance was placed on drug-induced ecstasy, and this was often linked to Zen Buddhism, a cult that became very popular (especially on the West Coast of America) because its teachings allowed for 'accidental' enlightenment. After years of graft the truth might come like a blinding light at an unexpected moment, so why not jumble up your preconceptions with a little acid and make that state of mind more likely?

It was only a short step, therefore, to Timothy Leary announcing acid as a religious sacrament – despite the fact that

the eight-fold path (eight essential conditions to reach Nirvana) excluded drugs, which were believed to work against meditation. People giving up tea, coffee and meat but still dropping acid were not uncommon. True seekers of Nirvana were also required to give up all relationships and family as mere worldly illusions to be stripped away. This idea had a certain romantic appeal to a generation that didn't trust adults, but it rarely went further

For the diligent searcher after the One Truth, the only path to follow was the long and hard one of prayer and meditation (bottom). Many hippies found a convenient shortcut through drugs like cannabis (below).

than a few months away on the Marrakesh Express.

The denial of the world in Buddhism and Hinduism was conveniently taken to mean the Western world only. Eastern religion was used to legitimise the hippie revolution – music, drugs and the non-competitive lifestyle – in much the same way as puritanism had legitimised the English Civil War. It provided a moral authority to throw at old people and politicians. Seen from afar, it appeared to be a very attractive religion. But it seemed attractive *precisely* because it was seen from afar, a standpoint that enabled converts to pick and choose their beliefs. The fact that Eastern religion was outside the Western set-up was a great attraction, encouraging

1399

the idea of a freak society in exile. It is also interesting, given the political climate of the time, that America was fighting a war in Asia, and adherence to religions popular in Vietnam was an ideal way of siding with the oppressed.

Nothing lasts

The implications of the fusion between rock and Eastern ideas were largely social rather than directly musical. A few communes survived in the Eighties, leading a ragged existence in northern California or the Welsh hills, but the significant result has been the growth of the ecology movement. The migration of hippies to the countryside, in an attempt to love and cultivate the earth, stemmed from the Eastern belief that there is one life in all things. Flowers, for instance, have always been a symbol of the divine in Eastern mandalas. This underlying principle of life also discouraged people from eating meat and made vegetarianism respectable rather than cranky. None of these ideas would have gained prominence had they not been aligned to rock music.

At the time, the religious fascinations of the East may have provoked an opposing response in the work of musicians as diverse as Loudon Wainwright III ('Guru') and Jethro Tull (1971's *Aqualung* album), but in the long term they 'legitimised' the stars' individual beliefs. Rock musicians like Pete Townshend and Carlos Santana

stayed with their respective gurus well into the Seventies, while others, like Richard and Linda Thompson and Cat Stevens, were converted to Islam.

There is also an ever-increasing band of born-again Christians, of whom Bob Dylan is the most famous convert. As for the saffron-robed followers of Guru A. C. Bhaktivedanta, heavily subsidised in the past by George Harrison, they still dance up and down city streets on occasion, but no-one takes them very seriously.

Below: Why don't we do it in the road? The hippies' sublime disregard for the material world could prove exasperating to those less enlightened souls intent on getting to work. Bottom: A service at the Krishna Temple.

For a brief period, however, Eastern ideas gave a revolutionary new lifestyle a certain cultural context and moral authority. They helped music expand its frontiers both structurally and lyrically, and, aligned with drugs, forced people to look at the natural world in a new way. The net result of these years was to destroy the illusion that life is ordered on any kind of logical, consecutive plane – something rock'n'roll always instinctively felt but never had the vocabulary to articulate.

But why, in the end, were there no other far-reaching effects? Firstly, the movement was incredibly naive in its belief that the world could be changed simply by changing people. Moreover, combining a social conscience with a world-denying religion was in effect trying to reconcile contradictory aims and, in any case, it wasn't possible to graft one culture on to another by some kind of cerebral sleight of hand. In the end, the two just didn't fit. Westerners were rarely trying to absorb the real thing, and those who eventually took a hard, close look at Eastern culture – like John Lennon – often found they couldn't bear it. The ex-Beatle eventually had to throw out the group of Hare Krishna freaks he'd allowed to live around his house at Tittenhurst Park because, as he pointed out, only half-jokingly: 'I just couldn't get any bloody peace with them walking around chanting and smiling all the time.'   COLIN SHEARMAN

Paint it Black

Psychedelia inspired black music to stand up and adopt different colours

POPULAR MYTHOLOGY has the precocious child, rock, cannibalising black culture for profit and acclaim while the originators languish in undeserved obscurity. The truth is rather more complex; as progressive rock and the singer-songwriter boom grew in the late Sixties, so a new breed of black star appeared—one that was not slow to take advantage of rock's new freedoms. But this was only the most obvious manifestation of a cross-fertilisation process between black and white music that had its origins nearly half a century before.

Musicians have never respected boundaries – country singers recorded many authentic blues in the Twenties and early Thirties. Similarly, bluesmen relished Jimmie Rodgers and many recorded in his shadow. Cross-fertilisation continued throughout the Thirties, notably when Texan Bob Wills fused country with jazz and blues to produce Western swing, while in Kentucky, bluegrass exponents like Bill and Charles Monroe unleashed their own brand of blues.

The immediate postwar years saw blues-soaked country music played in juke-joints throughout the segregated South. The flowering of rockabilly – the so-called genesis of rock – was hardly new, but Presley carried it beyond the South to the world at large. Between 1956 and 1963 Presley had 28 entries in *Billboard's* R&B chart, including four Number 1 hits, and was the most popular white artist with black audiences worldwide. He was the first rock singer significantly to affect black music, and his extravagant vocal stylings were continually copied. Whatever he assimilated of blues or gospel was transformed and returned to the R&B mainstream.

Soul brothers

By the early Sixties, Memphis provided racially integrated house bands at Stax where white session men, like Steve Cropper and Donald Dunn, exerted considerable influence on the development of soul. Some had even seen service in the old Sun studios, but now backed new black attractions like Otis Redding, Wilson Pickett and Aretha Franklin. Redding had tasted success in Europe with the Stax tour package and realised that he could reach a wider audience. He had already covered the Stones' 'Satisfaction' in 1966: his next move was to play the Monterey Festival the following year alongside Jimi Hendrix, a black guitar king who fitted in well with white rock usage of blues tradition. Just before his untimely death in late 1967, Redding was courting the white pop audience with 'Dock Of The Bay', significantly his biggest hit.

The new look of soul music as it moved into the Seventies was epitomised by Sly Stone (right) – funky, irreverent and outrageously attired.

It was an era of restless creativity and rapid change. An educated and newly affluent middle class were rampaging across the campuses of America, questioning received values and re-vamping a culture. If Fifties R&B and redneck equivalents spoke to the body, student youth of the Sixties were determined to address the head as well. Bob Dylan was the first to make the point and the acid rock explosion of San Francisco rammed home the new ethos.

The first soul figures to entertain psychedelia seriously were Sly and the Family Stone, who played the Bay Area. Discarding any idea that they were token blacks on the liberal rock scene, Sylvester Stewart and his aptly-named group seized the time. In a storm of spikey, rock-fused funk, they pulverised America with the injunction 'Dance To The Music' in January 1968. Just over a year later the chart-topping 'Stand!' electrified the Woodstock generation, becoming simultaneously an anthem for liberal hippiedom and impatient blacks. A succession of accomplished albums like *There's A Riot Going On* (1971) and *Fresh* (1973) then

succeeded in bringing protest, surrealism and Sly's supernova personality to an R&B audience, and left a rash of racially mixed bands in his wake. Peacock posturing and quirkily elusive lyrics were soon to reach their apotheosis with Nona Hendryx's work for LaBelle and the theatrical antics of George Clinton's bands Parliament and Funkadelic.

Politics to pin-ups

With the rise of the Civil Rights movement, black artists saw the possibility of using music as a political tool. 'Don't Be A Drop-Out', pleaded James Brown in 1966 adding, with clenched fist, 'Say It Loud – I'm Black And I'm Proud' in 1968. Curtis Mayfield quietly em-braced the message song, first as a member of the Impressions and then under his own name.

In Jamaica the rise of Bob Marley owed much to Mayfield. Rocking R&B stars like Roscoe Gordon, Fats Domino and Shirley and Lee fed the roots of reggae in the Fifties, but it was not until the Sixties that the Impressions, with Mayfield's songs of raised consciousness, sowed

Booker T. and his multi-racial MGs (above) epitomised the fertile – if sometimes uneasy – relationship between black and white in Sixties music.

In the Seventies, the worlds of black and white music meshed in complex ways. Reggae star Peter Tosh recorded with Mick Jagger (below right), while Sylvester (below left) could outcamp Bowie (below).

the seeds of Marley's later militant lyrics. The cool harmonies and delicate singing of the Impressions and their Chicago peers left an indelible – and more immediate – mark on the Wailers' own delivery. When they signed with Chris Blackwell's Island label in 1971, the Wailers became the first reggae band to employ the full range of modern rock technology.

The Sixties also witnessed a remarkable shift from the two-minute venom of rock'n'roll as artists like Cream, the Grateful Dead and Jimi Hendrix insisted on their right to stretch out on disc, sometimes drawing one track over a full album side. This dangerous freedom was embraced rather late in the day by black musicians in the popular arena. Isaac Hayes led the way with discursive, sumptuously orchestrated, marathon work-outs on *Hot Buttered Soul* (1969). Marvin Gaye took matters one stage further with concept albums like *What's Going On* (1971) which dared suggest that there was more to life than being a stud. When Hayes' 'symphonic' talents led him into the cinema with the score for *Shaft* (1971), the

floodgates opened. Curtis Mayfield added new dimensions with *Superfly* (1972) and other soundtracks followed fast as Hollywood cashed in with stereotyped pictures of black lowlife. Musically the best offerings were Marvin Gaye's *Trouble Man* (1972), Willie Hutch's *The Mack* (1973) and Bobby Womack's *Across 110th Street* (1973).

The final legacy inherited from rock was a desire to shock. The romantic fantasies erected by Hayes in the late Sixties to satisfy a newly arrived, sophisticated black audience with money to burn on albums, rapidly came under attack. Following the sexually ambivalent, androgynous examples of Lou Reed, Mick Jagger and David Bowie came youngbloods like the Ohio Players with their sado-masochistic imagery, liberated ladies like Betty Davis and teasing transexuals like Sylvester. In the last analysis black conservatism needed shaking, but in hugging rock to their bosom the black progressives embraced the idea of a youth culture that was to prove something of a mixed blessing.   CLIVE ANDERSON

STONED SOUL

Sly Stone's revolution took no prisoners

IT IS AUDACIOUS achievement enough that a musician should at one time fundamentally alter the state and style of music in his chosen field. To do so twice is quite remarkable. That, in essence, is what Sly Stone did in the three years between 1968 and 1971. He first shook a somewhat predictable, conventionalised black music by upturning preconceptions about arrangements, instrumentation and musicians' roles, race and sex, following this by marrying black music to rock – a move that alerted white bands to the adaptability of black rhythms to rock and vice versa.

Below: Family outing. Standing, from left: Freddie Stewart (guitar), Sly, Greg Errico (drums), Rose Stewart (keyboards), Cynthia Robinson (trumpet). Seated: Larry Graham (bass) and Jerry Martini (sax and keyboards). Left: Sly Stone, rhinestone cowboy, shoots from the hip.

Born Sylvester Stewart in Dallas, Texas on 15 March 1944, he was raised from the age of nine in Vallejo, California, a Bay Area industrial town. Like most black families, the Stewarts had a church background. According to Sly himself, he made a record with a gospel group at the age of four, singing 'On The Battlefield For My Lord'. At 16, he cut 'Long Time Away', a local hit on the G&P label. He and Freddie Stewart subsequently formed the Viscanes who scored another moderate success with 'Yellow Moon', produced by George Motola on the VPM label. Motola was later to licence a clutch of previously unissued Sly Stone doowop performances to the Nashville Subbarao label in 1978. At the turn of the Fifties, Sly and Freddie Stewart had recorded rock'n'roll as the Stewart Brothers for Ensign ('The Rat') and Keen ('Yum Yum'), adding yet another influence that would surface, alongside gospel and doowop, in Sly's later work.

Sly studied music theory and composition at Vallejo Junior College, enrolled at a school of broadcasting, met pioneer FM

radio DJ Tom Donahue in 1964 and began writing and producing records in San Francisco for Donahue's Autumn label. Sly wrote pop hits for the Beau Brummels (America's answer to the British invasion of the Sixties) and Bobby Freeman, while his production assignments included the Mojo Men, the Vejtables and some of his own sides such as the instrumental 'Buttermilk'. He was responsible for the lion's share of Autumn's output, including Grace Slick and the Great Society's 'Somebody To Love' on North Beach.

Stone starts a-rollin'

When the company ran into cash-flow problems, Sly became a DJ on the black KSOL and KDIA stations, where his unpredictability won a loyal, intrigued and entertained following. It was then, in 1966, that he started to pull together his band, first named the Stoners. After several false starts, he settled on a nucleus drawn from his family, brother Freddie (born 5 June 1946) on guitar and sister Rose (25 March 1945) on keyboards. His brother had been in a band with drummer Gregg Errico (1 September 1946) and his cousin, Jerry Martini (1 October 1943), played reeds and keyboards and they were duly recruited. To these he added trumpeter Cynthia Robinson (12 January 1946) and bassist Larry Graham (14 August 1946). The group first recorded for the local Loadstone label.

With this outfit Sylvester Stewart became his hip dude alter ego, the street-smart Sly Stone and made a stew of white rock, new psychedelic ideas, hippie philosophies of love, peace and brotherhood, family feelings and the fundamentals of black R&B, soul and funk.

Black music was susceptible to new influences at the end of the Sixties because, although by no means utterly moribund, it had settled into a pattern in which certain sounds and styles dominated. Motown and Stax, Detroit and Muscle Shoals had become hit factories with all the faults that production-line music-making can perpetuate. The years 1968 and 1969 saw those factories turn out such records as Wilson Pickett's 'Funky Broadway', Gladys Knight and the Pips' 'I Heard It Through The Grapevine', Sam and Dave's 'Soul Man', and Smokey Robinson and the Miracles' 'I Second That Emotion'. All topped the R&B charts, so clearly there was still a market for 'straight' soul music.

Sly took the instrumentation of the rock band, the vocal power of gospel harmony groups, the driving funk rhythms of James Brown, the horn arrangements of Stax and shuffled the pack. The band he carefully selected to play around with this 'melting-pot music' also confounded expectations. The two women instrumentalists in the multi-racial band wore clothes of eye-damaging garishness, mixing satin and leather, velvet and denim, plumes and flares. Vocals were shared between the band and, while lacking the purity and technical skill of traditional black singers

(although bassist Larry Graham's deep voice had a resonance worthy of the best baritones), they had an undeniable vitality and freshness. Combined with the fact that they played their own instruments and weren't dressed in the identikit matching suits of the normal black singing groups, Sly and the Family Stone broke most of the rules of black music.

Signing with manager David Kapralik and the CBS label, the resulting single, 'Underdog', and album, A Whole New Thing, were by no means outstanding. Encouraged to produce a poppier, more light-hearted, positive and accessible sound and message, Sly offered 'Dance To The Music' in January 1968. The record's infectious, enthusiastic delivery and acappella vocal section caught the imagination and took the record to Number 8 in the Hot Hundred. The double-sided hit 'Everyday People'/'Sing A Simple Song' later that year was Sly's first Number 1 in the US, and presaged a number of hits, all in typical exultant style: 'Stand!'; 'I Want To Take You Higher' – the performance of which at Woodstock was one of the Festival's most vivid images; 'Hot Fun In The

Summertime'; and 'Thank You (Falettinme Be Mice Elf Agin)', which showed signs of the coming change in style.

A pilgrim's progress

Having turned out a succession of optimistic good-time hit singles, Sly Stone swung violently to the left and released not the promised 'up' album, The Incredible And Unpredictable Sly And The Family Stone, but the delayed and costly There's A Riot Goin' On, a dark, brooding vision of the blacks' life in America ameliorated only by his wry humour. Instead of the good vibes and party spirit that had infused Sly's first hits, he suddenly bared the troubled mind and soul of an artist who realised the contradictions of encouraging celebration, as he had been doing so effectively, when the country – and most particularly his people – were plainly in neither the mood nor the condition to enter into the festivities.

A combination of the blacks' long-standing ills – discrimination, poverty, their crime and drugs escape-routes, the numbers being conscripted to die in a futile war in Asia – were in no way minimised by

concert at a sell-out Madison Square Garden, one of the gigs he *did* turn up for. His marriage and child were celebrated on *Small Talk*, an album that revealed music of increasing slightness. It gave him two minor single hits, 'Time For Livin'' and the raucous 'Loose Booty'.

High on Sly

By the mid Seventies the Family Stone had all but disintegrated. Drummer Errico and bassist Graham had quit during the making of *Fresh* (Graham formed the excellent Graham Central Station and later became a successful solo artist) and while Rose, Cynthia, Jerry and Freddie were still in the band and Vanetta Stone increased the sense of the Family Stone in both name and numbers, the special spirit that prevailed in the band at the beginning had gone and the music's spirit had waned too. 1975's *High On You* was a retread LP; superficially promising, but the songs couldn't sustain the old power. *High Energy*, a double set of old material containing none of the hit singles, was a peculiar addition to his discography shortly afterwards. A year later *Heard Ya Missed Me, Well I'm Back* was issued, a thoroughly dreadful set of songs that represented the nadir of Sly's recording career.

Sylvester Stewart remained silent for the following three years. By 1979 he'd left CBS for Warner Brothers and, with producer Mark Davis, put out *Back On The Right Track*, a fairly accurate title – but then *Missed Me* had been so far off-beam that one expected little else than an improvement. Also in 1979 CBS had producer John Luongo remix Sly's old dance hits for the then-booming disco market. The album, *Ten Years Too Soon*, was itself approximately three years too late; not an appropriate tribute.

Despite the flagging inspiration that characterised most of Sly Stone's music from 1974 onwards, there can be no question of his central importance to the development of popular music, predominantly black, from 1969 onwards. The intricacies of arrangement in his music between 1968 and 1971 finally gave the lie to the white rock audience's assumptions about the simplistic nature of black music when compared with the increasing pretensions of progressive rock. Such artists as the Isley Brothers, Prince and the Parliament/Funkadelic combine built on the foundations laid by Sly's extravagant image and stage act with some success. And, though he may not be participating, the musical riot Sly Stone instigated was still going on in the Eighties. GEOFF BROWN

---

the increase in affluent, middle-class blacks whose ranks Sly had joined since his success. It was as though he had toured the ghetto streets again in remembrance of his roots, made a personal pilgrimage, and that the irrefutable conclusions of this journey had forced him to turn his back on the solid successes of the previous years in the white marketplace and produce music that mirrored lives far less comfortable. Far from damaging record sales, this 'topical' introspection lifted *Riot* to Number 1 in the LP charts.

There was a two year gap before 1973's *Fresh*, which was indeed a brisker, brighter affair siring three subsequent hit singles ('If You Want Me To Stay', 'Frisky' and 'If It Were Left Up To Me'), plus a version of the old Doris Day hit 'Que Sera Sera'. That prophetic version of an unlikely song was one of a series of wayward events that now peppered Sly's somewhat frantic, very public 'private' life. An audience expects stars to lead a hectic social life, but becomes less enchanted with it as soon as it affects their work or they begin simply to look ridiculous, for that makes the public look fools too.

Above: Sly and the Family Stone's stage performances often resembled riotous fancy-dress parties. Sly's ubiquitous cowboy gear landed him on the wrong side of the law, however, when his toy gun was mistaken for the real thing in a New York shop, and he was promptly arrested.

The maverick Sly, even before *Riot*, was beginning to earn a reputation for late appearances at concerts, often not showing at all; one concert in Washington in 1970 culminated in a genuine riot. Rumours of his increasing dependency on drugs and pressure being exerted by black political groups proliferated. He was arrested for possession of cocaine. Ridiculous episodes combined to make Sly seem less of the innovative musician linking the James Brown era of the Sixties with the many emerging funk bands of the Seventies and more of a shambling buffoon. A woman passing by a shop in New York saw Sly, dressed in his by-now customary cowboy gear, brandishing a toy gun which she believed to be real; he was arrested again.

In 1974 he married Kathy Silva in the most public of circumstances, during a

---

**Sly and the Family Stone
Recommended Listening**

Greatest Hits (CBS 32029) (Includes: Stand!, Hot Fun In The Summertime, Dance To The Music, Sing A Simple Song, Life, Fun, M'Lady); *There's A Riot Goin' On* (Epic 64613) (Includes: Thank You For Talking To Me Africa, Brave and Strong, Africa Talks to You [The Asphalt Jungle], Runnin' Away, Family Affair).

Rhythm'n'heat: the gospel according to Isaac

THE STORY OF Isaac Hayes is an archetypal saga of the South, a rags-to-riches story of improbable events and even wilder excess. The son of Isaac and Eula Hayes, he was orphaned early and raised by sharecropping grandparents near Covington, Tennessee, some 30 miles north of Memphis. His earliest years are shrouded in convenient mystery which his various record companies have done little to dispel. Accordingly, his date of birth is variously given as 6 August 1938 and 20 August 1943.

Hayes moved to Memphis in the late Forties and took an active interest in music at high school. Among his fellow students was a local boy, David Porter, born on 21 November 1941. At the age of six, Porter sang in a gospel group at Rose Hill Baptist Church along with Maurice White, later of Earth, Wind and Fire. At night he performed in a string of Memphis clubs as Little David, and by 1961 had made his recording debut with 'Chivalry'/ 'Farewell' for the tiny local Eagle label. (In 1963, he recorded in Memphis with the Mar-Keys. These recordings appeared not on Stax but on the Newark-based Savoy label.) Porter first met Isaac Hayes at a talent show at the Palace Theatre on Beale Street. By then Hayes was leader and bass singer with the Teen-tones; Porter worked with the Marquettes. Anxious to make their mark, they began writing together.

Porter joined Stax as a staff writer in 1961, while in 1962 Hayes recorded for the local Youngstown label. These sides would also be re-issued on San-American and Brunswick. Hayes mastered piano, guitar and sax, and was soon proficient enough to join the Mar-Keys in jam sessions. Thus he attracted the attention of Stax company president Jim Stewart.

The result was regular session work for Stax and Atlantic, starting in 1963. In the halcyon days that followed, and particularly the three years from 1965 to 1967, Hayes' keyboard playing graced classic records from Otis Redding, Wilson Pickett, Don Covay and Eddie Floyd. The sessions with Redding were especially important, as they enabled Hayes to watch a master of improvisation at close quarters. He saw songs evolve in the studio and began to appreciate the inevitability of the arrangements to which they were wedded. From Redding's singing he learned how to milk a song for every nuance, and how words and syllables themselves were the combustible elements of pure music.

The soul man cometh

With David Porter, Hayes' writing and production skills became a key factor in the success of Stax as the premier Southern R&B company. The duo nurtured Carla Thomas, Sam and Dave, Johnnie Taylor, the Emotions, the Soul Children and many more; two of the biggest hits of the period were 'Hold On I'm Coming' and 'Soul Man', R&B chart-toppers for Sam and Dave in 1966 and 1967 respectively.

A desultory appearance on Volt as Sir Isaac and The Do-Dads (1965), followed in September 1967 by the slapdash Atlantic album *Presenting Isaac Hayes*, hardly prepared the record business for the events of 1969. In that year executives of Gulf and Western, who had taken over Stax in May 1968, realised that marginally more affluent black audiences were switching from singles to albums. 28 LPs were commissioned immediately, and Hayes and Porter spent two arduous weeks recording all the big names at Stax. Then, realising that they were still an album short, Isaac Hayes took the Bar-Kays rhythm section into the studio and cut *Hot Buttered Soul* as a loose-limbed workout.

From its inception it was little more than an

Above: Hayes in unfamiliar garb at a Grammy Award ceremony. His stage gear was somewhat less formal (left).

afterthought and received scant promotion after its release on the Stax subsidiary label, Enterprise. Imagine the astonishment, then, when it promptly outsold the company's entire roster and from August 1969 topped the jazz and soul charts. More important, it reached Number 8 in the pop album charts, made rapid inroads on MOR broadcasting schedules and opened up new avenues for black artists. Their music could break loose from the ghetto into the lucrative pastures of middle America. True, there had always been a coterie of white jazz aficionados buying albums, but the excursions of a larger, pop-oriented audience into R&B had been sporadic and confined to singles. Hayes changed all that at a stroke.

Rapping roots

Curiously enough, *Hot Buttered Soul* had its roots in a typically conservative Southern soul tradition. Rhythm'n'grit emotion collided with R&B, country and pop in a *mélange* that echoed the sentiment, if not the form, of the blues. Even the extended rap at the outset of 'By The Time I Get To Phoenix' was not without precedent. Hayes had employed it successfully on night-club audiences in Memphis for some years, combining gospel sermonising with street-corner jive and a ready wit to notable effect. Such monologues freed Hayes from the strictures of conventional singing, allowed him to give simple songs a deeper resonance and still retain the common touch. Audiences throughout America were able to respond to his colourful blend of soap-opera cliché and ghetto chic.

To some extent it was a formula anticipated by Solomon Burke and Joe Tex in the early Sixties. As an arranger and producer, however, Hayes was able to raise it to positively Gothic proportions. Strings, for example, had been used on R&B recordings by Carla Thomas, William Bell and Johnnie Taylor, but never with such shimmering extravagance. Hayes unleashed whole sections of the Memphis Symphony Orchestra on cuts that could run for 18 minutes or more. Cunningly he set the gutbucket fire of a progressive rhythm section – the newly-constituted Bar-Kays – against the silky sophistication of classical players. With multi-tracking and high-fidelity sound, Hayes took R&B to new levels of technical sophistication and applied his colours as he wished. It was a development echoed only by Motown's Norman Whitfield – but where the latter achieved diamond-hard psychedelia, Hayes retained warmth and soul amid the innovation.

Bald is beautiful

By recording romantic pop from the pen of Jimmy Webb, Hayes smashed a number of neuroses. Black artists had long recorded versions of white hits – Ray Charles with 'I Can't Stop Loving You', for instance – but the process had become difficult in a decade preoccupied with black identity. And, in any case, these artists had seldom taken the dangerous step of casting themselves in a primarily romantic role for white audiences. Now, suddenly, they could incorporate pop material without compromising their blackness and even play the stud for women across the United States, white or black. After Hayes, skin colour didn't matter. Why, you could even be bald and of indeterminate age and still ooze sex appeal. Gone were the airbrushed photographs and light make-up used in some vain bid to emulate Harry Belafonte or Johnny Mathis.

The biggest problem with Hayes was how to edit lengthy album tracks for release as singles. But the butchers triumphed, as ever, and 'By The Time I Got To Phoenix', backed with a sensuous version of Burt Bacharach and Hal David's 'Walk On By', again suitably truncated, was a double-sided hit on the R&B chart.

Issued in March 1970, *The Isaac Hayes Movement* served the same mixture of standards and steamy orchestral soul. The album emulated its predecessor's crossover success, peaking at Number 8 in the LP charts. Again the accent was Southern, florid and overripe, but there was no denying the power of cuts like 'I Stand Accused'. Hayes subjected Jerry Butler's classic to a painfully protracted rap before delivering cool country soul in the best traditions of

Toussaint McCall and O. V. Wright. Although Willie Mitchell had started producing Al Green with a similar combination of delicacy and symphonic opulence, Isaac Hayes' position as soul superstud remained unassailable.

November 1970 brought *To Be Continued* and the first hint of stagnation. 'Ike's Rap', intoned in a semi-articulate Marlon Brando mumble against a backdrop of cicadas in the sultry Memphis night, did little to dispel fears of decline. His mooning delivery of 'Our Day Will Come', capped by Bacharach and David's sickly 'The Look Of Love', made matters worse and the set – a Number 11 pop album – was redeemed only by the urgent 'Runnin' Out Of Fools'. April 1971 saw his slow version of 'Never Can Say Goodbye', a single that reached Number 22 nationally and served as a trailer for the *Black Moses* album. That it succeeded as a 45 was surprising, since the Jackson Five had taken it to Number 2 only weeks before.

Shaft – can you dig it?

Hayes' career was recharged when film director Gordon Parks asked him to score *Shaft* (1971) for MGM. Hayes' music dominated and sold the picture by catching exactly the hustling mood of the day. Here come Isaac Hayes or John Shaft – take your pick – upwardly mobile and afire with black pride, straining to dump whitey on his backside at the hint of a sneer and leaving foxy ladies down the line. Black audiences cheered every screening, international audiences were entranced. From August 1971 the double album climbed to Number 1 in the American charts and miraculously settled at Number 12 in the UK. The title track fared even better when it was released as a single in October, topping the US Hot Hundred and reaching Number 4 in Britain. It also won the 1971 Best Song Oscar.

Overnight *Shaft*'s chattering wah-wah guitar became obligatory for private-eye movies, rapidly permeated the advertising world and enlivened countless soul records for a decade. Hollywood scrambled to make films about blacks and soul progressives queued to write soundtracks. The results were generally derivative, however, honourable exceptions being Curtis Mayfield's *Superfly*, Marvin Gaye's *Trouble Man* (both 1972) and Willie Hutch's *The Mack* (1973).

Unfortunately Hayes began to believe his own publicity and, although the *Black Moses* album from November 1971 sold heavily and rose to Number 10 in the rankings, it nonetheless represented the beginning of the end for Isaac Hayes as a major force. An affluent lifestyle and a penchant for supporting black community projects do not of themselves qualify someone for the role of shaman, especially when that person combines calculated eroticism with a whiff of the pimpwalk. Hayes' appearance at the August 1972 Wattstax festival in Los Angeles, decked out as Moses in chains and replete with codpiece, was

faintly ridiculous; his performance paled beside allegedly lesser acts. Stax continued to milk *Shaft* and pushed Hayes into woeful film scores like *Three Tough Guys* and *Truck Turner* (in which he also starred as a freelance bounty hunter), both issued in 1974.

By now the Stax empire was falling and Hayes was involved in costly litigation accusing them of misrepresentation, falsification of sales and withholding royalties. He settled out of court when the label agreed to release him to ABC. Unfortunately the ensuing albums, *Chocolate Chip* (1975), *Groove-A-Thon* and *Juicy Fruit* (both 1976), failed to restore his reputation. Meanwhile Barry White, assisted by arranger Gene Page, stepped in with a particularly vulgar – and popular – dilution of Hayes' style. Hayes elected to change direction, producing the Isaac Hayes Movement and the Masqueraders with modest success.

To be continued . . .

Despite six acceptable albums of his own, cut for Polydor between 1977 and 1981, Hayes has remained aloof. On *Royal Rappin's* (1979) he consented to share vocal honours with Millie Jackson, while elsewhere he has preferred to write, arrange and produce for Linda Clifford, Dionne Warwick and Donald Byrd.

Although Hayes entered the Eighties still smouldering on the sidelines, it is for the years 1969-71 that he will be remembered. His tortuous raps licensed the Soul Children, Laura Lee, Millie Jackson, Margie Joseph, Shirley Brown, Barry White and many more. His arrangements affected everyone from Gene Page to MFSB and underpinned the entire disco explosion. His insistence that an album should be a unified whole, not just a collection of tracks, did for black music what the Beatles had achieved earlier in rock. His emphasis on total control as writer, producer and performer enlarged that achievement, but this – combined with the longer tracks he pioneered – gave room for a dangerous degree of self-indulgence hitherto rarely found in black music. His legacy is mixed.

CLIVE ANDERSON

Hayes graduated from writing and producing other artists with partner David Porter (above) to the solo spotlight (right).

MOVE ON UP

THE CAREER OF Curtis Mayfield has spanned over a quarter of a century, both as a group member and a solo artist. During this time, he has proved a crucial influence on his chosen field of soul music. While never prolific, his recorded output has always been distinguished by a certain spiritual integrity, his occasional commercial successes only serving to highlight the vast wealth of his material that has remained sadly unrecognised.

Born in Chicago on 3 June 1942, Mayfield was already known as an accomplished guitarist when he was invited to join the Roosters (later the Impressions) in 1958. Since then, he has pioneered many breakthroughs in vocal and musical arrangements, while his own distinctive vocal style – brittle, yet tough – and versa-

Curtis Mayfield: from Impression to superstar

tile approach to the guitar have been much admired and imitated by other soul artists.

His career with the Impressions is bright with masterly compositions, arrangements and performances, and it is not surprising that some of them became massive hit singles. Hitmaking seems to have been a secondary consideration for the Impressions, but when the hits *did* come, they were superb. 'It's All Right' (1963), 'Woman's Got Soul' (1965) and 'You've Been Cheating' (1965) were soul/R&B songs of depth and character, and the gospel flavour of 'I'm So Proud' (1964) and 'Amen' proved Mayfield's songwriting

versatility to be unequalled by anyone else in the field.

'Amen' was a Top Ten hit in America in 1965 – and it was also the turning-point in Mayfield's writing career. Its committed basis inspired him to write and record 'We're A Winner', the first of his many songs to deal with black society in the United States. Although its social comment was mild (especially when compared with Mayfield's later solo work in the early and mid Seventies) it was banned by many radio stations in America.

He later described the situation to *Melody Maker*: 'Of course when you make such statements you run into programme directors who feel that this isn't what they want their audiences to hear, even though it might be true. I look upon "We're A

Winner" as a song that anyone could listen to and take pride in being a part of, especially those minority groups who are actually experiencing the problems we have in our country.' 'We're A Winner' was one of the Impressions' last releases on ABC Records – although they had enjoyed the bulk of their commercial success with this label, Mayfield decided to set up his own operation.

After setting up his own record companies, Windy C Records in 1966 and Mayfield Records in 1967, he finally formed the Curtom label, on which the Impressions released 'Fool For You' in 1968, scoring a Number 22 hit. This was followed by another political song, 'This Is My Country'. The quality of these songs and the subsequent 'Seven Years', 'Choice Of Colours' and the magnificent 'Mighty Mighty Spade And Whitey' pushed back the frontiers of soul music as nothing before.

Mixing social comment with a musical dexterity unequalled by anyone else working in the field, the Impressions influenced many of the new, post-Motown and Stax-era soul singers to adopt a more radical lyrical stance while leaving the music with its traditional integrity. Mayfield, however, was getting restless as his lyrical brilliance outgrew the Impressions' more melodic intent. He left them in 1970 to pursue his own career, leaving behind *Check Out Your Mind* and the brilliant but sadly neglected *Young Mod's Forgotten Story*, two LPs that pointed the way forward into a more uncompromising treatment of socially uncomfortable themes.

Head-on attack
The radical themes of black power, militancy and violence were becoming more popular within American soul music at the time Mayfield went solo. Sly and the Family Stone, following Mayfield's own lyrical influence, had delivered *There's A Riot Goin' On*, and Marvin Gaye's *What's Going On* was in the making. In this turbulent atmosphere Curtis released his first single under his own name on the Buddah label. 'Don't Worry (If There's A Hell Below, We're All Going To Go)' came as a shock even to those who expected innovation from Mayfield. The mild politicising of his later lyrics for the Impressions had been abandoned in favour of a head-on attack. The music held no comforts for the listener either, its vicious fuzz-bass and screaming electric lead guitars combining with Henry Gibson's conga work.

'Don't Worry' was not a hit, but the following single, 'Move On Up', was a massive seller on both sides of the Atlantic. It was dance-floor genius with a lyrical statement exhorting black Americans to 'move on up to a greater day' – a song of hope with a shifting, exciting rhythm and a promise of even greater things to come. The full

Curtis Mayfield (above left and right) made his impression on soul music with a new political directness.

versions of both songs graced *Curtis*, his first solo LP, and served to give a deeper clarity and perspective to the rest of the material. The LP was magnificent, ranging from the gay abandon of 'Wild And Free' to the considered structure of 'Miss Black America'. Mayfield's arrangements breathed life and vigour into the songs and his grasp of melody, especially when delivered with that characteristic rasping falsetto, was a revelation.

A commercially successful future looked certain, but Mayfield's integrity immersed him more deeply into his music at the expense of his public image. Then, in late

1971, followed a double LP, *Curtis Live*, on which Gibson's conga-playing was again outstanding. Recorded live at the Bitter End, a New York club, the album presented versions of Mayfield's songs from the Impressions' repertoire as well as his newer solo tracks. For the second time he met radio censorship with the song 'Stone Junkie'. Mayfield commented: 'I believe that anything that is happening should be told as it is. I could sit around here all day singing love, love, love, and shake it, shake it, and we're all having a good time, but the young are not fools. There's no need to play games today.'

At this time Curtis and his now-regular working group paid a lightning visit to Britain and made an unofficial debut at the Speakeasy before opening the tour proper at the Rainbow Theatre. Despite the fact that the latter show was greeted with universal acclaim, the general feeling was that the intimacy of Mayfield's music was better suited to the smaller, more club-like venue. An appearance on BBC-TV's 'Old Grey Whistle Test' further enhanced his reputation in the UK.

Back in America, his second studio LP, *Roots*, took Mayfield even further away from traditional soul music and towards a hybrid of rock and funk. Only one song on the LP was under four minutes long, reflecting the trend of extended improvisation in rock. The fuzz guitars were again in evidence and on the song 'Underground', Mayfield arranged the lead electric guitar to play phrases more suited to a saxophone. But he was not making conventional soul music. He used Impressions arranger Johnny Pate for *Roots*, and even recruited Leroy Hutson, who had replaced him when he left the Impressions, to contribute backing vocals. The single 'We Got To Have Peace' failed and, just when it seemed that his approach would alienate even his most staunch admirers, Mayfield was invited to write the score for the film *Superfly* (1971).

Back to the world
Isaac Hayes had enjoyed phenomenal success with his music for the first of the black detective films, *Shaft*, a year earlier and perhaps Mayfield saw *Superfly* as a way of regaining a more orthodox credibility among soul fans. Whatever his motives, the result was a success. The more traditional elements of funk were re-introduced into the music to produce a soundtrack LP that stood up on its own – a rare achievement. The *Superfly* LP, with its juxtaposition of songs and instrumentals, provided the violence of the film with an unusual counterpoint. The title track was a big hit, and the power of the words reflected Mayfield's social concerns.

Despite the film's concentration on the world of drugs, Mayfield's lyrics were scathing in their attacks on pushers and users. 'Freddie's Dead' was also released as a single and nominated for an Oscar as best song, but it was eventually withdrawn because of its lyrical content. The film was a huge success and even included footage of Curtis performing 'I'm Your Pusherman' in a nightclub.

When his next LP, *Back To The World*, was released in the summer of 1973 rock overtones had been eased out in favour of strings and brass. It was Mayfield's finest solo record to date, the title song dealing with repatriation for a veteran after returning from Vietnam, and 'Future Shock' developing his obsession with the place of the black man in American society. The album's successor, *Sweet Exorcist*, failed badly as a commercial venture, however, although its music was as good as ever. The single, 'Kung Fu', was tight and funky, the

Above: Curtis backs up his songs of racial harmony by jamming with white bluesmen Canned Heat. Below: Mayfield the businessman. Curtom Records played an increasingly important part in his musical life through the Seventies, but failed to sign or discover major artists of Curtis' calibre.

rest of the LP sparing in its intensity but full to the brim with evolutionary ideas.

The soulful *Got To Find A Way* in 1975 and the doom-laden *There Is No Place Like America Today* in 1976 also failed to re-establish Mayfield as a major contender, and although the critical acclaim never receded, commercial success failed to materialise. Mayfield, however, had little cause for worry as his other venture, the Curtom Record Company, had been steadily gathering momentum. Curtom had been originally distributed by Buddah Records, on which all of Mayfield's early solo material had been released, and its

main role was to provide an outlet for Mayfield's formidable output of songs with little-known artists who deserved wider attention. However, the more successful Curtom ventures were the already-established Impressions' *Finally Got Myself Together* and *Leroy Hutson; The Man*.

Celluloid sounds
In 1977 Mayfield was signed for another film venture, *Short Eyes*, which told a brutal story about prison life. Again he composed all the music and sang all but one of the songs, as well as making an appearance in the film. Other films for which Mayfield wrote songs included *Claudine* (1974), *Let's Do It Again* (1975) and *Sparkle* (1976). *Let's Do It Again*'s box-office receipts made it one of the most successful black films of all time.

His releases subsequently became more sporadic; *Do It All Night* (1978) and *Heartbeat* (1979) were followed by a flirtation with disco music, which proved artistically disastrous. An album with Curtom artist Linda Clifford called *The Right Combination*, was primarily intended to promote his record label – an accusation that could not be levelled at his 1982 release, *Honesty*. Released through the Boardwalk label, this was hailed as a true return to form, with Mayfield in his element both as a social observer and balladeer.

Mayfield's influence endured more in the Eighties in the UK, where he performed regularly and guested on a single by admirers the Blow Monkeys. But despite a dearth of new music, his past track record already ensured Curtis Mayfield pride of place in the history of soul music.

TED GIBBONS

LaBelle
WITH LOVE

**The space-age soul of
Sarah, Nona and Patti**

*Birds of an exotic feather: Sarah Dash,
Nona Hendryx and Patti LaBelle.*

OF ALL THE SOUL acts to greet the Seventies
with a display of space-age chic, LaBelle
seemed least likely. To their old followers,
it seemed that they had been on the chit-
terling circuit too long to undergo such a
rigorous transformation. Lead singer Patti
LaBelle was born Patricia Louise Holt-
Edwards in Philadelphia on 4 October
1944, and rapidly absorbed the gospel
tradition, joining Cynthia 'Cindy' Birdsong in a local group called the Ordettes
in 1959. The following year, promoter

Bernard Montague introduced them to Sarah Dash and Wynona Hendryx, who had been part of another Philly group, the Del-Capris. The new quartet moved to Harold B. Robinson's Newtown label where they recorded some dozen sides as Patti LaBelle and the Bluebelles.

They had their first real hit in August 1963 when 'Down The Aisle' appeared in the R&B charts. Then Newtown was swallowed by the burgeoning giant Cameo-Parkway; the new label failed to develop their talents, preferring cheerful pop performers like Chubby Checker to R&B. The Bluebelles secured only one minor R&B chart hit on the label in January 1964 with a tired show-tune by Rodgers and Hart, 'You'll Never Walk Alone'. If nothing else, it showed how Patti LaBelle could take a song from a whisper to a scream, giving it a thrilling new resonance. Such dynamic presence kept them in the public eye when they were booked for a string of shows at the Uptown, Philadelphia and the Apollo, New York – engagements that finally brought them to the attention of Atlantic Records.

Their first work for the label consisted of live recordings made at the Uptown and the Brooklyn Fox in July and December 1964. Incredibly, they had to wait until October the following year before they were granted a studio session. This produced the soulful 'Patti's Prayer' and a minor hit in 'All Or Nothing'. But Atlantic did little more than take the group as they found them, and the Bluebelles marked time with a clutch of unsuccessful singles until their departure from the label in October 1969. Only 'I'm Still Waiting' (1966) and 'Take Me For A Little While' (1967) had created any ripples. Cindy Birdsong, frustrated with their lack of success, left to replace Florence Ballard in the Supremes in 1967. The end of the Sixties saw the Bluebelles reduced to a trio and stagnating on the small club circuit.

A fortuitous meeting with Vicki Wickham at Buddah Records in New York

The colourful plumage modelled by Patti (above left) and Sarah (above right) transformed Patti LaBelle and the Bluebelles (opposite) into LaBelle (above far right).

changed everything. Wickham readily recognised R&B talent, and, ever since her days in British TV with the production team of 'Ready, Steady, Go!', had proved herself adept at presentation. There was a glut of predictably glamorous black girl groups in soul, but none were making inroads in rock. Wickham became the Bluebelles' manager, changed their name to LaBelle and pushed both their image and their music in the 'progressive' direction of Sly and the Family Stone.

The refurbished trio made their first appearance at New York Town Hall in 1970, clad in denim and wrapping their tongues around improbable lyrics. Conservative Patti worried because she felt that sharply-dressed soul audiences would fail to relate to their new image and songs. Nona, on the other hand, was desperate for change. She didn't share Patti's gospel roots and was more sympathetic to rock. By process of natural selection she became lyricist and spokeswoman for the group.

Their new career got off to a slow start; the albums *LaBelle* (1971) and *Moonshadow* (1972), both recorded for Warner Brothers, were limply promoted. 1971 also saw them contributing backing vocals to Laura Nyro's *Gonna Take A Miracle*. They registered more strongly with *Pressure Cookin'* (1973), their sole album outing for RCA. With the inclusion of 'Open Up Your Heart', a song specially commissioned from Stevie Wonder, and Gil Scott-Heron's 'The Revolution Will Not Be Televised', they established an incisive new image with the potential to reach both rock and soul fans.

Their debut album for Epic, neatly titled *Nightbirds*, and produced under the aegis of Allen Toussaint in New Orleans during 1974, was a remarkable fusion of funk, rock and gospel. Leo Nocentelli of the

Meters provided tormented lead guitar over Toussaint's swirling keyboards. Bob Crewe's voodoo pastiche, 'Lady Marmalade', perverted the Creole tradition to provide the sexual invitation: 'Voulez-vous coucher avec moi ce soir?'. A smash hit, it introduced the notion of LaBelle as sexually liberated necromancers, an image which was reinforced by dark ballads like Nona's title track and by their bizarre stage costumes, funky spacesuits of feathers and armour plate. After their 'Nightbirds' extravaganza at the Metropolitan Opera House New York and at London's Drury Lane, they became the essence of chic, attracting fervent admirers of every sexual persuasion.

Ashes to ashes

The next year's LP, *Phoenix*, again produced by Toussaint, marked time. The space fantasies were enlarged, with a richer sound and overwrought vocals, while Nona Hendryx introduced a disturbing mysticism on songs like 'Slow Burn'. The album contained no surprises, however; LaBelle were faced with the problem of how to move forward before their extraordinary theatre of rock'n'soul became utterly dated. After *Chameleon*, slickly produced by Pointer Sisters mentor David Rubinson in California during 1976, the three decided to pursue solo careers. This final album was arguably their finest, and it certainly represents the flowering of Nona's remarkable writing talent. The title track, 'Come Into My Life' and 'A Man In A Trenchcoat' were powerful, idiosyncratic songs, while the gospel-based 'Going Down Makes Me Shiver', a daring celebration of oral sex, was particularly perverse in its combination of sacred music and sexual lyrics.

All three Labelle members cut solo records after the group's demise in 1977. Nona Hendryx couldn't find the hit formula, despite contributing to Talking Heads' *Remain In Light* (1980). Sarah Dash delivered three polished soul sets to the

Kirschner label without setting the charts ablaze.

But the most successful solo was Patti Labelle herself, whose film theme duet with Michael McDonald, 'On My Own', was a 1986 US chart-topper, pulling her *Winner In You* album to Number 1 with it. The track made Number 2 in the UK, where 'Oh People' also hit following her Live Aid appearance.

CLIVE ANDERSON

LaBelle
Recommended Listening

Nightbirds (Epic EPC 80566) (Includes: Lady Marmalade, Are You Lonely, It Took A Long Time, Space Children, All Girl Band, Don't Bring Me Down, Somebody Somewhere).

PUTTING ON THE STYLE

The ever-changing image of black stars

WHEN THE SOUND of rock'n'roll broke out over America in the mid Fifties, it spread the phraseology, music and dress of the black ghettoes. The shock that swept the United States was largely dependent upon white youth adopting the ways of a race still considered by many white Americans to be ignorant and inferior. By defining rock 'n'roll's style – with its flamboyance, its rhythmic drive, its overt sexuality and its critical look at authority – as black style, its participants made the music an unashamedly rebel one that could not immediately be absorbed into establishment showbusiness.

The black singer's dress and his attitude in song were embodiments of the fact that his race was at odds with white authority.

The importance of the singer's image was nothing new – it had been crucial in the growth and popularity of both jazz and the blues. These genres presented two sides of life for the American black – jazz was the music of the city slicker and the ghetto sophisticate, blues that of the poor and barely literate farm or factory worker.

By the Forties, jazz was as concerned with style as it was with music. The jazz audience identified itself with the atti-

Top left: Seductive Sonny Til looms over his Orioles. Their visual style, however, remained impeccably smooth, as did that of fellow doowoppers the Five Willows (above left). Seventies funksters Parliament (above) provided an outrageous contrast.

tudes inherent in a jazzman's playing by copying his lifestyle, his clothes and habits and by talking his barely comprehensible jargon. Musicians of the calibre of Charlie Parker and Lester Young were role models for young blacks and white bohemians unwilling to support the mainstream jazz of Nat King Cole. Their style was taken up as a rejection of conventionality and the restrictions of society's rules.

Lyrics and lifestyles
Whereas the jazz image conjured up a certain amount of luxury and reflected a society that had the resources to buy clothes and drink and visit nightclubs, the blues was concerned with a presentation of self within social confines; the bluesman

was inescapably part of poor society, and could only fight against it. Rather than craving the expensive lifestyle he lacked, the bluesman often concentrated his anger into the hostile shouted lyrics and the incessant rhythmic drive of the postwar urban era.

When rock came along, it took elements from both jazz and blues and welded them together with something all its own – a powerful, aggressive sexuality. The performance of the black vocal group was centred around a commitment to sensual pleasure that, to a white audience, was exotic and somewhat frightening. Black lyrics sold the promise of true love, but they were concerned rather with the white heat of passion than the rosy glow of romance. And the singers were not afraid to demonstrate it. Sonny Til of the Orioles was one of the first performers to bring explicit sexuality into his act – he moved seductively and caressed the air with his hands, so that his black audience responded with a series of ribald comments.

Clothes reinforced the idea that the singers were sexual predators. Suits were smart, shoes were sharp; the singer was smoothly groomed. Instead of neutralising the singer's potency, the well-dressed look emphasised it by contrast – and was also useful in making the black musician acceptable to whites. Chuck Berry, in the Fifties, was one such star. Immaculately

dressed in a white suit, he proceeded to taunt his audience with knowing leers, using his guitar as a blatant sexual symbol. Even in films like *Go Johnny Go!*, in which he played Uncle Tom to Alan Freed's Master, he managed to imply that he was unwilling to accept any rules other than his own.

Dance stance

The sexual innuendo that Chuck Berry had implied in the handling of his guitar was developed more explicitly in the dance routines and gymnastics used by Jackie Wilson and James Brown. Dance had always been part of a black musical act's presentation, even with vocal groups like the Cadillacs, but both Wilson and Brown used dance less as a visual entertainment than a primitive courting ritual. The sheer athleticism of their movements was wedded to a sinuous sexuality. The public image of black singers exuded confidence; in all they did, their movements, dress, their stage display, and in their lyrics, they proclaimed the message that the days of black oppression were long gone – and that, in the field of sexuality, they were masters.

Fearing that the frontiers of what a black performer could present to a white audience had been pushed too far forward, the record industry found a singer who could present a new style in a more acceptable form. Chubby Checker, unlike the athletic James Brown, was portly – cuddly rather than sexy – with an ever-ready grin that indicated friendliness and warmth rather than rebellion. But the mainstream of black rock continued to assert its sexuality with an outrageous dress sense, symbolised by the plaid suits and ill-matching waistcoats James Brown adopted in the mid Sixties. The suit remained in vogue, but it took on an exotic character – flashy colours and shimmering fabrics glinted under the stage lights. The women used the same technique of combining the formal with the far-out, wearing cocktail dresses that would have been conventional but for their gaudy colours.

Dressed like this, artists from Motown, the biggest black-owned label, could aim at the pop market, and at white as well as black record buyers. Commercially successful singers could not rely on a style that was aimed solely at the black ghettoes, and an image had to be constructed that was true to black heritage and at the same time fitted in with white expectations and prejudices. Whereas earlier black singers could content themselves with the knowledge that their outrageous and rebellious individuality was a prime reason for their success in the white market, the Motown image had to be more universal, and therefore more respectable. For the first time, the record company it-

Reflections . . . Duke Ellington (below left) and LaBelle (bottom left) brush up their images. Marvin Gaye (below) went for a more relaxed look in the Seventies, adopting the suit and sweater of the mature man of leisure.

The new clothes style was associated more with the rock community than with the black population. Sly Stone merged rhinestoned country clothing with psychedelic rock; Isaac Hayes presented himself as a sophisticated white-slave trader; and Curtis Mayfield and Marvin Gaye adopted a more casual, leatherware look – sweaters, jeans and suede jackets. Sly Stone and Isaac Hayes took fantasy roles unassociated with ghetto realities, while Gaye and Mayfield strengthened the universality of their lyrics through a visual image that was not racially specific.

From the beginnings of rock to the Eighties, the public image presented by black performers has developed from an aggressive sneer at white values into the first flowerings of a self-evaluation that no longer threatens white morality – one that stresses black pride rather than black anger. This softening is part of the greater musical and stylistic integration that has come with an increased cross-fertilisation between black and white music. PAUL FRYER

The image of Motown's stars underwent a big change in the late Sixties and early Seventies. The Temptations and Diana Ross and the Supremes (left), early subjects for Berry Gordy's grooming, had a smooth, nightclub air about them. The Jackson Five (below), no less professional, wore afros and chunky, if matching, fabrics.

self came to control the public image presented by its singers.

The rise of the Stax label in the mid Sixties coincided with the peak of two trends in black rock – on the one hand the singer as hustler, and on the other a more middle-class presentation of the black self. The first group was represented by Wilson Pickett, Joe Tex and Solomon Burke, and the second by Otis Redding, who adopted the polo-necked sweater – never a style popular in the ghettoes – and combined it with the more traditional suit to suggest a relaxed man of leisure. The adoption of white dress conventions was an aid to Redding in his move towards a white audience, and he was taken up by them as a black hero.

Shopping for clothes

New styles not associated with the ghettoes gained rapid acceptance towards the end of the decade. Whether this meant going towards African roots, or towards integrationist America, the pose of the hustler was ignored in favour of the 'natural man', a man with deep feelings about his past. The overt Africanisms in clothing and ideology were found most commonly within the jazz community, where dashikis and Afro hairstyles became the norm. In soul, the Afro was sported by artists as diverse as Aretha Franklin, Michael Jackson and Stevie Wonder. The greased, coloured and straightened hair, and the suits that had been the fashion up until the mid Sixties were rejected as copies of white fashion.

All that Glitters

**Image and imagination ran riot
in the glam-rock revolution**

*Marc Bolan traded his kaftan
and acoustic guitar for glam
glad-rags and a rabid teenage
fan-following.*

DESPITE ALL the media approval of progressive rock in the late Sixties, not everyone regarded it as reverentially. Many pop fans were alienated by the self-indulgent approach of leading progressive musicians and by the pretentious noise that often passed for innovation. However much the new rock may have pleased sixth formers and college students, it rarely found favour with the majority of the pop audience – the singles-buying teenagers, and in particular those under 14 who favoured precisely those qualities of showmanship, glamour and fun that the progressives scorned. By 1971, an assault on the progressive ethos and a return to more traditional pop values seemed long overdue. The 'glam-rock' movement provided the impetus for both.

The backlash began, ironically, with the steady rise to chart fame and teenybopper stardom of one of the early heroes of the British progressive scene, Marc Bolan of Tyrannosaurus Rex. With his background in male modelling and the mid-Sixties Mod scene, Bolan had always had a good nose for a gimmick and a strong understanding of the importance of image. His strange wailing voice and Tolkien-inspired pseudo-mystical songs won his two-man group (formed with fellow bohemian Steve Peregrine Took) a cult following and moderate album sales in the post-1967 period, but he became frustrated at their failure to expand further. In 1970, he made a quite deliberate bid for commercial success, dropping his acoustic guitar for an electric sound that was strongly influenced by Chuck Berry, and concentrating on singles. The records sold, initially, because they were good radio and dance discs, but spots on BBC-TV's 'Top Of The Pops' gave T.Rex a new kind of exposure and attracted screaming girls to their concerts for the first time.

All crazee now

Quite predictably, Bolan was accused by many former fans and colleagues of 'selling out' to commercialism. John Peel, the first to play Tyrannosaurus Rex records on the radio back in 1967, now refused to play them. Bolan remained unrepentant, telling one interviewer: 'I'm probably more ethnic now than I ever was, much more, because I'm more involved with the art of producing good funky energy rock music. I'm very aware of the people that I'm playing for now. Before I wasn't really sure who I was playing for.' Yet he was also just a little *too* aware for his own good, too calculating and manipulative in his stage act and far too garrulous on the subject of his own fame. He spoke candidly of the sexual nature of his appeal – 'the whole thing is a game of seduction between me and the audience . . . an orgiastic exercise,' he told Donald Zec of the *Daily Mirror*. 'I've sort of become a rock'n'roll James Dean.' But Bolan failed to recognise that his popularity was not sufficiently broadly based to last; the young

Left, from top: Chicory Tip, middle-of-the-road glam-rockers who had a Number 1 hit with 'Son Of My Father'; Hot Chocolate, who shed their glam trappings to become pop veterans in the Eighties; the Sweet in Red Indian chic for a TV appearance; Slade playing to the gallery. Opposite: Gary's glittering prizes.

teenage girls who formed the largest part of his audience soon moved on to other, prettier faces with a much more conventional 'boy-next-door' appeal, like Donny Osmond and David Cassidy.

Bolan was a catalyst, a trailblazer for the likes of Slade, Gary Glitter, Sweet and even David Bowie, who enjoyed his first sustained commercial exposure in 1972 following the release of his *Ziggy Stardust* album. Slade had been a professional band for years, working mainly in their native West Midlands, and had flirted briefly with the progressive scene before allowing manager Chas Chandler to promote them as a 'skinhead' band. The image worked against them at first because of the skinheads' reputation for violence, but it wasn't entirely misplaced: the band identified strongly with the more positive aspects of the sub-culture, its view of pop music as *dance* music, its tribal loyalties, its sense of teenage solidarity, its anti-intellectual stance. Their music came to express all these qualities, though it was not so much the skinheads as their younger brothers and sisters, working-class youngsters fresh into their teens, who provided Slade with their main following.

Costume capers

The kids came to Slade via television appearances, Radio One airplay and hit records, but the relationship between band and audience was cemented in live performance. From the start of their chart career, Slade *belonged* to their fans and identified with them in a way that Marc Bolan with his sequinned ego never could. At its simplest, Slade's audience identification found expression in the deliberately misspelled record titles – 'Look Wot You Dun', 'Gudbuy T'Jane', 'Take Me Bak 'Ome' and so on – which were designed to win the sympathy of every put-upon schoolkid. But their appeal went far deeper: in performance, they seemed to transmit and absorb pure teenage energy, making the gig itself a celebration of teenage community, letting the fans dictate the atmosphere.

Slade represented the 'good-time' aspect of glam-rock. Noddy Holder and guitarist Dave Hill dressed up to the nines in costumes that could have been borrowed from the set of *A Clockwork Orange*. Yet this was really all part of a shared joke with the fans, who, in their turn, lost no opportunity in dressing even more outrageously than their idols.

Glam-rock inevitably became a bandwagon for groups to jump on, fuelled by the huge boom in teen magazines and the big increase in singles sales that T.Rex and Slade encouraged. The approach of acts like Sweet, Chicory Tip, Wizzard and others was to find a halfway house between the ribaldry of Slade and the posturing of Bolan, but frequently the result was simply a camp parody. Gary Glitter made a feature out of camp, basing his act on the gaudiest aspects of Fifties rock'n'roll – hence the gold lamé suits, mock-Presley gyrations and, of course, the name. His discs had little in common with vintage rock, his one musical gimmick being a sparse, reverberating guitar sound over a familiar stomping beat, and his appeal was almost entirely visual; with each 'Top Of The Pops' appearance his clothing became more outlandish and his stage act more theatrical. If

his image was laughable, it was meant to be

Gary Glitter's real name was Paul Gadd; he had been around the UK pop scene for years making periodic bids for stardom and failing every time. He was one of a number of faded or forgotten stars who found the climate of the early Seventies particularly favourable. In seeking to cater for the newly re-emergent teen market, the artists and the UK record industry could look back on their own past and put the lessons they had learned into practice. And when established acts weren't dipping into the past for ideas, newer stars were busy imitating their contemporaries. After Gary Glitter came Barry Blue, after Slade came Geordie, after the Faces came Nazareth. The Sweet, an unpretentious minor bubblegum group, rejigged their whole sound in homage to David Bowie – their 'Blockbuster', for instance, showed a remarkable similarity to 'The Jean Genie' – and feigned bisexuality, again in imitation of the master.

Glam and post-glam

Glam-rock strongly influenced the pop scene as a whole, even encouraging a new generation of groups with college-student appeal to rethink their attitude to image and stage presentation. Bowie, with his art and drama-school background, was especially important in this – his *Ziggy Stardust* show was rock theatre at its most powerful, while the album of the same name was itself a shrewd statement on the attractions and pressures of rock stardom. Bands such as Roxy Music, Mott the Hoople, Sparks, Cockney Rebel and Queen (who first appeared during 1974 with 'Seven Seas Of Rhye') all owed something to his initial breakthrough, while even Elton John, once marketed as a moody singer-songwriter, was inspired to don flamboyant costumes and cavort around his piano like a space-age Jerry Lee Lewis.

The glam-rock boom lasted well into 1975, with Mickie Most's RAK label having claimed an increasing share of the market with a series of manufactured teen acts. Significantly, it was an eight-week strike by 'Top Of The Pops' technicians in the middle of that year that signalled the beginning of the end. Denied their regular TV spots, Mud, Suzi Quatro, Slade and many others found their sales dropping alarmingly and none quite recovered. During their absence from the screen, it became apparent that the kids were outgrowing their former idols and that the glitter-glam scene was fast losing its novelty value.

Glam-rock did nevertheless leave an important commercial legacy. It was the small labels like RAK, Magnet, UK and Bell who had espoused the trend wholeheartedly, and their success gave an early indication of the power of the independent label in the market-place. In addition, glam re-established the single as the unit currency of pop and the teenager as its prime consumer. It also had important repercussions visually, giving expression to the kind of ideas that Adam Ant, Gary Numan, Japan and a whole batch of 'new romantics' would explore anew at the beginning of the Eighties. Finally, as a trend peculiar to the United Kingdom, it marked the beginning of a widening schism between British and American tastes.

STEPHEN BARNARD

ROCK '71

1969 and 1970 had been dull years for teen-oriented pop. While the era of 'progressive' rock had brought with it a boom in album sales, few new stars had emerged to take advantage of the young singles-buying public. But 1971 was to mark the beginning of a pop revival as a fresh generation of teen idols began to assail the charts. In Britain, T.Rex scored the first of four Number 1 hits with 'Hot Love', while Slade began their remarkable run of Top Ten entries with 'Coz I Luv You'. Sweet, too, announced their arrival with 'Funny Funny' and for the next three years their releases – together with those of T.Rex, Slade and the glitter stars that followed in their wake – were to dominate the UK hit parade. In the States, meanwhile, the Osmonds (in all their permutations) and David Cassidy arrived to cater for teenage tastes.

On the rock front, the singer-songwriter trend continued to prevail. The outstanding success story of the year was Carole King, whose *Tapestry* album was greeted with unanimous critical acclaim and became the year's top-selling LP in the US, while James Taylor, Cat Stevens, Gordon Lightfoot, Joni Mitchell and Melanie also released best-sellers. And while such technical virtuosos as Emerson, Lake and Palmer, Led Zeppelin and newcomers Yes still dominated in the 'progressive' field, a new form of more theatrical rock – the 'decadent' school spearheaded by David Bowie, Roxy Music and Alice Cooper – was just around the corner.

January

9 'Grandad', a sentimental song by television actor Clive Dunn, reaches Number 1 in the UK.
15 George Harrison's 'My Sweet Lord' is released. The song borrows heavily from the Chiffons' 'He's So Fine', a hit in 1963, and Harrison is subsequently sued for plagiarism.
16 Aretha Franklin volunteers to stand bail of up to 250,000 dollars for Angela Davis, a black activist imprisoned in California and awaiting trial accused of supplying guns used in a robbery.
18 Eric Burdon and War appear at the Midem Festival in Cannes, France. Though they have been allotted 15 minutes, the band play on for over an hour and cause Elton John, who is due to follow them on stage, to depart in a rage.

February

1 A riot breaks out at the Palais des Sports, Paris, during a concert featuring Iron Butterfly, Yes, Soft Machine, Gong and Kevin Ayers and the Whole World. During Ayers' set, members of the audience begin to bombard one another with bottles, causing the police to retaliate with tear gas.
6 Writing in the *Santa Barbara News Press*, rock critic Bill Hilton comments: 'Led Zeppelin has a rhythm that is unbeatable – plus one of the best girl singers in the business.'
13 The Osmonds reach Number 1 in the

Left: 'Dad's Army' star Clive Dunn made Number 1 with 'Grandad'. Above: Ex-Beatle George Harrison's 'My Sweet Lord' was a worldwide hit with unexpected repercussions. Above right: Diana Ross was 'Still Waiting' for her UK Number 1 to take off Stateside. Below: Eric Burdon and friends kept Elton John waiting – 'It's War!', said the pianist. Far right: Louis Armstrong departed this Wonderful World.

US with their first single, 'One Bad Apple'.
27 Paul McCartney's first solo single, 'Another Day', enters the UK Top Fifty. It later reaches Number 2.

March

Carole King's *Tapestry* is released in the US and soon reaches the top of the album charts. By the end of 1973, the LP has sold over 12 million copies around the world, making it the highest-selling record ever by a female artist.

5 *Cry Of Love*, the last studio album to be recorded by Jimi Hendrix, is released.

7 Harold McNair, flautist and sax player with Donovan and Ginger Baker's Airforce, dies from lung cancer.

13 Iron Butterfly split up.

April

2 The Rolling Stones perform at London's Marquee Club for the shooting of the film *Ladies And Gentlemen The Rolling Stones*. The invited audience includes Eric Clapton and Jimmy Page.

Ringo Starr's 'It Don't Come Easy' is released. It becomes the former Beatle's first big hit, reaching Number 4 on both sides of the Atlantic and eventually selling over a million copies.

3 T.Rex are at Number 1 in the UK for the first time with 'Hot Love'.

24 Russ Ballard, guitarist with Argent, is rushed to hospital in Frankfurt after being electrocuted by a live microphone at the Zoom Club. He survives.

May

1 Fleetwood Mac replace guitarist Jeremy Spencer, who quit the group to join religious sect the Children of God, with American Bob Welch.

8 'The Battle Hymn Of Lieutenant Calley', by C Company featuring Terry Nelson, peaks in the US charts at Number 37. The record, a song in praise of Lieutenant William L. Calley, recently convicted for the premeditated murder of 22 Vietnamese at My Lai, is awarded a gold disc the following April.

Bill Graham, disillusioned with the current music scene, announces the closure of his Fillmore East and West venues. 'In the early days of both Fillmore East and West, the level of the audience seemed much higher in terms of musical sophistication,' he comments. 'Now there are too many screams for "more" with total disregard for whether or not there was any musical quality.'

12 Rolling Stone Mick Jagger marries Nicaraguan beauty Bianca Perez Moreno de Macias in St Tropez.

June

11 Rioting erupts at a Livingstone Taylor and Jethro Tull concert at the Red Rocks Amphitheatre, Denver. 24 people, including four policemen, are taken to hospital; 20 are arrested for drunkenness, weapons violation and narcotics charges.

26 The final show takes place at the Fillmore East. The star-studded bill includes the Allman Brothers, the J. Geils Band, the Beach Boys, Country Joe and the Fish and Edgar Winter's White Trash.

July

3 Jim Morrison, singer with the Doors, is found dead in a bathtub by his wife Pamela while on holiday in Paris.

The Newport Folk Festival comes to a premature close when hundreds of youths run amok, causing thousands of dollars' worth of damage to equipment and seating.

6 Jazzman Louis Armstrong dies in New Orleans aged 71.

August

1 The Concert For Bangladesh, organised by George Harrison, takes place at New York's Madison Square Garden. Performers include Harrison, Ravi Shankar, Billy Preston, Eric Clapton, Leon Russell, Badfinger, Ringo Starr and Bob Dylan.

3 Paul McCartney announces that he is forming a touring band named Wings.

13 Sax player King Curtis is stabbed to death in New York.

21 Diana Ross reaches the top of the UK singles charts with 'I'm Still Waiting'; in the US, however, the song can only make Number 63.

September

4 At a Wishbone Ash concert in Texas, Francisco Carrasco, a sandwich vendor, is murdered.

21 'The Old Grey Whistle Test', a show devoted to 'serious' rock music, is aired for the first time on BBC television.

25 Guitarist and singer Peter Frampton announces his departure from Humble Pie.

30 Keyboard player Rick Wakeman makes his performing debut with Yes at Leicester's De Montfort Hall.

October

1 John Lennon is awarded a gold disc for US sales of *Imagine* on the eve of its UK release.

9 Chicago's *At Carnegie Hall*, the first four-album set to be released by a rock group, appears. Despite the hefty price tag, it soon sells over a million copies.

12 Rock'n'roll legend Gene Vincent dies at the age of 36 in California.

29 Guitarist Duane Allman of the Allman Brothers is killed in a motorcycle accident near his home in Macon, Georgia.

November

8 Led Zeppelin's fourth album, with its unusual 'title' of four rune-like symbols, is released.

13 'Coz I Luv You', by Wolverhampton stompers Slade, reaches Number 1 in the UK, beginning an incredible run of twelve consecutive Top Five hits.

17 The Frank Zappa film *200 Motels* is premiered at the London Pavilion.

18 Herman 'Little Junior' Parker, blues harpist and singer, and writer of the Elvis Presley classic 'Mystery Train', dies while undergoing a brain operation in Chicago.

December

10 Frank Zappa is attacked by a fan's jealous husband as the Mothers of Invention are playing a concert at London's Rainbow Theatre; the singer/guitarist falls from the stage and breaks a leg.

11 John Lennon and Yoko Ono appear at a benefit concert for John Sinclair in Ann Arbor, Michigan. Sinclair, manager of the MC5 and leader of the radical White Panthers party, is in prison on drugs charges.

25 Comedian Benny Hill's humorous song 'Ernie (The Fastest Milkman In The West)' is Number 1 in the UK, while Melanie's 'Brand New Key' tops the US charts.

31 The Band perform at the New York Academy of Music; the concert is recorded for the double album *Rock Of Ages*.

TOM HIBBERT, JENNY DAWSON

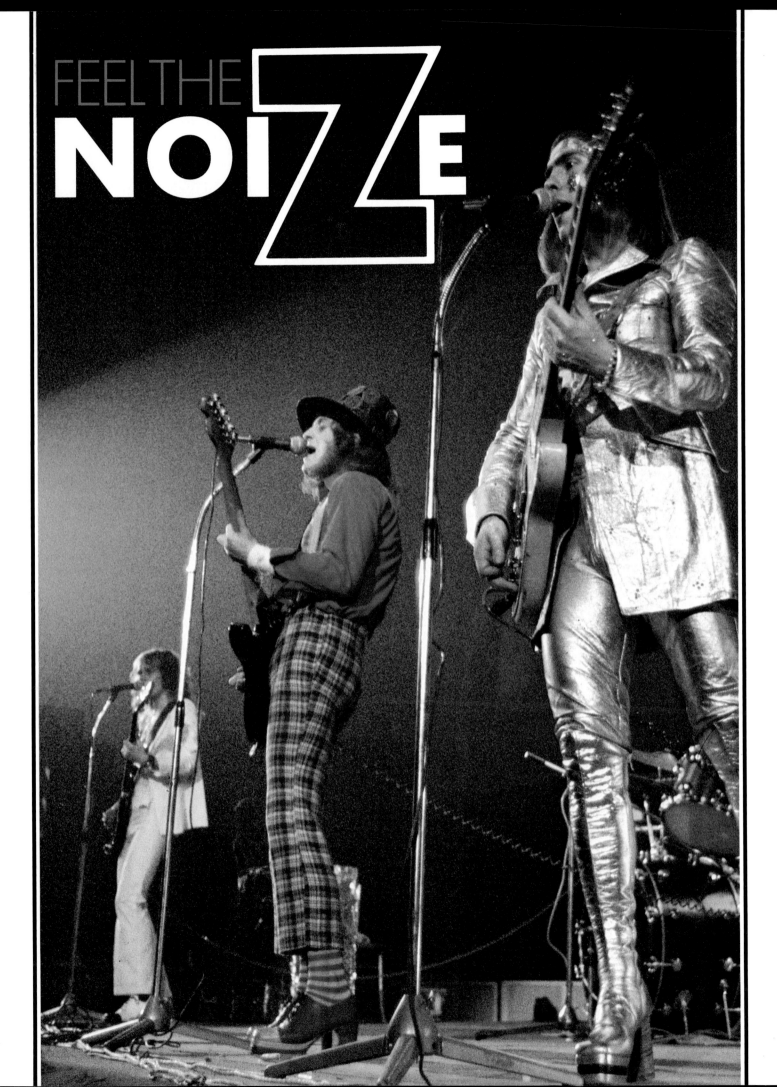

FEEL THE NOIZE

How Slade stomped their way to the top

'THE FANS are fed up with paying to sit on their hands while watching musicians who clearly couldn't care less about the customers.' Thus commented Slade's singer Noddy Holder in 1971. 'What is wanted is more of a party atmosphere.' And that is exactly what Slade provided, with a brash, vulgar, loud and cheery sound untainted by any hint of subtlety. Along with T.Rex, Sweet and the other glitter stars, Slade spearheaded the teen pop revival of the early Seventies; but whereas the appeal of their contemporaries was restricted largely to female teenage consumers, Slade attracted a wider following.

Unlike the vast majority of their rivals, their image was based not on effete sexuality and lip-gloss but on a warm-hearted, boozy 'working-class' fellowship: at a Slade concert, the sound of adolescent screams would be drowned beneath that of football-terrace chants and stomping boots. The group's good-time music was raw, crude and simplistic – music not for listening to but for shouting with and waving scarves at – and between 1971 and 1974, it provided Slade with 12 consecutive UK Top Ten entries (six of them Number 1 hits) and three Number 1 albums, making them commercially the most successful British act of their time.

Black country rock

Neville 'Noddy' Holder was born in Wolverhampton on 15 June 1950 and formed his first group, the Rockin' Phantoms, while still at school. The band were little more than an amateur R&B combo but they were young and keen, and so when singer and Midlands celebrity Steve Brett lost the services of his backing group in 1965, he replaced them with Holder's outfit. The Rockin' Phantoms thus became the Mavericks.

Meanwhile, guitarist Dave Hill (born Devon, 4 April 1952) and drummer Don Powell (born Wolverhampton, 10 September 1950) were playing in another youthful Wolverhampton-based band, the 'N Betweens, along with Johnny Howells (vocals), Mickey Marston (guitar) and Dave Jones (bass). The 'N Betweens also played R&B – but not very well – and, late in 1965, Jones quit the group following an argument concerning his musical ability (or lack of it). The band held auditions for a replacement and Jimmy Lea proved to be the successful candidate.

Lea (born Wolverhampton, 14 June 1952) was already an accomplished musician. He had begun to study the violin at the age of seven and had played with the Stafford Youth Orchestra for three years before taking up the bass guitar.

Soon after Lea's recruitment to the 'N Betweens, Mickey Marston followed Jones out of the band and Noddy Holder, bored with playing Jim Reeves and Roy Orbison

numbers behind Steve Brett's crooning, came in on second guitar. And when Howells also departed in April 1966, Holder, with his hoarse, grating and sturdy voice, took over on vocals.

The 'N Betweens were by now gigging regularly around the Black Country and points beyond. They had rejected R&B for an odd mixture of soul – Otis Redding and Motown – together with rock oddities such as Moby Grape's 'Omaha' and Procol Harum's 'The Milk Of Human Kindness', which all received hard-rock arrangements and, unusually for the time, twin lead guitars. In the summer of 1966, the group were playing at Tiles Club in

Slade attracted hostile attention for their skinhead look (above), but their image later mellowed (opposite).

London's Oxford Street before an enthusiastically bopping crowd when they were spotted by American producer and pop manipulator Kim Fowley. 'He came in the dressing room and he was totally over the top – a real freak,' Holder recalled in 1983. 'He did the usual thing, saying "You guys are the most original band I've ever seen. I'm gonna make you guys stars." But he actually followed it up. The next day he took us walking round London and he's taken us into the bank with him to cash a cheque and he'd say to the bank teller: "Look at these four guys' faces. One day they're gonna be stars. And don't forget – Kim Fowley was the first to tell you."'

Fowley took the 'N Betweens to Regent Sound studios in Denmark Street where they recorded two numbers, 'You Better Run', a US hit for the Young Rascals, and 'Evil Witchman' which, according to Holder, was 'some song that Fowley ripped off someone and wrote some stupid new words to.' With a potential single in the can, Fowley negotiated a one-off deal with Columbia and 'You Better Run' was released in August 1966. It sold reasonably well, particularly in the group's native Midlands, but it failed to chart and the Kim Fowley connection was severed.

Bad news in the Bahamas

Still without a long-term contract, the 'N Betweens continued to gig throughout 1967, and the following year their agency secured them a six-week residency at a club in the Bahamas. Unfortunately, the club went out of business five weeks into the engagement, was taken over and the group were forced to stay on until they had paid off a massive hotel bill and could afford to ship their equipment home. For a further two months, the 'N Betweens played at the club seven nights a week backing fire-eaters, limbo dancers, strippers and third-rate soul singers. But the experience did have its advantages, for the musicians were still not writing original material and in the Bahamas they heard records that had never been heard in England – numbers like the Amboy Dukes' 'Journey To The Centre Of Your Mind', Nazz's 'Open My Eyes' and Steppenwolf's 'Born To Be Wild' – which they incorporated into their act.

Back in England towards the end of 1968, the group's agent obtained them an audition with Fontana Records. The label's head, Jack Bavistock, was highly impressed with the sound and offered them a deal. Bavistock wasn't so impressed with the band's name, however, and proffered an alternative. It was as Ambrose Slade that the group's first album was released in April 1969. *Beginnings* was composed largely of cover versions – songs by Jeff Lynne, Frank Zappa, the Moody Blues and the Beatles – although the single lifted from the LP, 'Genesis', was a group-composed instrumental.

Both album and single flopped, but they did at least catch the attention of London agent John Gunnell who took ex-Animal Chas Chandler to see Ambrose Slade performing at Rasputin's club. Chandler had recently stopped managing Jimi Hendrix and was on the lookout for fresh talent – and the enthusiasm of the audience and the vitality of the group convinced him that he'd found it. Chandler signed the band to a management deal, shortened their name to Slade and produced their next single, 'Wild Winds Are Blowing'.

The record was another failure, but by now Slade were attracting a good deal of media attention – much of it hostile – because of the new image they had adopted. Searching for a look that would single them out from the long-haired, loon-panted masses, the members of Slade had cropped their hair, donned braces and 'bovver' boots and gone skinhead. Associations with skinhead violence led to cancelled bookings and a backlash in the music press – but it also led to TV interviews and national press coverage.

Suddenly, Slade were mildly notorious, and when their next single, a version of Mann and Weil's 'Shape Of Things To Come', emerged in March 1970, the band were invited to appear on BBC-TV's 'Top Of The Pops'. The exposure failed to assist sales of the record, however, and by the time their third single, 'Know Who You Are' (which was 'Genesis' with an added lyric), had flopped in September, the group had rejected the skinhead look and were growing their hair once more.

Boots for dancing
By 1971, the Slade controversy (and hence the band itself) had been forgotten by the media. But then in June, 'Get Down And Get With It' – a version of a song by New Orleans singer Bobby Marchan performed in raucous, relentless, stomping fashion – entered the UK Top Twenty, reaching Number 16. Despite lack of airplay, Slade had finally come up with a hit.

It was now that Chas Chandler insisted that the group start writing their own material. All that was lacking was self-confidence, he argued – and Jim Lea and Noddy Holder soon proved him right. 'Once we finally got down to it, "Coz I Luv You" came like a piece of cake,' Holder has said. 'It was just a jamming beat written in half an hour and to make it different – more *us* – we put stomping boot sounds all over it.'

In November 1971, 'Coz I Luv You', an infectious plodder dominated by Lea's electric violin and Holder's rasping tones, made the UK Number 1 position and established the formula that would keep Slade at the top for the next three years. It was a simple formula but a thoroughly effective one: a stomping rhythm, noise, jollity and immediate riffs, misspelled song titles and a garish image.

Spelling success
The formula proved more successful than Slade or Chandler could have ever imagined. 'Look Wot You Dun', the follow-up to 'Coz I Luv You', reached Number 4 in February 1972; 'Take Me Bak 'Ome' and 'Mama Weer All Crazee Now' both made the top slot; 'Gudbuy T'Jane' reached Number 2 and in March 1973 'Cum On Feel The Noize' entered the charts at Number 1. Meanwhile, the band were proving equally successful in the album market; *Slade Alive*, released in April 1972, climbed to Number 2, while *Slayed?* (1972) and *Sladest* (1973) both topped the LP charts.

The sound of Slade's pop chants echoed around drunken parties, football terraces, pubs at closing time and the concert halls of Britain, where the group were still gigging constantly. By the time they provided the country with its anthem for Christmas 1973, 'Merry Xmas Everybody', Slade had become a national institution.

Something had to give, however, and the end of 1974 brought with it signs of decline. For after an unbroken sequence of 12 Top Ten hits, the group were feeling the need to expand their boundaries – and so they made a movie. *Slade In Flame* ('the nitty gritty, behind-the-scenes story about your average rock'n'roll band,' according to Noddy Holder) was, as rock films go, a commendable effort. However, Slade were supposed to be a *people's* band, working-class and down to earth; in trying to become movie stars they were alienating a proportion of their audience.

In 1975, they lost more fans by embarking on a concerted and lengthy effort to 'break' the United States, where they had never found success. When they returned to Britain two years later, having failed in their mission, the group found that they had been all but forgotten. Punk had brought with it a new generation of 'people's bands' and Slade were now has-beens and definitely unhip. An album released in March 1977 was wryly titled *Whatever Happened To Slade?*.

Back to the roots
Slade still had energy to spare, however, and the will to play and win; for the next three years they toured ceaselessly around clubs and even pubs, slowly rebuilding grass-roots support. Then in the summer of 1980, the band were booked, at the last minute, to appear at the Reading Festival – and their rowdy, barnstorming set turned out to be the event's sensation. Slade were as raucous, rude and hyperactive as ever and while Dave Hill's screeching guitar added an element that appealed to the heavy-metal contingent, the group was otherwise devoid of the strutting pomp of most other acts on the heavy metal-oriented bill. Warmth and humour were, as always, in evidence.

A live EP of their festival performance, *Slade Alive At Reading*, entered the UK Top Fifty at the end of the year and the band continued to work into the Eighties, attracting a growing following of denim-jacketed youths and older fans re-converted to the cause. With gutsily euphoric workouts of the hits, jovial, crowd-stirring yells from Holder, utterly tasteless, high-volume guitar from Hill and rampant audience participation all round, Slade's live performances (captured on the 1982 album *Slade On Stage*) had become, if anything, more vibrant than they had been a decade earlier.

Despite a run of three UK Top Twenty singles in four months (including 'My Oh My', a 1983 Number 2, and the third re-entry of 'Xmas'), Slade were destined to rely on live work—always their forte—for their daily bread.   TOM HIBBERT

*Mama Weer All Crazee Now: Breezy
bearers of bonhomie and bluster (above),
Slade made their mark with infectious
dance-hall stomps and crazy antics
(below). Below left: Noddy Holder surveys
his flying circus.*

Slade
Recommended Listening

Sladest (Polydor 2442 119) (Includes: Get Down
And Get With It, Coz I Luv You, Take Me Bak 'Ome,
Mama Weer All Crazee Now, Gudbuy T'Jane, Cum
On Feel The Noize, Skweeze Me Pleeze Me).

Gary Glitter: a success story in sequins

SUCCESS – particularly in the fad-conscious world of pop music – often depends on being in the right place at the right time. Paul Gadd's musical career began in the Fifties and had spanned 12 years of performing in clubs (and the release of a number of unsuccessful singles) before the emergence of glam-rock in Britain in the early Seventies catapulted him to stardom in the guise of Gary Glitter. He sustained a rigorous publicity campaign during his heyday, ensuring that the sparkle did not fade before he had emblazoned his sequinned pseudonym across the pages of rock history. Glam-rock was as much about image as music; Gary Glitter's musical legacy amounts to a mere handful of singles, but his outrageous persona and lavish stage act remain memorable.

He was born in the small town of Banbury in Oxfordshire, and gives his date of birth as 8 May 1944. One of the first musical influences in his young life was his Uncle John, who performed in clubs and pubs, accompanying himself on his guitar. While in his early teens, Gary gained his second major influence – Elvis Presley – on a visit to the local cinema to see *Loving You* (1957).

The youngster returned every day for a week, perfecting his impersonation of the King in front of a mirror with a tennis racquet. When his teachers asked him what he wanted to be after he left school, he answered without hesitation: 'A rock 'n'roll star'.

He saved up for a white Hofner Senator guitar by selling newspapers and formed a skiffle group before adopting his stepfather's name of Russell to front a school rock band, Paul Russell and the Rebels. By the age of 13, he was earning up to £45 a week singing nightly; his venues included the Safari Club in London's Trafalgar Square and the 2 Is coffee bar in Old Compton Street, where he rubbed shoulders with the likes of Adam Faith and Bruce Welch of the Shadows.

Shopping for clothes

Even at that age, Gary had no difficulty deciding what to spend his money on – clothes. He would turn up at school in the latest Italian fashions – pointed leather shoes and 'bum-freezer' jackets. The 'in' place to shop for clothes then was Al Kazura (later Johnson's) on the King's Road, Chelsea, from whom he later commissioned his extravagant glitter costumes.

Leaving school at 14, Gary worked for a week in a theatre-ticket agency before deciding to concentrate solely on his musical career. Fronting his first pro band – Paul Raven and the Vibraphones – as vocalist, he dropped guitar because it restricted his movement on stage. He toured in 1960 and 1961 as a bottom-of-the-bill singer, doing Buddy Holly covers, with a show that included comedians Bernard Bresslaw and Ronnie Corbett. Then came his first venture onto vinyl when he was spotted by film-producer Robert Hartford Davis. He became Gary's first manager, and shortly afterwards the Decca label released 'Alone In The Night', a pop ballad in a minor key, with which the

singer made his TV debut in 'Cool For Cats'. Two further singles for Parlophone under his second manager Vic Billings were equally unsuccessful.

Then Gary's talent for involving the audience in his stage act, persuading them to sing and clap when required, landed him the job of warm-up man on the TV show 'Ready, Steady, Go!'. He was in the right place for meeting the right people, and one of these was Mike Leander, a prominent songwriter and producer who had worked with many top names and was to become Gary's main collaborator during the Glitter years. But first came an interlude in Germany, when Gary formed a band with John Russell, later to become the sax

THE GANG

On stage, Gary Glitter was a larger than life performer . . . but the sequin-laden trousers of his tailor-made suit were a little on the small side.

and trombone player with the Glitter Band. With the Merseybeat invasion in full swing in Britain, they decided to follow the Beatles' lead and head for Germany to serve their apprenticeship on the club circuit in Hamburg.

The glamour game

By 1971 a new craze was sweeping the commercial music scene back in England – glam-rock. The time was right for a novelty act with the right ingredients to break into the charts. Sitting around with a group of friends one night, the singer dreamt up a list of suitably alliterative names, eventually settling on Gary Glitter.

Gary had remained in touch with Mike Leander while in Germany and, on his return to the UK, the duo teamed up to record 'Rock And Roll (Parts One And Two)' for Bell Records. The formula was a neat one: to a basic drum rhythm were added simple, catchy riffs and easily memorable, repetitive lyrics, with plenty of shouting and handclapping to ensure maximum audience participation at a live performance. It stripped rock music back down to the bare bones.

The rock audience of the late Sixties had veered towards underground bands and the record-buying public had become increasingly album-oriented. But the typical teenage pop music fan's pocket-money did not stretch to LPs, and there was a gap in the singles market. After the protest songs of the Sixties, the introspection of the singer-songwriters and heavy rock, the early Seventies heralded a return to sheer fun in pop music – bopping songs to play at parties and discos.

However, 'Rock And Roll' was by no means an instant chart success for Gary Glitter. It had the kids on their feet in the discos, but it took four months for it to get radio airplay. The record reached Number 2 in the UK and Number 7 in the US, but it was the B-side – with sporadic shouts and handclaps over the backing track – that was listed as the hit. Eventually, it sold over three million copies, won Gary his first gold disc and a songwriting award (he co-wrote the song with Leander).

After years as a warm-up man and small-time performer, success had come at last. But in the competitive glam-rock field of the early Seventies, he could not afford to rest on his laurels. Subtlety was not a word to be given much consideration; to outshine the other acts, Glitter had to push the image to the verge of parody – more camp, more sparkles, more make-up, more hair-spray, more inches on the platform shoes, more sequins and lurex. Meanwhile, he confirmed his hit formula with the release of 'I Didn't Know I Loved You (Till I Saw You Rock'n'Roll)', a UK Number 4 hit that was unashamedly cloned from its predecessor.

Rest in peace?

From appearing at the Rock'n'Roll Revival concert at Wembley Stadium in the summer of 1972 alongside Chuck Berry and Jerry Lee Lewis, Gary Glitter kept up the momentum with a breathless tour schedule covering concert halls all over Britain, Europe and Australia. As a publicity stunt in 1973, he took a boat out onto the River Thames and lowered a coffin into the water; it contained photos and discs of Paul Raven and the ceremony, attended by DJ Alan Freeman, represented Glitter's symbolic burial of his old image. He went on to perform at the Rainbow and at the London Palladium – for the latter, Bell Records flew 10 American underground rock journalists, at a cost of 10,000 dollars, to see him.

In a review in *Rolling Stone* in March 1973, Paul Gambaccini described the event: '"My God, it's Marlene Dietrich!" exclaimed one of the 10 as the star slinked

down a golden staircase in a black robe and plumage-covered hat. Glitter flung the robe aside and proceeded to moan and gyrate through an hour of thump-thump-thump rock'n'roll. "Do you want to touch?" Glitter asked the shrieking girls. Then he gave them "Do You Wanna Touch Me (Oh Yeah)", complete with pelvic thrusts and robot-like movements, occasionally turning his back on the throng to readjust the zipper on his pants.'

The staircase had been rented from Pinewood Studios for Gary's elaborate set; he had to be hoisted to the top of it to make his dramatic entrance, tottering on his nine-inch platform shoes. His performance of 'I'm The Leader Of The Gang (I Am!)' was equally spectacular, employing up to eight motorbikes as stage props. A busy promotions and publicity team saturated

the media with material, while his fan club cut up his old glitter suits to post snippets to his followers. Gary rehearsed his stage act with fanatical enthusiasm, right down to perfecting the knack of raising one eyebrow to stare quizzically at the audience, one of his many self-parodying gestures.

Behind him, his band had developed a basic leg-stepping routine. John Russell was still with Gary on sax and trombone; the rest of the band comprised Harvey Ellison (also on sax), Gerry Shephard (guitar), John Springate (bass) and Pete Phipps and Peter Gill on drums. In 1973 Tony Leonard replaced Peter Gill, who went on to join Saxon. The Glitter Band were to register seven UK Top Twenty hits under their own name – including a 1975 Number 2 with 'Goodbye My Love' – in the early and mid Seventies before finally splitting in 1977.

Above: Gary rode the charts in the glitter era, towering above his fellow glam-rockers. Inset above left: Gary's first professional photo as Paul Raven. Opposite: Glitter gets down on stage.

Platinum productions

Gary Glitter had 11 Top Ten hit singles in the UK between June 1972 and July 1975. 1973 was his most prolific year: two Number 2 hits with 'Do You Wanna Touch Me (Oh Yeah)' and 'Hello Hello I'm Back Again' preceded his first chart-topper in July with the playground chant 'I'm The Leader Of The Gang (I Am!)', which sold a million worldwide. Its success was topped, however, by 'I Love You Love Me Love' in November when this slower-paced but equally persistent song entered the charts at Number 1 to register his third million-

charts for a couple more years, however: 'Remember Me This Way' reached Number 3 in March 1974; 'Always Yours' gave him his third Number 1 in June; and 'Oh Yes! You're Beautiful' made Number 2 in November. The following year saw his last Top Ten hits with 'Love Like You And Me' and 'Doing Alright With The Boys'.

Gary Glitter's heyday was over. At the peak of his success, his £250,000 house in Sussex had seen weekend guests arrive in their hundreds; it boasted a marble bathroom with bronze and silver wallpaper flown specially from New York, and an octagonal bedroom – the Glitter Suite – dripping with gilt, chandeliers and mirrors. But Gary's singles output was beginning to dry up, and his tour costs soared as he experimented with such gimmicks as hydraulic lifts and, on one occasion, 25 Gary Glitter lookalikes. A number of unsuccessful business ventures and the attentions of the taxman left Gary with little to show, materially, for his stardom. In March 1976, he announced that he was quitting, sold his house and went to live in Paris. From there, he travelled to Thailand, where he developed an interest

in Buddhism. After a spell on a Pacific island, his passion for the stage drew him back to star as Frank N Furter—in fishnets and false eyelashes—in a production of the *Rocky Horror Show* in New Zealand, and to attempt a series of comebacks.

He re-entered the UK Top Thirty in 1984 with 'Dance Me Up' (Number 25) and 'Another Rock'n'Roll Christmas' (Number 7), while in 1988 a thinly disguised version of 'Rock and Roll (Part Two)' was taken to the top of the UK charts by the Timelords as 'Doctorin' The Tardis'. Glitter got his royalties. Meanwhile in the United States, his songs crept back into the charts with Joan Jett's cover of 'Do You Wanna Touch Me (Oh Yeah)'. The enthusiasm of the old trouper seemed hard to quell; perhaps rock'n'roller Little Richard's self-accolade could be pinned equally well to Gary Glitter's spangled breast: 'I'm just the same as ever – loud, electrifying and full of personal magnetism.'

ANNETTE KENNERLEY

seller. Gary picked up four silver discs in 1973; the following year he became the first British artist to be awarded a platinum record by the British Phonograph Society, and by the end of 1975 he had sold 18 million records. In addition to his successful singles, he released four albums and a hit compilation.

But the diamanté on the glam-rock bandwagon had already begun to tarnish. In December 1973, Marc Bolan had declared: 'Glam-rock is dead ... it was a great thing but now you have your Sweet, Chicory Tip and Gary Glitter ... what those guys are doing is circus and comedy.' New fads were taking a grip on the fickle pop audience – notably the Monkees-mould Bay City Rollers, whose tartan-and-terraces image was upstaging the glitter and eyeshadow. Gary managed to ride the

Gary Glitter
Recommended Listening

Gary Glitter's Golden Greats (GTO GTLP 021) (Includes: Rock And Roll Part One, Hello Hello I'm Back Again, I'm The Leader Of The Gang (I Am!), I Love You Love Me Love, Do You Wanna Touch Me (Oh Yeah), Oh Yes! You're Beautiful).

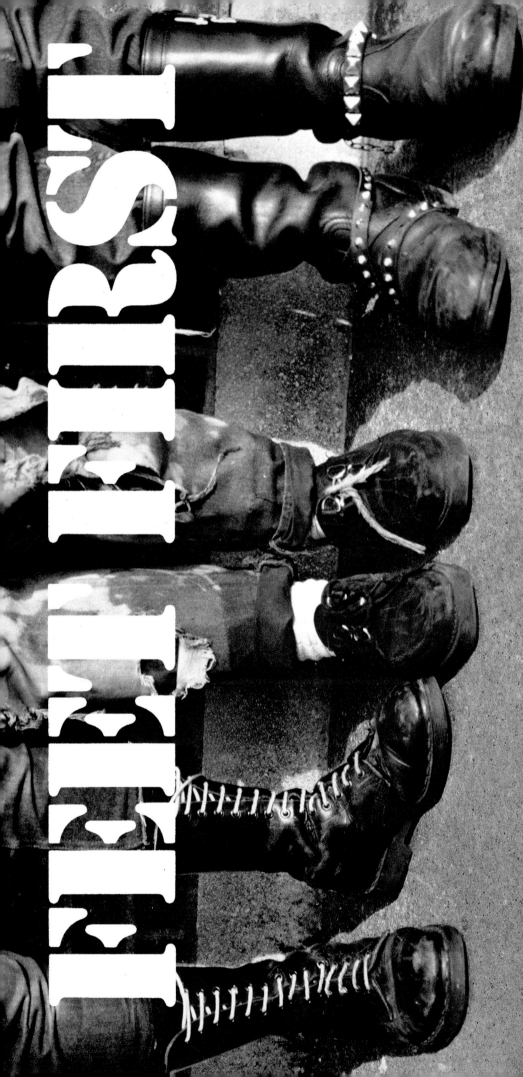

FEET FIRST

Rock steps forward in different styles

ROCK FASHIONS start at the feet upwards. Whatever clothes fans have opted for, their choice of footwear has always been the most conspicuous indicator of their taste, style and musical allegiances. This may be simply because feet are especially 'eloquent' in dancing to rock – but shoe-power probably resides in the *symbolic* importance of footwear: bovver boots, for example, represent skinhead aggression; pixie boots represent new romantic pea-cockery. Moreover, shoes have always been a sign of rock's unwillingness to conform.

Breaking step . . .

When Elvis Presley warned his fans not to step on his blue suede shoes, he was doing more than merely stating his sartorial standards. Those powder-blue shoes signalled a break away from traditional male footwear which, no matter how flamboyant the rest of a performer's outfit might be, tended towards practicality and classic, conservative lines. Women had long suffered for the sake of fashion – teetering on spindly stilettos to turn a shapely ankle – but men's feet had been blessed with comparative kindness by footwear trends.

In the late Fifties, Jerry Lee Lewis would plump for a pair of handmade two-tone Oxfords – or 'co-respondents' as they were called in the Thirties, while Chuck Berry, even in the late Sixties, would complement his stylish appearance with real crocodile shoes. The Teddy Boy look in the Fifties had sparked off an interest in more adventurous styles of footwear, with ever more far-reaching points to the winkle-pickers. In the Sixties, the elastic-sided Chelsea 'Beatle' boots oddly combined with the new thin trouser leg. The higher heel now returned to men's shoes – for the first time since the eighteenth century.

The utterly clothes-conscious Mods made a number of new shoe styles fashionable. Buckles and side laces came in, the snub-toed winklepickers or 'chisels' came and went, Hush Puppies were favourites with both sexes (they were considered good to dance in), as were Clarks' desert boots, running shoes and even bowling shoes. Raoul shoe shop in London's Carnaby Street was *the* place to buy your shoes.

Shaw footed

Feet were often overlooked when pop stars dressed for performances, however. Even a dedicated follower of fashion like Ray Davies of the Kinks would wear a nondescript pair of 'brothel creepers' – suede lace-up ankle-huggers – with a snazzy red tartan suit. Some stars have made an impact by complete non-conformity – Sandie Shaw became famous for appearing barefoot. Women's footwear seems to adhere to the rest of their stage image – the Supremes had to complete their slinky, glamorous outfits with high-heeled, strappy shoes; Lulu closed the gap between her mini skirts and the floor with white knee-length boots; and Tina Turner added inches to her stage presence with towering platform sling-backs.

The hippie movement brought a more relaxed fashion to rock music in the late Sixties. In the States, there was a reaction against the commercial aspects of the promotion business, which involved the hyping of mediocre performers, restyling their looks with appropriate clothing. Many 'rebel' rock artists donned their oldest clothes and scuffed sneakers. Leather-thonged sandals, 'Jesus' boots and – in a more ethnic style – moccasins were also popular. For an extravagant look, some performers – Captain Beefheart, for instance – would have shoes and boots hand-made for them, in soft, coloured leathers, with appliquéd motifs, or cowboy boots with elaborate top-stitching decorations scrolled on the sides.

Height of fashion

Certain fashion and music trends have determined more strictly than others what young people should wear on their feet. At the start of the Seventies, platforms soared to previously unimagined heights as glam-rock flourished. Bolan, Bowie, Slade, Roxy Music, the Sweet, Rod Stewart and Gary Glitter all tottered on-stage on soles that added up to nine inches onto their height, their boots and shoes made from glittering silver and gold leather, often decorated with stars, moons or other motifs. If one person in particular is to be remembered from the early Seventies for his shocking shoes, it must be strutting dwarf Elton John, whose knee-length brightly-coloured boots and sculptured platform shoes became as much a trademark for him as his equally noticeable gimmicky specs.

In the second half of the Seventies, punk manacled together various elements of footwear fashion; if you could afford it, leather boots rattling with zips, buckles and chains were uniform – the predominant colour being black; for penniless punks, grubby plimsolls à la Sid Vicious, showing the maximum amount of daylight, would do just as well. In London in the Eighties, any style of shoe could be purchased to complete the specific look desired, be it Ted, Mod, punk or hippie. Carnaby Street was still the Mods' Mecca; a trip down the King's Road, Chelsea, would kit you out in jangling leather bondage boots, Woolworths could supply you with elasticated plimsolls for the Haircut 100 look, and dear old Hush Puppies were always there to ease your tortured soles.

FRANCES KENNETT

These boots weren't made for walking: Gary Glitter takes the weight off his feet (right). Elton John's stacks were more modest (above right). Opposite, from top: Motorcycle boots with studs, suede brothel-creepers and Doc Martens.

BORN TO BOOGIE

The electrifying rise of Marc Bolan and T.Rex

MARC BOLAN IS commonly considered the originator of glam-rock, although his career spanned the decade from Mod to punk and encompassed acoustic flower-power, modelling and hosting a TV chat show. His stylish image whipped up fan hysteria on a scale not seen since the Beatles' heyday and, from 1970 to 1977, he was responsible for T.Rex's 15 Top Twenty hits in the UK and one US Top Ten entry. Bolan was a star – one of the few really glamorous pop heroes.

He was born Marc Feld in Hackney, London, on 30 September 1947. The son of an East End lorry driver, Marc learned his street savvy in the playgrounds of Stoke Newington and helping out on his mother's barrow in Soho's Berwick Street market. His parents encouraged his early musical ambitions by buying him a drum kit and guitar. He played in a school trio called Susie and the Hula Hoops behind Helen Shapiro, who was to become a star some two years later.

Bolan used to skip school to 'hang out' around Soho and the 2 Is coffee bar, where skiffle had its first flowering. He listened to records and spent all his earnings from after-school jobs and the market stall on clothes. His first suit (which his mother paid for) was made to his own design by Burtons. He read poetry and mixed with the fringes of bohemia, where he was accepted for his child-like good looks and sharp dress-sense. At 14 he was a proto-Mod; talented and ambitious, he nevertheless lacked direction.

It was his photogenic qualities that gave him his first taste of success. Through an acquaintance, journalist Angus McGill, Marc was chosen as a representative of the Mod generation and, photographed with typical gritty realism by Don McCullin, appeared on the cover of *Town* magazine. Further modelling work led to Marc's image appearing throughout the country as a cardboard cutout in the windows of the John Temple tailoring chain and in various mail-order catalogues. He also flirted with the idea of an acting career, playing a small role in an episode of the children's TV series 'Orlando'.

The idea gradually crystallised that the music business might be the answer. While sharing a flat with Alan Warren, a young helper on ITV's 'Five O'Clock Club', Marc cut an acetate of a Betty Everett number, 'You're No Good', under the name of Toby Tyler. Warren had some publicity photos done by Mike McGrath and tried to

sell the package to Rediffusion TV, but got nowhere. Marc decided that he had to write some of his own material, improve his guitar-playing and come up with a distinctive sound.

During the period 1964-65 he did just that. His extremely fertile mind started to weave the fantasies that appeared in his lyrics and in his life story. His imagination could transform a fortnight in Paris with actor Riggs O'Hara into a six-month stay with a French wizard in a magical castle learning the black arts – a story that cropped up again and again in Bolan's early publicity material. Impressed by Dylan's technique of packing his lyrics with images, Bolan began to evolve a similar style of his own. He also set out to capitalise on his thin voice by developing a unique wavering nasal delivery, which he went on to use throughout his career. His guitar work, always a weak point, improved with hours and hours of arduous strumming practice.

Childish antics

As Marc Bowland, he had his first official release with 'The Wizard' on Decca in 1965, produced by John Economedies and complete with bass, drums, orchestra and chorus. Although slightly out of the ordinary, and critically well-received, the single failed to chart. It did, however, lead to an appearance on 'Ready, Steady, Go!', where Marc first encountered the electric guitar-playing of Jimi Hendrix – an experience that was to influence his long-term development. At the same TV show, Marc also met B. P. Fallon, who was to become a life-long friend, publicist and general sounding-board for ideas. A second, equally unsuccessful Decca single, 'The Third Degree'/'San Francisco Poet', followed, and was the first to feature the name Marc Bolan. In 1966, he appeared again on 'Ready, Steady, Go!' to promote 'Hippy Gumbo' (on Columbia), but it was to be another critically-acclaimed flop.

It was at this time that Bolan walked into the life of the Yardbirds producer/manager Simon Napier-Bell, who spotted the potential of Bolan's unique songs but, with hindsight, was perhaps not the man

Rake's progress: Marc Bolan's path from fresh-faced youth as a model (above left) to the dizzy heights of T.Rextasy (right) took him through the quiet acoustic idyll of the hippie years, when he and Steve Took made up the duo Tyrannosaurus Rex (left).

to handle them. He recorded Marc singing with acoustic guitar accompaniment and did the rounds of the record companies to no avail – nobody liked Marc's high-pitched, quavering whine of a voice. Napier-Bell then persuaded Marc to join John's Children, a band that he managed; the idea was that Marc would write all their material, play electric guitar (learning as he did so) and be heard by a ready-made audience.

The band John's Children, one of the first signings to Kit Lambert's Track label, were a bizarre and virtually talentless outfit that myth and dim memory have endowed with pretensions as a precursor of both glam-rock and nihilist punk. Their carefully contrived stage show featured more fighting, destruction and general mayhem than actual playing and ultimately resulted in their being fired from supporting the Who on a tour of West Germany when they incited a full-scale riot that had to be suppressed by troops.

Bolan's role in this drunken, brawling outfit was equally bizarre; most of the time he remained the introverted, intense song-writer/poet, but for gigs he would emerge briefly to play basic psychedelic lead guitar, dance around and whip his equipment to pieces with lengths of chain. Although most of the songs they played live were Bolan originals, John's Children's recorded output was small. They had a minor hit with 'Desdemona' in June 1967, and released a supposedly live album *Orgasm* (a studio album, in fact, with audience screams lifted from a Beatles film).

A monster success?

John's Children remained at best an *ad hoc* outfit in tune with the happy-go-lucky ethos of 1967, but Bolan was frustrated by the lack of recognition for his own role and advertised in the music press for musicians to join a band of his own. As he intended it to be the biggest musical phenomenon of all time, he called the band Tyrannosaurus Rex after the world's largest-ever carnivore. The first recruit was a drummer called Steve Peregrine Took, probably chosen as much for his name (from *The Lord Of The Rings*) as for his ability. Together with a guitarist and bass player, the electric Tyrannosaurus Rex played one disastrous, unrehearsed gig at the Electric Garden (later Middle Earth) in London's Covent Garden. Marc should have realised, after all his false starts, that success would not come in such an off-the-wall fashion. The debacle was further compounded by Track Records repossessing Marc's electric guitar equipment and Steve having to sell his double drum kit. Out of necessity, therefore, the acoustic duo of Tyrannosaurus Rex emerged, with Bolan on a cheap acoustic guitar and Steve Peregrine Took on bongos.

The cross-legged, long-haired pair with their songs full of the magical imagery of mystical lands, elves and pixies became a well-known sight in the hippie era of 1968,

although at gigs they were virtually un-amplified and sat almost out of view below head height on a prayer mat. The first person to help them reach a wider audience was DJ John Peel. Post-pirate and pre-Radio One, Peel was at that time reduced to running a travelling roadshow. He was so impressed by Bolan (having frequently played a two-year-old copy of 'Hippy Gumbo') that he arranged a gig format with Tyrannosaurus Rex playing acoustically between Peel's own sets of the latest recorded sounds.

A helping hand came from American producer Tony Visconti (later to do major work with Bowie). He signed them to the Regal Zonophone label and in 1968 they released two singles, 'Debora' (which reached Number 34) and 'One Inch Rock' (which made Number 28), together with two albums, *My People Were Fair And Had Sky In Their Hair, But Now They're Content To Wear Stars On Their Brows* and *Prophets, Seers and Sages/The Angels Of The Ages*. Bolan's love of the sheer sound of words – as suggested by the titles – and the shimmering imagery he was able to conjure up shone through the simple songs and complex delivery of these records.

During this period Bolan became more sure of himself. His naive faith was being replaced by absolute certainty. Technically he was more proficient, although he still resisted Visconti's urgings to electrify the sound and re-introduce bass and drums. Domestically he finally made the leap of leaving home and settling into a flat with June Child, who had met Marc through her job at Blackhill Enterprises – the concert-promotions company that handled Pink Floyd's shows – when Marc had asked them to look at Tyrannosaurus Rex. The group slowly built up their following and their price rose from £10 to £150 per night while Marc wrote streams of poetry and songs in his little music room in their small Notting Hill flat.

The transitional years in Bolan's career were 1969 and 1970. During 1969 Tyrannosaurus Rex released their best album, *Unicorn*, and a transitional single, 'King Of The Rumbling Spires', that featured electric guitar. At the end of a US tour, Steve Took – heavily into LSD at the time – decided to quit; Bolan replaced him with another tall and gentle bongo player, Mickey Finn. Bolan completed the album *Beard Of Stars* almost single-handedly, using a good deal of electric instrumentation, and began introducing his Strato-caster for the final numbers at concerts.

Bolan's breakthrough came in autumn 1970 with 'Ride A White Swan', a single that was to become a pop classic. He was hell-bent on becoming a star, and in this song he brought together all the elements of a good commercial hit – a chugging boogie beat, simply delivered sing-song lyrics and a catchy melody. It was also the first release by the more pronounceable T.Rex. One airplay was enough to set the sales rolling, and the disc went on to reach Number 2 in the UK charts.

Left: Metal Guru Marc dominates the studio on the London Weekend Television show, 'Supersonic'. Inset below left: Bolan spreads his wings with Mickey Finn.

Getting it on

To hang on to the success that 'Ride A White Swan' brought him, it was necessary for Bolan to promote his image and material through live gigs. The tour of the States the previous year had highlighted the limitations of the acoustic duo format – they simply could not play large venues. So Bolan recruited Steve Currie on bass, Bill Fyfield (nicknamed Legend after his former band) on drums and engaged former Turtles Howard Kaylan and Mark Volman as backing singers, a role they had already fulfilled on the *T.Rex* album, released in 1970. Bolan then got to work on his image, vamping up his appearance with the corkscrew hairstyle, the gold suits, sequins and mascara that were to become his and glam-rock's trademarks.

With T.Rex's next single, the even more commercial 'Hot Love', hitting the Number 1 spot early in 1971, and his subsequent appearance in satin and stardust on 'Top Of The Pops', many of Bolan's former underground followers slammed him for 'selling out'. But Bolan was up where he wanted to be, and was now reaching a wider audience. T.Rex's singles success reads like a dream: following on the trail of 'Hot Love' in 1971 came 'Get It On' (Number 1) and 'Jeepster' (Number 2), while the following year saw two Number 1 hits with 'Telegram Sam' and 'Metal

'The only times I've really been shook lately is like at the weekends there's probably three or four hundred chicks outside, you know. Well, I don't know where they got the address from, but they appear, you know, and suddenly I look out of the window and they all sort of scream and I think well, it sounds very naive, I mean sometimes I'm really not aware of it at all.'
Marc Bolan

Guru', two Number 2 singles with 'Children Of The Revolution' and 'Solid Gold Easy Action' and a Number 7 with 'Debora'/'One Inch Rock'. In 1973 '20th Century Boy' made Number 3 and 'The Groover' peaked at Number 4. 'Get It On', retitled 'Bang A Gong' to avoid confusion with a 1971 chart hit by Chase, also called 'Get It On', made Number 10 in the US in 1972.

T.Rex were also instrumental in bringing commercial pop into the album charts. Their next two LPs, *Electric Warrior* (1971) and *The Slider* (1972), both hit the top of the UK album charts – and the former began many a pop fan's album collection. And Bolan capitalised on his immense success by making a film. In collaboration with Ringo Starr, he starred in an exploitative but successful documentary, *Born To Boogie*, using footage from the sellout concerts at the Empire Pool, Wembley, in 1972.

Coke and cognac
Bolan's halo was beginning to slip, however. Young fans were being tempted away by fresh new idols like Donny Osmond and David Cassidy. Bolan's excesses were starting to show in his spreading waistline and bloated face. BBC-TV's 'Nationwide' unkindly spliced together a medley to demonstrate how similar many of T.Rex's singles were. Always able to give an interviewer good copy, Marc had been the darling of the rock press, but they, too, began to turn against him as he became increasingly egotistical and self-opinionated.

The problem was not so much success as the habits it brought with it. Cocaine and cognac, which he could now afford in large quantities, resulted in schizophrenia and paranoia. Screaming bouts of temper, selfishness and general high-handedness not only alienated the press, but also destroyed his private life. Old friends like John Peel and Tony Visconti were discarded as no longer useful; Bill Legend and Mickey Finn left the band (Mickey bought an antique shop in the King's Road, Chelsea); and June Child, whom Bolan had married in 1970, left him after finally losing out to extra-marital affairs.

His recorded work suffered; after 'The Groover' (1973), T.Rex's singles failed to make the Top Ten; *Zinc Alloy And The Hidden Riders Of Tomorrow* (1974) received bad reviews and sales were poor. The resilient Bolan bounced back, however, as his relationship with singer/songwriter/producer Gloria Jones, whom he had met in LA in 1973, blossomed and a son, Rolan, was born to them in 1975. He cut down on drugs and drink and concentrated on serious musical work. A self-mocking ballad, 'Whatever Happened To The Teenage Dream', had preceded a UK tour with a revamped and more professional T.Rex in 1974, featuring Gloria Jones on vocals and clavinet, Steve Currie (bass), Davey Lutton (drums) and former Beach Boy sessioneer Dino Dines on keyboards. The albums of the period – *Bolan's Zip Gun* (1974) and *Futuristic Dragon* (1976) – were patchy flops, although he still managed to squeeze into the UK Top Twenty with the singles 'New York City' and 'I Love To Boogie'.

Bolan's career seemed to be picking up. He did a series of interviews for ITV's *Today* programme and, in his more familiar role with T.Rex, made regular appearances on Mike Mansfield's 'Supersonic' for London Weekend Television, using all the flash, trash and over-the-top presentation he could muster. But rock 'n'roll was still his avowed priority, and by 1977 he had put together the most technically proficient T.Rex line-up ever, with Herbie Flowers (later with Sky) on bass, Tony Newman on drums, Dino Dines on keyboards and Miller Anderson on guitar.

Above: Marc struts in the limelight. Never one to stay in the shadows, he tenaciously revived his flagging fortunes in 1976.

They worked on an album, *Dandy In The Underworld*, and toured with the Damned.

The last boogie
For years, Bolan had been describing himself as a 'street punk', so he welcomed the punk revolution as a return to basic rock 'n'roll and an exorcism of glam-rock. Somewhat plumper, with his hair peroxided at the front, Bolan found a renewed confidence, playing to a new generation of fans who acknowledged both his past contribution to music and his current mastery. He was working on a new album and there were rumours of a deal with RCA; he also had a regular column in *Record Mirror*. It was from this position that he embarked upon his last venture – a series of shows for Granada TV. The final episode, featuring a duet with David Bowie, had not even been screened when Bolan died. On 6 September 1977 he and Gloria were returning from an evening out at Morton's nightclub in Berkeley Square, London, when Gloria, who was driving, lost control of their purple Mini and hit a tree. Bolan was killed instantly; he was not yet 30. Three years later, in 1980, Steve Took, who had had a spell with the Pink Fairies since leaving Bolan, died a drugs casualty; Steve Currie died in 1981.

Since Bolan's death there has been the inevitable managerial exploitation, with Simon Napier-Bell releasing acoustic tapes from 1966 with a rock backing added. However, such has been the interest of loyal fans that the Marc Bolan Fan Club (the second largest in Europe) has been able to buy up EMI's tape catalogue and supervise a controlled series of new releases and reissues.

What set Marc Bolan aside from other stars was his drive, ambition, savvy, charm and – as one of his friends put it – 'his incredible sense of style'. Britain's most celebrated star of the early Seventies, he brought glamour, fun and teen-appeal back into rock – and his influence remained current into the Eighties.

CHRISTOPHER NORTH

T.REX
Discography (to 1977)

Singles
Debora/Child Star (Regal Zonophone, 1968); One Inch Rock/Salamanda Palaganda (Regal Zonophone, 1968); Pewter Suitor/Warlord Of The Royal Crocodiles (Regal Zonophone 3016, 1969); King Of The Rumbling Spires/Do You Remember? (Regal Zonophone 3022, 1969); By The Light Of The Magical Moon/Find A Little Wood (Regal Zonophone 3025, 1970); Ride A White Swan/Is It Love/Summertime Blues (Fly BUG 1, 1970); Hot Love/King Of The Mountain Cometh/Woodland Rock (Fly BUG 6, 1971); Get It On/There Was A Time/Raw Ramp (Fly BUG 10, 1971); Jeepster/Life's A Gas (Fly BUG 16, 1971); Telegram Sam/Baby Strange/Cadillac (T.Rex 101, 1972); Debora/One Inch Rock/The Woodland Bop/Seal Of Seasons (Magnifly Echo 102); Metal Guru/Lady/Thunderwing (EMI MARC 1, 1972); Children Of The Revolution/Jitterbug Love/Sunken Rags (EMI MARC 2, 1972); Solid Gold Easy Action/Born To Boogie (EMI MARC 3, 1972); 20th Century Boy/Free Angel (EMI MARC 4, 1973); The Groover/Midnight (EMI MARC 5, 1973); Truck On (Tyke)/Sitting Here (EMI MARC 6, 1973); Teenage Dream/Satisfaction Pony (EMI MARC 7, 1974); Jasper C. Debussy/Hippy Gumbo/The Perfumed Garden Of Gulliver Smith (Track 2094013, 1974); Light Of Love/Explosive Mouth (EMI MARC 8, 1974); Zip Gun Boogie/Space Boss (EMI MARC 9, 1975); New York City/Chrome Sitar (EMI MARC 10, 1975); Dreamy Lady/Do You Wanna Dance?/Dock Of The Bay (EMI MARC 11, 1975); London Boys/Solid Baby (EMI MARC 13, 1976); I Love To Boogie/Baby Boomerang (EMI MARC 14, 1976); Laser Love/Life's An Elevator (EMI MARC 15, 1976); The Soul Of My Suit/All Alone (EMI MARC 16, 1977); Dandy In The Underworld/Groove A Little/Tame My Tiger (EMI MARC 17); Celebrate Summer/Ride My Wheels (EMI MARC 18, 1977).

EPs
Bolan's Best Plus One (Ant 1, 1977).

Albums
My People Were Fair And Had Sky In Their Hair, But Now They're Content To Wear Stars On Their Brows (Regal Zonophone SLRZ 1003, 1968); *Prophets, Seers And Sages/The Angels Of The Ages* (Regal Zonophone SLRZ 1005, 1968); *Unicorn* (Regal Zonophone SLRZ 1007, 1969); *A Beard Of Stars* (Regal Zonophone SLRZ 1013, 1970); *T.Rex* (Fly Hi-Fly 2, 1970); *Electric Warrior* (Fly Hi-Fly 6, 1971); *The Slider* (EMI BLN 5001, 1972); *Tanx* (EMI BLN 5002, 1972); *Zinc Alloy And The Hidden Riders Of Tomorrow* (EMI BLNA 7751, 1974); *Bolan Zip Gun* (EMI BLNA 7752, 1975); *Futuristic Dragon* (EMI BLN 5004, 1976); *Dandy In The Underworld* (EMI BLN 5005, 1977).

Numbers in *italics* refer to illustrations.

U.S. HIT SINGLES

1972

JANUARY

1   BRAND NEW KEY   *Melanie*
8   BRAND NEW KEY   *Melanie*
15   AMERICAN PIE   *Don McLean*
22   AMERICAN PIE   *Don McLean*
29   AMERICAN PIE   *Don McLean*

FEBRUARY

5   AMERICAN PIE   *Don McLean*
12   LET'S STAY TOGETHER   *Al Green*
19   WITHOUT YOU   *Nilsson*
26   WITHOUT YOU   *Nilsson*

MARCH

4   WITHOUT YOU   *Nilsson*
11   WITHOUT YOU   *Nilsson*
18   HEART OF GOLD   *Neil Young*
25   A HORSE WITH NO NAME   *America*

APRIL

1   A HORSE WITH NO NAME   *America*
8   A HORSE WITH NO NAME   *America*
15   THE FIRST TIME EVER I SAW YOUR FACE
    Roberta Flack
22   THE FIRST TIME EVER I SAW YOUR FACE
    Roberta Flack
29   THE FIRST TIME EVER I SAW YOUR FACE
    Roberta Flack

MAY

6   THE FIRST TIME EVER I SAW YOUR FACE
    Roberta Flack
13   THE FIRST TIME EVER I SAW YOUR FACE
    Roberta Flack
20   THE FIRST TIME EVER I SAW YOUR FACE
    Roberta Flack
27   OH GIRL   *Chi-Lites*

JUNE

3   I'LL TAKE YOU THERE   *Staple Singers*
10   THE CANDY MAN   *Sammy Davis*
17   THE CANDY MAN   *Sammy Davis*
24   THE CANDY MAN   *Sammy Davis*

JULY

1   SONG SUNG BLUE   *Neil Diamond*
8   LEAN ON ME   *Bill Withers*
15   LEAN ON ME   *Bill Withers*
22   LEAN ON ME   *Bill Withers*
29   ALONE AGAIN (NATURALLY)
    Gilbert O'Sullivan

AUGUST

5   ALONE AGAIN (NATURALLY)
    Gilbert O'Sullivan
12   ALONE AGAIN (NATURALLY)
    Gilbert O'Sullivan
19   ALONE AGAIN (NATURALLY)
    Gilbert O'Sullivan
26   BRANDY (YOU'RE A FINE GIRL)
    Looking Glass

SEPTEMBER

2   ALONE AGAIN (NATURALLY)
    Gilbert O'Sullivan
9   ALONE AGAIN (NATURALLY)
    Gilbert O'Sullivan
16   BLACK AND WHITE   *Three Dog Night*
23   BABY DON'T GET HOOKED ON ME
    Mac Davis
30   BABY DON'T GET HOOKED ON ME
    Mac Davis

OCTOBER

7   BABY DON'T GET HOOKED ON ME
    Mac Davis
14   BEN   *Michael Jackson*
21   MY DING-A-LING   *Chuck Berry*
28   MY DING-A-LING   *Chuck Berry*

NOVEMBER

4   I CAN SEE CLEARLY NOW   *Johnny Nash*
11   I CAN SEE CLEARLY NOW   *Johnny Nash*
18   I CAN SEE CLEARLY NOW   *Johnny Nash*
25   I CAN SEE CLEARLY NOW   *Johnny Nash*

DECEMBER

2   PAPA WAS A ROLLING STONE
    Temptations
9   I AM A WOMAN   *Helen Reddy*
16   ME AND MRS JONES   *Billy Paul*
23   ME AND MRS JONES   *Billy Paul*
30   ME AND MRS JONES   *Billy Paul*

1973

JANUARY

6   YOU'RE SO VAIN   *Carly Simon*
13   YOU'RE SO VAIN   *Carly Simon*
20   YOU'RE SO VAIN   *Carly Simon*

FEBRUARY

3   CROCODILE ROCK   *Elton John*
10   CROCODILE ROCK   *Elton John*
17   CROCODILE ROCK   *Elton john*
24   KILLING ME SOFTLY WITH HIS SONG
     Roberta Flack

MARCH

3   KILLING ME SOFTLY WITH HIS SONG
     Roberta Flack
10   KILLING ME SOFTLY WITH HIS SONG
     Roberta Flack
17   KILLING ME SOFTLY WITH HIS SONG
     Roberta Flack
24   LOVE TRAIN   *O'Jays*
31   KILLING ME SOFTLY WITH HIS SONG
     Roberta Flack

APRIL

7   THE NIGHT THE LIGHTS WENT OUT IN
     GEORGIA   *Vicky Lawrence*
14   THE NIGHT THE LIGHTS WENT OUT IN
     GEORGIA   *Vicky Lawrence*
21   TIE A YELLOW RIBBON ROUND THE OLE
     OAK TREE   *Dawn*
28   TIE A YELLOW RIBBON ROUND THE OLE
     OAK TREE   *Dawn*

MAY

5   TIE A YELLOW RIBBON ROUND THE OLE
     OAK TREE   *Dawn*
12   TIE A YELLOW RIBBON ROUND THE OLE
     OAK TREE   *Dawn*
19   YOU ARE THE SUNSHINE OF MY LIFE
     Stevie Wonder
26   FRANKENSTEIN   *Edgar Winter Group*

JUNE

2   MY LOVE   *Paul McCartney and Wings*
9   MY LOVE   *Paul McCartney and Wings*
16   MY LOVE   *Paul McCartney and Wings*
23   MY LOVE   *Paul McCartney and Wings*
30   GIVE ME LOVE GIVE ME PEACE ON
     EARTH   *George Harrison*

JULY

7   WILL IT GO ROUND IN CIRCLES
     Billy Preston
14   WILL IT GO ROUND IN CIRCLES
     Billy Preston
21   BAD BAD LEROY BROWN   *Jim Croce*
28   BAD BAD LEROY BROWN   *Jim Croce*

AUGUST

4   THE MORNING AFTER   *Maureen McGovern*
11   THE MORNING AFTER   *Maureen McGovern*
18   TOUCH ME IN THE MORNING   *Diana Ross*
25   BROTHER LOUIE   *Stories*

SEPTEMBER

1   BROTHER LOUIE   *Stories*
8   LET'S GET IT ON   *Marvin Gaye*
15   DELTA DAWN   *Helen Reddy*
22   LET'S GET IT ON   *Marvin Gaye*
29   WE'RE AN AMERICAN BAND   *Grand Funk*

OCTOBER

6   HALF BREED   *Cher*
13   HALF BREED   *Cher*
20   ANGIE   *Rolling Stones*
27   MIDNIGHT TRAIN TO GEORGIA
     Gladys Knight and the Pips

NOVEMBER

3   MIDNIGHT TRAIN TO GEORGIA
     Gladys Knight and the Pips
10   KEEP ON TRUCKIN'   *Eddie Kendricks*
17   KEEP ON TRUCKIN'   *Eddie Kendricks*
24   PHOTOGRAPH   *Ringo Star*

DECEMBER

1   TOP OF THE WORLD
     Carpenters
8   TOP OF THE WORLD
     Carpenters
15   THE MOST BEAUTIFUL GIRL
     Charlie Rich
22   THE MOST BEAUTIFUL GIRL
     Charlie Rich
29   TIME IN A BOTTLE   *Jim Croce*

U.K. HIT SINGLES

1972

JANUARY

1 ERNIE (THE FASTEST MILKMAN IN THE WEST *Benny Hill*
8 I'D LIKE TO TEACH THE WORLD TO SING *New Seekers*
15 I'D LIKE TO TEACH THE WORLD TO SING *New Seekers*
22 I'D LIKE TO TEACH THE WORLD TO SING *New Seekers*

FEBRUARY

5 TELEGRAM SAM *T. Rex*
12 TELEGRAM SAM *T. Rex*
19 SON OF MY FATHER *Chicory Tip*
26 SON OF MY FATHER *Chicory Tip*

MARCH

4 SON OF MY FATHER *Chicory Tip*
11 WITHOUT YOU *Nilsson*
18 WITHOUT YOU *Nilsson*
25 WITHOUT YOU *Nilsson*

APRIL

1 WITHOUT YOU *Nilsson*
8 WITHOUT YOU *Nilsson*
15 AMAZING GRACE *The Royal Scots Dragoon Guards*
22 AMAZING GRACE *The Royal Scots Dragoon Guards*
29 AMAZING GRACE *The Royal Scots Dragoon Guards*

MAY

6 AMAZING GRACE *The Royal Scots Dragoon Guards*
13 AMAZING GRACE *The Royal Scots Dragoon Guards*
20 METAL GURU *T. Rex*
27 METAL GURU *T. Rex*

JUNE

3 METAL GURU *T. Rex*
10 METAL GURU *T. Rex*
17 VINCENT *Don McLean*
24 VINCENT *Don McLean*

JULY

1 TAKE ME BAK'OME *Slade*
8 PUPPY LOVE *Donny Osmond*
15 PUPPY LOVE *Donny Osmond*
22 PUPPY LOVE *Donny Osmond*
29 PUPPY LOVE *Donny Osmond*

AUGUST

5 PUPPY LOVE *Donny Osmond*
12 SCHOOL'S OUT *Alice Cooper*
19 SCHOOL'S OUT *Alice Cooper*
26 SCHOOL'S OUT *Alice Cooper*

SEPTEMBER

2 YOU WEAR IT WELL *Rod Stewart*
9 MAMA WEER ALL CRAZEE NOW *Slade*
16 MAMA WEER ALL CRAZEE NOW *Slade*
23 MAMA WEER ALL CRAZEE NOW *Slade*
30 HOW CAN I BE SURE? *David Cassidy*

OCTOBER

7 HOW CAN I BE SURE? *David Cassidy*
14 MOULDY OLD DOUGH *Lieutenant Pigeon*
28 MOULDY OLD DOUGH *Lieutenant Pigeon*

NOVEMBER

4 MOULDY OLD DOUGH *Lieutenant Pigeon*
11 CLAIR *Gilbert O'Sullivan*
18 CLAIR *Gilbert O'Sullivan*
25 MY DING-A-LING *Chuck Berry*

DECEMBER

2 MY DING-A-LING *Chuck Berry*
9 MY DING-A-LING *Chuck Berry*
16 MY DING-A-LING *Chuck Berry*
23 LONG HAIRED LOVER FROM LIVERPOOL *Little Jimmy Osmond*
30 LONG HAIRED LOVER FROM LIVERPOOL *Little Jimmy Osmond*

1973

JANUARY

6 LONG HAIRED LOVER FROM LIVERPOOL
   Little Jimmy Osmond
13 LONG HAIRED LOVER FROM LIVERPOOL
   Little Jimmy Osmond
20 LONG HAIRED LOVER FROM LIVERPOOL
   Little Jimmy Osmond
27 BLOCKBUSTER   *Sweet*

FEBRUARY

3 BLOCKBUSTER   *Sweet*
10 BLOCKBUSTER   *Sweet*
17 BLOCKBUSTER   *Sweet*
24 BLOCKBUSTER   *Sweet*

MARCH

3 CUM ON FEEL THE NOIZE   *Slade*
10 CUM ON FEEL THE NOIZE   *Slade*
17 CUM ON FEEL THE NOIZE   *Slade*
24 CUM ON FEEL THE NOIZE   *Slade*
31 THE TWELFTH OF NEVER   *Donny Osmond*

APRIL

7 GET DOWN   *Gilbert O'Sullivan*
14 GET DOWN   *Gilbert O'Sullivan*
21 TIE A YELLOW RIBBON ROUND THE OLE
   OAK TREE   *Dawn*
28 TIE A YELLOW RIBBON ROUND THE OLE
   OAK TREE   *Dawn*

MAY

5 TIE A YELLOW RIBBON ROUND THE OLE
   OAK TREE   *Dawn*
12 TIE A YELLOW RIBBON ROUND THE OLE
   OAK TREE   *Dawn*
19 SEE MY BABY JIVE   *Wizzard*
26 SEE MY BABY JIVE   *Wizzard*

JUNE

2 SEE MY BABY JIVE   *Wizzard*
9 SEE MY BABY JIVE   *Wizzard*
16 CAN THE CAN   *Suzi Quatro*
23 RUBBER BULLETS   *10cc*
30 SQWEZE ME PLEEZE ME   *Slade*

JULY

7 SQWEZE ME PLEEZE ME   *Slade*
14 SQWEZE ME PLEEZE ME   *Slade*
21 WELCOME HOME   *Peters and Lee*
28 I'M LEADER OF THE GANG (I AM)
   Gary Glitter

AUGUST

4 I'M LEADER OF THE GANG (I AM)
   Gary Glitter
11 I'M LEADER OF THE GANG (I AM)
   Gary Glitter
18 I'M LEADER OF THE GANG (I AM)
   Gary Glitter
25 YOUNG LOVE   *Donny Osmond*

SEPTEMBER

1 YOUNG LOVE   *Donny Osmond*
8 YOUNG LOVE   *Donny Osmond*
15 YOUNG LOVE   *Donny Osmond*
22 ANGEL FINGERS   *Wizzard*
29 EYE LEVEL   *Simon Park Orchestra*

OCTOBER

6 EYE LEVEL   *Simon Park Orchestra*
13 EYE LEVEL   *Simon Park Orchestra*
20 EYE LEVEL   *Simon Park Orchestra*
27 DAYDREAMER/THE PUPPY SONG
   David Cassidy

NOVEMBER

3 DAYDREAMER/THE PUPPY SONG
   David Cassidy
10 DAYDREAMER/THE PUPPY SONG
   David Cassidy
17 I LOVE YOU LOVE ME LOVE
   Gary Glitter
24 I LOVE YOU LOVE ME LOVE
   Gary Glitter

DECEMBER

1 I LOVE YOU LOVE ME LOVE
   Gary Glitter
8 I LOVE YOU LOVE ME LOVE
   Gary Glitter
15 MERRY XMAS EVERYBODY   *Slade*
22 MERRY XMAS EVERYBODY   *Slade*
29 MERRY XMAS EVERYBODY   *Slade*